Clarification
Of The
Monetary
Standard

CLARIFICATION OF THE MONETARY STANDARD.

The Concept and Its Relation to Monetary Policies and Objectives

WILL E. MASON

The Pennsylvania State University Press

University Park / 1963

To
Frank D. Graham

PREFACE

My interest in the subject of this study began many years ago when, as a graduate student, I shuttled between the seminars on money and banking conducted by the late Professors Frank D. Graham and Edwin W. Kemmerer while assisting Professor Friedrich A. Lutz in the undergraduate course. The subject of the monetary standard came up in one form or another as I subsequently worked in other related fields. My continued study and research strengthened the apprehension that traditional doctrines in international monetary economics frequently reflected underlying conceptual obscurities. This impression has been reinforced by many recent discussions of monetary theory and policy. Further development of monetary theory and policy alternatives seems to me to require a reconsideration of basic concepts. The purpose of this study is to stimulate such a reexamination. It is hoped that the inquiry will help to move us toward a more workable conceptual framework for policy decisions. It is also hoped that the reinterpretation of the development of monetary theory presented here will motivate further review of the subject.

Much of the research was done under a fellowship granted by the Ford Foundation. Completion of the project was made possible by (1) grants from The Pennsylvania State University, (2) assistance from the Bureau of Business Research of the College of Business Administration, and (3) the cooperation of my superiors and colleagues which freed me from many academic duties.

My indebtedness to others is great. The concept of a monetary standard developed in this study as a workable alternative to received notions was suggested by conversations with Frank D. Graham. Friedrich A. Lutz influenced my thinking on monetary matters in more ways than I can now precisely identify. Stanley E. Howard's interest and encouragement has immeasurably helped to sustain my research efforts through the years. My students as well as my colleagues have helped clarify my thoughts on the range of topics covered by the present treatise. Lester V. Chandler, J. Herbert Furth, Marvin Rozen, and Jacob Viner have read portions of the manuscript. Their criticisms and suggestions resulted in the removal of many sources of potential confusion to the reader and embarrassment to the writer. I am especially indebted to Ervin P. Hexner, who read the entire manuscript. Without his encouragement and assistance the project might never have been brought to completion.

The depth of my gratitude to the institutions and persons who have helped me so generously should not, of course, be construed as in any way implying their agreement with my analysis or conclusions.

Will E. Mason

State College, Pa.
November 3, 1962

CONTENTS

Clarification
Of The
Monetary
Standard

I

INTRODUCTION

Gladstone once described the study of money as "a fruitful cause of insanity." [1] He was probably referring to the bullion controversy, which a participant compared to "fighting a shadow." This early nineteenth-century English dispute was the first battle in the "war of standards," which has raged inconclusively to this very day. "No generation since the beginning of the nineteenth century has escaped the sharp controversy over the question of the monetary standard." [2] The shifts in the battlefields, the forces, and the objectives have not been easy to follow—even from the vantage point of history, with the record before us. Nevertheless, the early battles were at least distinguishable: the bullion and currency controversies (Great Britain), the green-

1

back and resumption issues (United States), the battle of bimetallism (Europe and United States),[3] and the interwar parity struggle (primarily Europe). Although the victories were never decisive enough to end the war, the battles were at least concluded—if only by truces instead of treaties.

The renewal of hostilities during the great depression arrayed, on a worldwide scale, the "managed currency" revolutionists against the orthodox high priests of the "golden rules." The enlarged scope, the new weapons provided by improved technical knowledge, and the new tactics of propaganda, subversion, infiltration, and guerilla activities converted the heretofore two-sided war, with distinguishable battles capable of resolution, into a permanent global revolution in depth. The simple, nineteenth-century formula of the "good guys" against the "bad guys" ceased to apply to the real world. In modern monetary "multilateralism" the triumph of one side cannot be expected. Victories are as indistinct as the battles. A review of the war of standards reveals a progressive deterioration in the durability of the truces until it has become impossible to initiate, much less to maintain, one.

The waxing complexity of society helps to explain, but not to excuse, the inconclusiveness of our struggles. Evidence indicates that our comprehension has not kept pace with our creativeness. In the early battles of this war the opposing forces knew—or felt they knew—what they were fighting about. The issues were apparent. This became less and less true as hostilities "progressed." The armies broke into warring factions, with shifting coalitions, until the troops hardly knew whom they were fighting or for what. What appeared earlier to be "like fighting a shadow" has, to a very large extent, become just that. Not even the agenda for a peace conference can be drawn up until the opponents at least understand the issues that divide them. Such understanding insures neither a treaty nor constructive use of the resources liberated for non-military uses, but it makes both possible.

2

LACK OF ATTENTION TO GENERIC CONCEPT OF A MONETARY STANDARD

The war of standards degenerated into disconnected battles with conflicting objectives. The periodic skirmishes became all tactics and no strategy. Having developed different ideas of their objectives, coalitions lacked cohesiveness. Internal disagreements on tactics (policies) ultimately resulted from differences in the strategic conceptualization of the conflict. The classical consensus on the concept of a monetary standard was lost in the battles following the bullion controversy. The specific standards fought over, therefore, lost their specificity. Victory or defeat became undefinable; consequently the war of standards became unresolvable.

Unfortunately, the loss of the former consensus on the concept of a monetary standard did not inspire remedial action. Instead, the concept has been almost entirely neglected in modern literature.[4] Dictionaries and encyclopedias completely ignore the concept, despite their inclusion of articles on some (not all) of its subordinate manifestations. This is even true of the *Encyclopaedia of the Social Sciences* and of Palgrave's *Dictionary of Political Economy,* which neglect very little, if anything, else that was ever mentioned in connection with economics. Those most insistent upon the necessity of definitions in monetary discussions have defined virtually everything except the concept on which their homilies concerning monetary standards were based.[5] It was, for example, completely overlooked in W. A. L. Coulborn's chapter on definitions.[6] John Donaldson affirmed that "it would be desirable to define" such terms as the "monetary standard" before they are discussed.[7] Every term he mentioned except this one was forthwith defined under its own heading. Among these headings we find that the "monetary standard" became "Monetary Standards."[8] Thus the problem of defining the concept was neatly sidestepped, and the reader is confronted, without any further introduction, with the various kinds of standards.[9]

3

Even writers who prefaced their treatment of monetary standards with a purported delineation of basic concepts typically ignore *the* basic concept. Harold G. Moulton began his discussion of "General Principles" (of "the Standard Question") with definitions of "The Various Kinds of Standards."[10] Ray V. Leffler's introductory observations were limited to such topics as "Utility of a Monetary Commodity," "Money Value," and "Need for Use Commodity."[11] And Jay L. O'Hara dealt with such things as the choice between British and Spanish currency units.[12] Preliminary to consideration of the various monetary standards, William Howard Steiner addressed himself to "the standard question itself." However, this turned out to be not what is the meaning of a monetary standard, but rather which particular standard is best.[13] "General principles" relative to the monetary standard have been construed narrowly. This appears to be one area in which writers have not erred on the side of excessive generality.

Normally, authors of treatises on money (including textbooks for beginning students) plunge their readers into the morass of mechanical details relative to individual standards without even an attempt to explain what it's all about.[14] The ambiguity of these discussions is not surprising. It is the inevitable result of the procedure. If one does not have a precise idea of the concept of a monetary standard, he cannot define its various manifestations with precision. Consequently, even the specific standards are seldom specifically defined.[15] Most authors are content to describe their alleged characteristics.[16] Economists have shown a growing reluctance to define the various standards. Instead of saying "a . . . standard *is* . . . ," writers have resorted to such phraseology as "a country is *said to be* on a . . . standard *when*" such and such conditions prevail or when its monetary system possesses certain specified characteristics.[17] This tactic relieves the writer from responsibility both for the foolish things that have been said and for deciding what *should* be said.

Nevertheless, the paper standard(s), however it (they) may be labeled—inconverti-

4

ble, fiat, managed, forced, multiple, or any combination of these—defies (defy) the conventional approach. Its (their) characteristics cannot be described—cannot even be listed— because the absence of a generic concept of a monetary standard means that there is practically no limit to the variety of attributes that this (these) monetary arrangement(s)—for lack of a better term at the moment—may display. Textbook writers—those courageous souls who must deal resolutely with unsolved problems—are forced to reverse their technique and treat this range of phenomena negatively. In short, they simply admit that a noncommodity standard does not possess the characteristics of commodity standards—a truism that sometimes takes several pages to demonstrate. The basic methodological defect that accounts for the prevailing confusion is the attempt to identify the species before the genus.

Such unscientific procedure could yield only imprecise and inconclusive results, confusing rather than clarifying monetary issues. Not only are the different standards indistinguishable; they are unrestrained in their proliferation. The absence of a limiting genus means that the variety of alleged species is bounded only by the imagination of the observers. And for people not noted for their imagination—the discipline is not calculated to cultivate this quality—economists have produced some rather fanciful categories, e.g., "non-fixed inconvertible paper standard,"[18] "managed irredeemable paper standard based on silver,"[19] "irredeemable paper money" standard "based on gold" (also called a " 'provisional' gold standard"),[20] "managed inconvertible gold bullion standard,"[21] "gold insolvency standard,"[22] "inconvertible managed gold standard,"[23] "variable gold standard,"[24] "manipulated gold-loan standard,"[25] and "inconvertible paper money gold standard."[26] A reaction to this terminological tumefaction is observable in a recent tendency to call all monetary systems with bases broader than bimetallism, "multiple standards."[27] This is, at least, a recognition that the "standard" distinctions, however bizarre, have lost their distinctiveness.

But even abandonment of exotic terms would not restore communicability. A more

5

serious obstacle to the progress of thought and action in monetary matters has been the confusion of monetary standards, policies, and objectives that has been the inevitable result of the absence of any boundaries to the meaning of the "monetary standard." Most modern discussions convey the impression that various standards are merely different combinations of policies. In fact, they are customarily identified and differentiated by their policies.[28] Actually, the absence of a generic concept precludes any other procedure. But instead of remedying the deficiency, the trend for some time has been to identify standards and policies. Sidney Sherwood, for example, defined bimetallism as "the *policy* of using both gold and silver as money, the mints being open to the free coinage of both these metals . . ." [29] What this amounts to is that the standard is a policy of carrying out certain policies.[30] Little attention, however, has been given to the question as to which policies are *both necessary and sufficient*—and no attention has been devoted to the question as to whether all the customarily listed ones are sufficient—to constitute the particular standard under consideration.[31] Consequently, standard and policy issues have become confused. The confusion is not new.[32] But it has become more pronounced and pervasive with the rising importance of monetary policy (and the declining significance of the monetary standard? Or is such a question logically precluded by their identification?). "Standard" and "policy" have come to be used interchangeably, if not synonymously.[33] As a result, neither the similarity nor the difference, if any, is clear.

Monetary objectives, like policies, have become indistinguishable from standards—and for the same reason.[34] The terms "standard" and "objective" or "goal" are almost as substitutive in monetary literature as "standard" and "policy." [35] Consequently, experts often cannot even individually decide, much less collectively agree, as to what it is they are talking about. For some years now there has been much ado about price-level stabilization. But what is it? Those who should know appear to have counseled us that it is: (1) an objective inferred from a particular standard,[36] (2) a standard inferred from a particular ob-

6

jective,[37] (3) an objective unrelated (irrelevant?) to the standard, if any,[38] and (4) both a standard and goal.[39] Like Stephen Leacock's fabled character, the monetary economist has mounted his academic high horse and ridden madly off in all directions!

Our failure to determine precisely what *a* monetary standard is has left basic questions unanswered and unanswerable: (1) Is the United States, for example, on the (a?) gold standard or not? (2) If so, what are the implications for present questions relative to monetary policy? (3) If not, what *is* the present monetary standard,[40] and what are the policy inferences to be drawn therefrom? The inconclusiveness of the interminable arguments on these questions is too well known to need laboring.[41] But the fundamental reason has apparently escaped detection. The difficulty, as usual, is in the premises, which are seldom explicit and often sunk in the subconscious. The monetary standard means different things to different people. These issues can never be resolved until it is realized that the genus monetary standard must be established before the species can be identified.[42] Had biologists proceeded in the manner of monetary analysts, they would still be arguing as to whether the chestnut oak is a chestnut tree or an oak tree. If biologists had been as unscientific as the money doctors, there would be today no biological sciences—and the life-saving wonder drugs would probably be unknown! The policy issues of modern democratic societies—intensified by the tugging and hauling of countervailing pressure groups [43]—have been rendered unresolvable by the confusion of monetary objectives, policies, and standards resulting from neglect of the generic idea of a monetary standard.

What the "money muddle" cries out for is a concept of a monetary standard sufficiently precise, reasonable, and realistic to permit isolation of the phenomenon and identification of its species.[44] Achievement of this objective would enable us to distinguish the issues of substance from those of terminology. The distinction would facilitate the resolution of issues in both spheres. Some heretofore irreconcilable conflicts will disappear with the

7

banished haze of superfluous verbiage. When words no longer get in our way, there will be hope for more satisfactory progress toward solutions of "real" monetary problems.

Unfortunately, the textbook writers have not addressed themselves to this task.[45] Instead, they have generally proceeded along the following lines: First, they indulge in a ritualistic reiteration of the requisites of the material used as money,[46] or, at least, of standard money[47] —"cognizability," "divisibility," "malleability," "durability," "homogeneity," "high value relative to bulk," etc.—characteristics that are wholly unrelated to modern abstract debt money[48] and paper standards.[49] Second, they parade the traditional standards before us in their traditional trappings,[50] usually as a lesson in legislative history.[51] Finally, in the concluding chapters, they deal with current policy issues, typically, without even mentioning the "standard."[52]

Chapters on monetary policies and objectives not only ignore the chapters on standards, but often contradict them. Alternative policies and objectives are considered without any indication of the limitations that might be imposed on the range of choices by the monetary standard.[53] Moreover, in the past when people were more sure than they are now of what the "monetary standard" meant —and it was customary to "stand up and be counted" on the question—their stand on the standard in the early chapters was frequently contradicted by their policy recommendations in the later chapters. For instance, neither a policy of controlling gold production[54] nor policies for stabilizing the price level or maintaining full employment[55] appear to be compatible with the gold standard without making a mockery of the word "standard."[56] With the more recent practice of avoiding commitment in the chapters on standards, confusion has replaced contradiction. All these observations apply with equal force to the usual handling of monetary objectives.[57] "Goals" and "policies" are not clearly distinguished either from each other or from standards.

The difficulties with the concept of the monetary standard described above appear to be implicitly recognized in the present tendency to ignore the very idea of a *domestic* monetary standard. Having apparently consigned that subject to the historians, several texts of recent vintage deal directly with monetary standards only in connection with international finance in general and exchange-rate policy in particular.[58] Recent revisions of old texts have collapsed the detailed description of the historical development of standards included in previous editions, tending to subordinate the subject to policies, particularly international financial policies.[59] And here, too, "policies" are replacing "standards," which are also being relegated to history—though, in this case, recent enough history to be retained in money and banking textbooks.[60] Thus, so far as contemporary monetary issues, domestic or international, are concerned, the concept of a standard has practically disappeared.[61]

THE PROBLEM

Besides conflicting objectives, a basic reason for the public-policy paralysis plaguing modern economies is that current monetary problems are not well enough understood to permit the assignment of responsibility for their solution. Economists are not furnishing public officials with the assistance that might reasonably be expected because economists cannot even agree on the issues, much less on their resolution. One reason for this difficulty has been the confusion of substantive and terminological questions resulting from the lack of a consensus on the concept of a monetary standard. This vacuum has drawn the terms "standards," "policies," and "objectives" into a verbal whirlpool, with the result that the term "monetary standard" is all but lost and the others are not going any place or doing much of anything really useful. As a result, communication on monetary problems has virtually broken down.

Little progress can be expected in resolving the substantive monetary issues until the terminological obstacles have been cleared away. This requires answers to the following fundamental questions:

9

(1) What is *a* monetary standard? (2) Is it relevant to current monetary issues, or is the concept as well as its species passé? In the search for answers to these questions, some reasons for the above-mentioned methodological shortcoming of modern monetary analysis have been discovered. The basic difficulty is that classical terms have been retained without any apparent conscious awareness of how the corresponding concepts have been modified by intervening institutional changes. The implicit assumption of general agreement on an operational generic concept of a monetary standard, which had been true of classical economics, was apparently inherited with classical terminology. The growing obsolescence of the assumption generally escaped notice. Therefore, explicit identification of the genus, monetary standard, as distinct from its species, did not appear to be necessary.

Different views of the generic idea developed implicitly. All of them are irrelevant to present facts and inconsistent with modern value theory. The incompatibility with modern theory escaped attention because neoclassical misconstructions of classical monetary theory had produced a theoretical dichotomy which appeared to immunize monetary theory against the postclassical developments in value theory. Recent reinterpretations of the concept of a monetary standard have failed to reestablish its former relevance to policy. The difficulty is not removed by the present spreading practice of simply ignoring the term "monetary standard." The idea of a standard is probably as necessary in the field of money as in any other. Modern policy controversies are rendered unresolvable by implicit allegiance of the contestants to different notions of a monetary standard, none of which seems really relevant. Isolation and resolution of the substantive issues relative to monetary policy require a concept of a monetary standard that is compatible with the contemporary institutional and intellectual environment.

The following pages will demonstrate these propositions and suggest a workable concept of a monetary standard for the modern economy. It is hoped that a modest contribution will thereby be made to elimination of certain terminological obstructions to monetary analysis and clarification of some of the substantive issues in the realm of monetary policy.

ORGANIZATION OF THE STUDY

Chapter two demonstrates the unworkability of the received concepts of a monetary standard. The preclassical view of the standard as the material constituting standard money was not only consistent with contemporaneous economic facts and theory, but also relevant to concurrent policy issues. The same was true of the classical interpretation of the monetary standard as the material comprising the standard of value. But neither concept is presently useful. At best, the preclassical construction is, in the modern setting, an empty legalism of no substantive significance—benign but relatively meaningless. At worst, it represents a confusion of monetary policy with the monetary standard. For example, the provisions of the International Monetary Fund Agreement committing each member nation to define its monetary unit in terms of gold and to limit variations in the prices of gold and foreign exchange have been construed as establishing a "new" international gold standard. Recognition that members of the Fund pay little, if any, heed to gold in determining domestic monetary policy has inspired the notion that there is a categorical distinction between international and domestic monetary standards. The supposition that a nation's domestic standard may be different from, and unrelated to, the international monetary standard to which it is presumed to subscribe is the unfortunate consequence of confounding a gold policy with a gold standard. This confusion is the root of today's vexing monetary-policy dilemmas. On the other hand, the classical concept of the monetary standard as the material constituting the standard of value is not only irrelevant to present policy issues, but also incompatible with present economic theory and institutions. The postclassical image of a monetary standard, as distinct from the other two versions, was simply a combination of the preclassical and classical. It represented an at-

11

tempt to accommodate the idea to the conceptual and theoretical confusion that typified the transitions: (1) from specie to deposit currency, (2) from classical to modern value theory, and (3) from classical to neoclassical monetary theory. Completion of these transitions then brought a reversion to classical and preclassical concepts of a monetary standard—often a confusion rather than a combination of the two—which presently constitute serious obstacles to rational monetary analysis and realistic policy decisions.

Chapter three shows that the classical concept of a monetary standard was rendered obsolete by: (1) a gradual broadening of "money" to embrace all forms of credit media of exchange, including bank deposits, and (2) a modification of value theory, eliminating the notion of intrinsic value on which the classical concept of a "standard measure of value" was based.

Chapter four resolves the paradox in the retention of the classical concept of a standard measure of value by revealing the neoclassical dichotomization of economic theory, which appeared to render developments in value theory irrelevant to monetary theory. It will be argued, moreover, that misinterpretation of Jevons reinforced the immunization of monetary theory against postclassical developments in value theory.

Chapter five illustrates the confusion of monetary objectives, policies, and standards caused by continued use of obsolete concepts of a monetary standard. The resulting ambiguity of specific alternative monetary standards is offered as a basic cause of the communication breakdown in the area of money.

Chapter six demonstrates: (1) the unworkability of the recently suggested concept of a monetary standard as the principle limiting the money supply, and (2) the workability—as well as the widespread implicit use—of the concept as the criterion of monetary policy.

Chapter seven briefly summarizes the argument and develops some implications for the present and future.

II

CONCEPTS OF A
MONETARY STANDARD
IMPLIED IN
DISCUSSIONS OF
SPECIFIC STANDARDS

The absence of a limiting genus permitted proliferation not only of standard species, but also of descriptive tomes, tracts, and texts. Presumably, any person who purports to describe, defend, or attack a particular phenomenon has some idea, however nebulous, about the nature of the general class which includes his subject. This chapter will examine the received concepts of a monetary standard implicit in past discussions of specific (gold, bimetallic, paper, etc.) standards.

During the nineteenth-century bimetallic controversy, S. Dana Horton concluded that writers on money had imputed nine different meanings to the term "monetary standard." [1] He then demonstrated the unworkability of the classification by showing that it would put Holland, for example, on five standards at once. [2] Such a demonstration was possible because the list represented an overclassification with overlapping categories. Actually, there were not that many interpretations of the concept. Although each one could be supported by isolated statements to be found in the literature, consideration of contexts compels reduction (by combination) of Horton's list to four: (1) the fineness of standard metal, (2) the material constituting standard money, (3) the material used as the standard of value, and (4) the material making up both standard money and the standard of value.[3]

The first can be dispensed with quickly. The fineness of standard metal[4] was an issue only during the experimentation to determine the minimum percentage of alloy required to produce economical and practicable circulating coins of precious metals. The question was settled prior to the currency controversies of the nineteenth century.[5] The lack of a unanimous decision among nations—England's "legal standard" being eleven-twelfths,[6] whereas that of the United States was nine-tenths[7]—caused no difficulty. Par values were calculated fundamentally by the relative quantities of pure monetary metal; the value of the alloy was, in any case, negligible. Moreover, the fineness of "standard bullion" was never a serious issue because under a metallic standard the latitude was insufficient to permit serious controversy. In any event, acceptance of the term "paper standard" precludes interpretation of "monetary standard" as the fineness of "standard metal." The remainder of this chapter will be devoted to an examination of the other three interpretations.

THE MATERIAL CONSTITUTING STANDARD MONEY

The conception of the monetary standard as the material constituting standard money[8] has, perhaps, the oldest and the newest authoritative support. It was the received preclassical doctrine, and the waning of classical influence has brought its revival. This

14

version was the natural outgrowth of the early conception of the standard as the fineness of monetary metal.[9] Since the fine content of standard bullion had become traditional by the time modern monetary systems were established, the basic monetary problem was the standard-bullion content of the standard coin.[10] Preclassical legislators therefore viewed the problem of the monetary standard as that of defining the monetary unit in terms of standard metal—i.e., defining standard money.[11]

Evidence of this interpretation. This interpretation ended with the opening of the classical school and did not clearly reappear until the 1930's.[12] It is a simple, mechanistic construction, and its reemergence reflected a desire for order amidst the wreckage of the depression. It appealed to, and consequently was first revived by, the legalistically minded [13] and mechanically oriented.[14] They were supported by those who were unhappy about the fluctuations in the goods value of commodity money but too orthodox to consider the heretical alternative of cutting money loose from the commodity. The idea of a "standard" in the realm of money was preserved by applying it to values of moneys instead of goods. This meant that the monetary standard was not so much the standard for measuring the relative values of goods, as it was the standard for measuring the relative values of moneys, domestically or internationally.[15] Despite the economic chaos of the depression decade, the money value of moneys was "manageable." Indeed, at least domestically, it was—as a standard should be—fixed.[16]

Moreover, in the face of conceptual and theoretical controversies arising out of the depression experience, interpreting the monetary standard as the substance of standard money apparently appeared to more and more authorities as the only means of preserving the concept. Increasing awareness that credit money was money, not just a substitute for money, raised a question as to whether the causal sequence of value ran from gold to money—as had been traditionally assumed—or from money to gold. Associated with this question were unresolved theoretical issues which raised doubts about the validity (even the meaning) of

15

a metallic, much less paper, standard of value. Construing the monetary standard as the material comprising standard money no doubt appeared to many modern critics as a means of separating the mechanism of the monetary system from the substance of monetary theory. It was, perhaps, felt that in this way the resolution of theoretical issues would be obstructed least by terminological difficulties and institutional biases.

All this is implicit in the literature. In some recent instances this view of the monetary standard has been virtually explicit [17] and, in some, actually explicit. For example, F. M. Taylor defined "the monetary standard" as *that thing the value of which fixes the value of the monetary unit."* [18] Likewise, Major B. Foster introduced his chapter on "Monetary Standards" with the following statement: "The term, *monetary standard, refers to the type of standard money* used in a monetary system. Thus, if in a particular country gold is the money or material in which credits are ultimately redeemable, that country is said to be on a gold standard." [19] George Walter Woodworth defined "the ultimate monetary standard" as "a basic quantum of value to which the value of the monetary unit is always equated." [20] Since the concept of marginal utility precludes the notion of a "quantum of value," the latter term can mean only a quantum of a valuable commodity or group of commodities. Therefore, this definition boils down to the material constituting standard money.[21] Lawrence Smith said, "The standard in a monetary system is that with which all forms of money are, in general, maintained at a parity." [22] This means the same thing.

Thus, the preclassical view of the monetary standard has returned under distinguished auspices, seeking our allegiance. Before we climb on the bandwagon with whatever instruments we have at hand, let us pause to look at the score and listen to the band. Was the music written for modern instruments, and are the artists following the composition? In short, how well does this interpretation of the monetary standard serve its purpose? What *is* its purpose? The purpose of any generic concept is to identify the common characteristic by which all varieties of

16

the phenomenon may be recognized and distinguished from specimens of a different order. It must enable us to accomplish both inclusion and exclusion. The "standard-money" construction of the monetary standard is deficient in both respects.

Limited application. This conception of a monetary standard fails to identify the distinctive characteristic common to all monetary arrangements generally known as standards. Moreover, it has been ignored—even by its professed proponents—in the process of describing the various species of standards. Being of antique origin, it applied very well to the museum pieces known as the "traditional (pure) gold standard" and "bimetallism" of the same vintage. But the standards considered in contemporary discussions have, for some time, had little if anything to do with "standard money."

For instance, standard money is wholly unrelated to the "tabular standard" and the "limping standard." These standards do *not* "take their names from" their respective standard moneys. If they did, the standard moneys would be "tables" and "limpings," respectively! [23] And these "standards" have been an integral part of the literature since the first and third quarters of the last century [24] —long before the revival of the definition of a monetary standard under discussion. Actually, neither the originators nor the propagators of the "tabular standard" had any idea of making any change whatsoever in the existing standard money.[25] The plan had nothing to do with standard money and would have operated, for better or worse, whatever the nature of the latter.[26] The "limping standard" did arise out of confusion about what was standard money during the transition from bimetallic to gold standards,[27] but this conceptual cripple merely obscured what was already confused. And the signification of the term "limping standard" was progressively beclouded by the multiplicity of meanings that became attached to it.[28] It is no wonder that exponents of the pre-post classical conception of the monetary standard had difficulty with the "tabular" and "limping" standards.[29] These notions were inferences from an alien premise.[30]

17

The "compensated standard" gave the same people trouble for the same reason. Its authors, conceiving the monetary standard as the standard of value (instead of standard money), sought to stabilize the standard of value by destandardizing money.[31] Consequently, the plan had *no standard money*.[32] The gold monetary unit was to be made variable in terms of gold in order to stabilize its value in terms of goods. While the innovators of the plan, because of their premise, could logically call this a monetary standard,[33] those who interpreted the monetary standard in terms of standard money could not. Some did, however, and involved themselves in the inevitable contradictions to be expected from the violence done to their concept of a standard.[34] If the monetary standard means the material comprising standard money, the proposal to stabilize the price level by varying the commodity content of the monetary unit cannot be called a monetary standard because, in such a scheme, there is no standard money.

Moreover, what *is* standard money in the (1) gold bullion standard,[35] (2) "limited" gold bullion standard (in all its unlimited varieties),[36] (3) gold exchange standard,[37] (4) gold settlement standard,[38] (5) gold parity standard,[39] (6) gold reserve standard,[40] (7) parallel standard,[41] (8) currency exchange standard,[42] (9) commodity reserve standard,[43] (10) stable-price-level standard (also called "price index" or "index number" standard),[44] (11) multiple standard,[45] (12) interest standard,[46] (13) credit standard,[47] and (14) labor standard? [48]

Even if the standard money of each of the above alleged standards could be identified, there would still be a fatal flaw in the interpretation of the monetary standard as the substance of standard money. Such a construction of the concept limits it to commodity (e.g., metallic) standards. There is a fundamental inconsistency in the attempt to include the paper standard: Metallic standard money is defined as a specific quantity of metal, but paper standard money is *not* defined as a specific quantity of paper.[49] Consequently, while descriptions of metallic standards are positive, characterizations of paper standards are nega-

18

tive, merely indicating what they are not.[50] The "paper standard," therefore, has no positive meaning. "Paper" merely connotes the abstract nature of an inconvertible monetary unit. It is not made of paper. It is not made of anything.[51]

Standard money is simply irrelevant to the paper, or inconvertible, standard. The term "standard money" originated as a means of distinguishing full-bodied coins from circulating media of exchange which were not full-bodied equivalents of the monetary unit. At first, the latter were coins of different metals having no fixed mint values and, therefore, circulating at their market values. The British Coinage Act of 1816 provided for token coins,[52] and the practice was later copied by other nations. By provisions well known to the conversant reader, token coins were made generally acceptable at face values exceeding the worth of their metal content. Thenceforward, "standard money" became merely the opposite of "token money."[53] "We must," said Jevons, "distinguish between coins according as they serve for *standard money* or for *token money*."[54] Now, in substance, paper money is the most token of all circulating media.[55] Therefore, under a "paper standard," all money is token.[56]

If all money is token, none is standard.[57] If the monetary standard is the material comprising standard money, and there is no standard money —then there is *no monetary standard*.[58] Thus, this concept of a monetary standard appears to be inapplicable to most of the postdepression monetary world.

The only alternative treatment of standard money under a paper standard is even less congenial to the standard-money interpretation of the monetary standard. All varieties of inconvertible paper money may be called standard, instead of token.[59] Consequently, this "analysis" of the paper standard reduces to the absurdity that the monetary standard is money.[60]

Not the basis of classification actually used. It is clear from what has been said that the standard-money concept of the monetary standard has not been generally used as the basis of identifying specific standards. This is not surprising as there are competing concepts of a monetary standard. What *is* surprising is its frequent neglect by the very persons who express or imply their allegiance to this concept. The particular standards discussed often have little, if any, correspondence with what has been professed (at least, by implication) to be the nature of a monetary standard.

Space does not permit a complete catalogue of these discrepancies, but the following sample is offered in evidence. The gold reserve standard is not directly related to gold standard money.[61] Even on the assumption that a paper standard is a legitimate offspring of the parent genus, a host of inconsistencies appear in specific cases. Descriptions and classifications of paper standards often involve an implicit substitution of "management" for the substance of standard money as the basis of comparison.[62] Moreover, what is managed is not just standard money, but nonstandard money as well; and the management is presumed to be unrelated to that which is assumed to be standard money.[63] Furthermore, distinguishing the "modified gold standard" from the "paper standard" on the basis of the point of view (international versus national, respectively) entirely ignores the concept on which differentiation of standards is purported to be based.[64] For exponents of the standard-money conception of the monetary standard, such labels as "drifting paper standard," [65] "stable-price-level standard" (also called "price index standard"),[66] "labor standard," [67] "discretionary standard," [68] and "fluctuating standard" [69] are contradictions of terms.

The mechanical, pre-classical construction of the monetary standard was reactivated as a benchmark in the post-1929 monetary flux. The concept, however, had little relevance to the "new economics." [70] Yet, there is an understandable reluctance to abandon it before a demonstrably superior replacement has been found. Sir Dennis Robertson has implicitly concluded that we can no longer attach any precise significance to the term "monetary standard" other than this purely mechanical and substantively meaningless one.[71] Before accepting this discouraging conclusion, let us explore the alternatives.

20

THE MATERIAL CONSTITUTING THE STANDARD OF VALUE

One alternative is the concept of a monetary standard as the material constituting the standard of value. Another is the combination of the two interpretations into a third conception of the monetary standard as the material comprising both standard money *and* the standard of value. Since the first concept (already discussed) does not necessarily imply the second, the combination is also a separate and distinct possibility. The standard-of-value conception of the standard will be discussed in this section, and the dualistic concept will be the subject of the following section of this chapter.

Distinction from previous concept. Although they are frequently confused, this construction of the monetary standard must be sharply distinguished from the previous one if the metamorphosis of the concept is to be understood. The term "standard (unit) of value" is used here in the normal sense of a standard by which relative values of goods are measured.[72] Application of the term to the measurement of the values of different moneys in terms of each other (instead of in terms of goods), on the other hand, simply implies the interpretation of the monetary standard as the material comprising standard money, instead of the standard of value. Such was the customary preclassical usage of the term "standard (unit) of value," [73] which was reflected in the provision of the United States Constitution conferring "upon Congress the power to coin money and to 'regulate the value thereof.' " [74] This was also the connotation of the language in Alexander Hamilton's report and the resulting Coinage Act of 1792.[75] Subsequent American monetary legislation was ambiguous enough to permit the synonymously used terms "unit of value" and "standard of value" to be interpreted either way.[76] A similar ambivalence has permeated economic literature; consequently the terms can be understood only in context, which in turn has changed with the nature of economic problems. Clear cases of applying "standard of value" to moneys (domestic or foreign) instead of goods are, however, discernible.[77]

21

Moreover, a standard of value for goods is not necessarily implied by a standard of value for moneys. Those who look upon standard money as the standard for rating different kinds of money usually imply that money, per se, or simply the monetary unit, is the standard by which the values of goods are measured.[78] Occasionally, this distinction is made explicit.[79] This treatment limits the problem of the monetary standard to one of mechanism (i.e., laws or policies) leaving the substantive issues of the goods value of money to the jurisdiction of monetary theory.[80]

On the other hand, criticisms of the gold standard as an "unstable standard"[81] implied the premised conception of the monetary standard as the standard of value (for goods), not as standard money (basis for rating moneys), because the latter, under the gold standard, was admittedly fixed. The same premise was implied by the orthodox defense of the gold standard as the least unstable of alternative standards.[82] These arguments indicate that something about the standard of value may change without any change in standard money, and this in turn implies a distinction between standard money and the standard of value.[83]

From these premises, several other differentiations are inferred. Proposals for "regulating the gold standard" to make it more stable obviously referred to the standard of value, not to standard money,[84] because gold standard money (defined as a fixed quantity of gold) was stable by definition. Irving Fisher argued that the standard of value could be indirectly stabilized by modifying standard money.[85] Others, however, have denied even this much connection between standard money and the standard of value, arguing that the former can be changed without affecting the latter.[86] Such reasoning leads inevitably to the possibility of a standard of value without any standard money: "It is theoretically possible to have as our standard *some commodity* not fit to be used as money at all."[87] Occasionally the standard of value is explicitly distinguished from standard money.[88]

Therefore, according to some writers, not only are the "standard of value" and

22

"standard money" different concepts; they are not even necessarily related. Thus, the "standard of value" and "standard money" versions of the monetary standard are to be distinguished, not confused.

Evidence of this interpretation. This concept has been illustrated by one of the rare exceptions to the general failure to delineate the genus monetary standard: "In a monetary sense the term standard refers to the substance (such as gold) to the value of which the value of money is adjusted, or according to the value of which the value of money is controlled." [89] This view has been implicit in the bulk of classical and neoclassical literature. Some modern analyses seem to support this concept of a monetary standard. It is implied in Webster's definition of "standard" and in extant encyclopedia articles on various specific standards.[90] It has been, perhaps, the most durable facet of classical doctrine.

Although preclassical roots are identifiable,[91] general acceptance of this interpretation of a monetary standard originated with the English bullion controversy of the Napoleonic era. The depreciation of the inconvertible pound shifted monetary discussions from mechanism to substance.[92] It was in these debates that the first headmaster of the classical school was prepared for his later responsibilities. The monetary standard was clearly and unequivocally interpreted by David Ricardo in terms of the *commodity* used as the *standard of value for goods:*

> No plan can possibly be devised which will maintain money at an absolutely uniform value, because it will always be subject to those variations to which the commodity itself is subject, which has been fixed upon as the standard.

> While the precious metals continued to be the standard of our currency, money must necessarily undergo the same variation in value as those metals. It was the comparative steadiness in value of the precious metals, for periods of some duration, which probably was the cause of the preference given to them in all countries, as *the standard by which to measure the value of other things.*[93]

Ricardo was not the first to explain the monetary standard in this manner. It had been shaping up as standard bullionist

23

doctrine since Walter Boyd's *Letter to the Right Honourable William Pitt, on the Influence of the Stoppage of Issues in Specie.*[94] Consequently, it was reflected in the *Bullion Report* of 1810 [95] and echoed by contemporaries as well as followers of Ricardo.[96]

Moreover, the bullionist concept of a monetary standard was not questioned by many of the antibullionists.[97] The two schools differed categorically in the species recommended, but *not* in the genus commonly recognized.[98] Antibullionists generally opposed the gold standard *because they regarded it as a variable standard of value.*[99] They naïvely thought that the standard of value could be fixed, or stabilized, like standards of physical measurement, simply by dissociation from any commodity, the value of which necessarily fluctuated with its supply and demand: "A natural fixed standard of value in exchange, or price, is impossible for the plain reason, that the market value of all things is constantly fluctuating. But an artificial fixed standard is perfectly practicable. This is obtained by adopting an ideal [i.e., abstract] measure, such as the pound sterling." [100] The recurrence, tenacity, and popularity of such views as this led James Mill to observe, "There is, unfortunately, something extremely fallacious in the study of money." [101] Indeed there was, but neither he nor his successors succeeded in making its exposure manifest; consequently it continued to prevent a resolution of the standard issue throughout this and subsequent monetary controversies. The fallacy was—and still is—that of "equivocation": the ambivalent use of a word capable of a double meaning. The word is "money." And its dual meaning includes: (1) the abstract monetary unit, and (2) the concrete embodiment of the monetary unit in a medium of exchange (and standard of value? Aye, there's the rub!).[102]

Classicists, keeping these two meanings separate throughout the bullion and currency controversies, insisted on the necessity for a commodity standard of value. Antibullionists and the extremist wing of the banking school, dissatisfied with the performance of a commodity (metallic) standard of value, sought its elimination and the absorption of the second meaning of money by the first. This appeared to classicists as an absurdity arising from ignorance not only of political economy, but also of language.[103] Ricardo joined the issue:

> This idea of a currency without a specific standard was, I believe, first advanced by Sir James Steuart,[104] but no one has yet been able to offer any test by which we could ascertain the uniformity in the value of a money so constituted. Those who supported this opinion did not see, that such a currency, instead of being invariable, was subject to the greatest variations,—that the only use of a standard is to regulate the quantity, and by the quantity the value of the currency—and that without a standard it would be exposed to all the fluctuations to which the ignorance or the interests of the issuers might subject it.[105]

Through default of a convincing antibullionist answer, a bullionist victory was crowned by the British Coinage Act of 1816, which officially named gold as the "Standard Measure of Value, and equivalent for Property." [106] Though nineteenth-century English law and its interpretation never deviated from this position,[107] the issue of the standard lived on through the currency controversy of the mid-nineteenth century. While the banking school included remnants of the antibullionist sect, the debate between the banking and currency schools generally turned on the proper implementation of the gold standard in the existent "mixed currency system." Notwithstanding their many differences, both sides agreed that the gold standard meant that a specified amount of gold was the standard for measuring the relative values of goods.[108]

The United States greenback followed the pattern of the inconvertible pound and, perhaps because the issue had been thrashed out in the earlier English experience, with much less discussion during the period of inconvertibility. A metallic standard was eventually restored and, as in the British case, it was generally construed as a metallic standard of value.[109] The American debate about resumption of specie payments and its consequences was not so much between metallic- and paper-standard advocates as between the proponents of monometallism and bi-

25

metallism, respectively. But again, there was general agreement on the concept of the monetary standard as the material constituting the standard of value. The protagonists differed simply in what they recommended to discharge this function. Monometallists wanted gold to be the sole standard of value.[110] Bimetallists advocated the use of both gold and silver.[111] The controversy culminated in the Gold Standard Act of 1900.[112] The report accompanying the House Bill for this legislation explained its purpose as follows:

> It is the intent of this bill to remove the 'limping' element, and to establish beyond doubt the *gold standard,* already adopted by the other great nations of the world.

> Why should it be so adopted? Perhaps the reason can not be better given than to quote from the able preliminary report of the Monetary Commission of 1898:

> "There must be some *standard of value.* The standard *must have a market value as a commodity* independently of any governmental fiat and of all legal-tender laws; it must be durable . . . , homogeneous [etc.] . . . Gold alone fulfills these conditions. The civilized world has, therefore, determined that the *standard shall be gold.* No government, however powerful, can in fact reverse that determination, or, without injury to the interests of all its people, attempt to establish any other *standard of value.*" [113]

Thus, the American lawmakers viewed their Gold Standard Act as formal recognition and legal establishment of gold as the standard of value.

Bimetallism never became the political issue in England that it was in the United States. Nevertheless, the din of the English currency quarrel included bimetallic overtones. However, the common agreement on the concept of a monetary standard was not disturbed.[114] English interest in the bimetallic question was more theoretical than political, and the discussion was, as might be expected, conducted on a more sober, academic level. The *gold standard of value* was upheld by such distinguished Englishmen as John Stuart Mill,[115] George Joachim Goschen,[116] W. Stanley Jevons,[117] John Elliot Cairnes,[118] S. Dana Horton,[119] Walter Bagehot,[120] Robert Giffen,[121] Henry Farquhar,[122] and the Right Honourable Lord Thomas Henry Farrer.[123] The *bimetallic standard of value* mustered an equally impressive roster of supporters [124] including H. S. Foxwell,[125] J. Shield Nicholson,[126] and Alfred Marshall.[127]

When the productivity of the new Alaskan and South African gold mines eliminated the bimetallic case against gold, the monetary standard ceased to be an issue. Attention was turned to completing the structure and perfecting the techniques of central banking. Sufficient progress had been made by the outbreak of World War I to be of material assistance in war finance. The postwar adjustment revived the monetary-standard question—or, rather, raised the following questions about the gold standard (the only alternative seriously considered): When, with what modifications, and at what parities should it be restored? These questions were answered in time for a few years (or few months, in the case of some countries) of "new era" exhilaration. The point here, however, is simply that throughout the changing scene of the twentieth century's first three decades one thing remained the same. That was the implicit conception of the monetary standard as the material constituting the standard of value.[128] It was not questioned by even the unorthodox critics of the time.[129]

The collapse of the international gold standard in 1931 produced no sharp general break in economic literature. Reflection on the implications took time. The general retreat to the simpler mechanical and legalistic conception of the monetary standard as the substance of standard money did not begin till the middle 'thirties.[130] An alternative interpretation based on classical premises came into fashion about the same time,[131] and a new monetary heterodoxy soon developed.[132] Meanwhile, the publication pipeline continued to disgorge traditional material through the depression decade. True to tradition, it faithfully echoed the classical standard-of-value construction of a monetary standard.[133] Some stalwarts held fast to the classical concept through the depression, war, and postwar readjustment.[134]

Limitations and inconsistencies of application. Attempts to encompass modern monetary standards by the classical concept of a standard in-

27

volve fundamental inconsistencies. In this classical frame of reference, the notion of a "paper standard" remains the same contradiction of terms that the classical economists exposed over a century ago.[135] Talk about metallic and paper standards of value contains a basic inconsistency: A metallic standard of value is concrete, whereas a so-called "paper standard of value" is abstract. A "paper standard of value" can mean only the absence of a concrete standard of value.[136] Attempts to make something positive out of this negation have generally been inferences from the implicit premise of the basic antibullionist error. This false premise was the confusion of the standard of value and unit of account.[137] The distinction, implicit in classical literature,[138] had been made explicit by Jevons' separation of "standard" and "measure" of value.[139] He, Walker, and others had sensed that what was used as a measure of value (for simultaneous comparison of values) was immaterial. Anything would serve equally well since, by definition, its value did not vary during use. This, they pointed out, was not the area within which the serious monetary problems of society were to be found.[140] Basic monetary difficulties arise from changes in the value of money through time. These problems fall within the province of the standard of value, not the Jevonsonian "measure of value," or unit of account. Unfortunately, Walker's modification of Jevons' terminology tended to obscure the fundamental distinction Jevons had made explicit.[141] The ultimate absurdity of the attempt to make something positive out of the negative notion of an inconvertible paper standard was reached with the statement that such paper money "became its own standard."[142]

The bimetallic controversy involved less serious, but nonetheless troublesome, difficulties. Despite interpretation of the monetary standard by both sides as the metal or metals constituting the standard of value, the opponents' terminology was not always consistent with this common premise. Perhaps one reason for the triumph of the gold standard was the fact that the case for a single standard of value was simple, obvious, and logical, whereas the argument for a dual standard of value was complex[143] and required some sophistication and considerable

28

subtlety of reasoning to avoid being identified with the absurdity of a "double standard of value."[144] Although it was easier for monometallists to be consistent, their characterization of bimetallism as a double standard,[145] failing to demonstrate a premium on either metal,[146] often appeared to mistake an alternating circulation for an alternating standard.[147] On the other hand, its supporters, failing to interpret bimetallism consistently as a *joint* standard,[148] were often caught in the terminological trap set for them by their adversaries: Many bimetallists, ironically, adopted the term "double standard" as a synonym for bimetallism.[149] In short, neither of the opposing camps in this battle of standards consistently applied their common conception of the monetary standard to their differences about specific standards.

The notion of a "multiple standard," which grew out of the bimetallic controversy, led to another inconsistency in applying the standard-of-value conception of the monetary standard to immediate monetary problems. The more logically minded bimetallists were inexorably led to symmetallism as a means of avoiding the pitfalls of a "double" or "alternating" standard of value and achieving a true joint standard.[150] Marshall left his proposed plan open-ended for possible inclusion of other storable, portable commodities of "universal demand."[151] The desire for a stable standard of value then led logically to the composite commodity-reserve standard.[152] The composite of commodities could be regarded as the concrete standard of value. However, only a minority of those desiderating a stable price level recommended this path to the objective. The majority interpretation of the "multiple standard" was merely an index number of the prices of a number of staple commodities.[153] This variety of standard does not, like the commodity-reserve standard, follow as a logical development from mono- and bimetallism. The latter are concrete standards of value; the index-number standard is not. The abstract "multiple standard" is therefore as incompatible with the standard-of-value conception of the monetary standard as the paper standard. Indeed, what is the difference between the "multiple standard" and the "paper standard"? The obvious overlapping of these

29

so-called standards reveals that the standard of value is not the criterion by which they are classified as monetary standards.

Another obstacle to logical classification of monetary standards has been the "tabular standard." This concept was developed by those implicitly defining the monetary standard as the material comprising the standard of value.[154] The "tabular standard of value"[155] is, therefore, a misnomer. The tabular standard was not conceived as a standard of value.[156] Its originators had no more intention of disturbing the standard of value than of changing the standard money.[157] The tabular standard was merely a device to permit equitable adjustment of time contracts, compensating for the inevitable variations in the goods value of the commodity (e.g., gold and/or silver) used as the standard of value.[158] It was suggested as an alternative to abandonment of the metallic standard in the quest for equity between debtors and creditors.[159] Jevons' use of the term "tabular standard of value" was not inconsistent[160] because this translated into the modern term, tabular "standard of deferred payments." By "standard of value" Jevons meant what has come to be known (since Walker) as "standard of deferred payments."[161] His label for what is generally "known" today as the "standard of value" was "measure of value."[162] Even after Walker's alteration of Jevons' terminological innovation, Jevons' terminology was often followed without any implication that the tabular standard was a "standard of value" in the Jevonsonian sense.[163] Confusion resulted from the failure to adhere consistently to the lexicons of either Jevons or Walker.[164] About the turn of the century, the relevant terms of both came to be ignored by some writers, who applied the tabular standard to the "permanent" standard of value, relevant to time contracts, as distinct from the "temporary" standard of value, pertinent to all other transactions.[165] Identification of the "tabular standard" with the "standard of value" then came about in two ways: (1) by adopting Jevons' term, "tabular standard of value," without a realization of its restricted meaning, or (2) by abandoning the artificial and arbitrary distinction between "temporary"

30

and "permanent" "standards of value." The first cause was inexcusable; the second, inevitable. But, in either case, the result was deplorable.

There seems to have been an irresistible urge to convert the tabular standard into the monetary standard. By connotative association, the abstract index number, known as a tabular standard,[166] became confused with the concrete commodities represented by the index number. This association without conception resulted in the mysterious birth of the "multiple standard." "It is," said Irving Fisher, "but a short step from such contracts in single-commodity standards to contracts in *multiple-commodity standards*. Under these the money payments are adjusted according to an index number, *or, to use the earlier designation, according to the 'tabular standard.'* "[167] Robert Giffen invested the abstraction with "substance" in the following manner: "A *fourth* kind of imperfect *monetary standard* . . . is where a selection is made of a *standard substance that is not an independent commodity* like gold and silver, having a natural use apart from money, but which is formed *ad hoc* by a compound of the two metals, gold and silver, or by a *compound of many commodities as in the tabular* standard of Jevons."[168] This appeared to effect the transition of the tabular standard from an abstract index number to a concrete standard of value composed of a number of commodities. M. K. Graham then completed the process by demonstrating that the "national tabular standard of value" was what later Grahams called the "commodity-reserve standard."[169] Although the latter could be interpreted as a standard of value, few followed the line of reasoning to this logical conclusion. Most of those who embarked on this journey arrived only at the paradoxical conclusion that an abstract index number is a concrete, composite commodity standard of value.[170]

Other inconsistencies may be noted in the application of the idea that the monetary standard is the material of which the standard of value is composed. First, the designation of the "compensated" monetary-unit proposal[171] as a "compensated standard"[172] is a contradiction of terms.[173] Second, talk of "control" of the gold

31

standard is inconsistent with this interpretation of a monetary standard.[174] Third, the notion of a "limited gold bullion standard" is equally inconsistent with the basic concept.[175] It differs from the second anomaly only in that it envisages control of the value of the standard of value by manipulation of the demand for, rather than the supply of, gold. Gold certainly ceases to be a standard of value when its own value is artificially manipulated in accordance with some other criterion.

Not the basis of classification actually used. The discrepancies already noted have demonstrated that monetary standards have not been consistently identified as species of the genus "standard of value" even by those who appeared to profess this conception of a monetary standard. Inconsistencies between the generic idea and its alleged manifestations—nonexistent among the early classicists—have progressively increased since the classical period. An important contributing factor was the growing desire for the realization of a stable price level, *vide:* "Stable general prices are essential to normal industrial activity. Any monetary system which seeks to realize either rising or falling general prices must of necessity result in disaster. The general social and industrial effects of rising or falling prices are an evil . . . Besides, a monetary system which seeks to realize either rising or falling general prices is arbitrary inasmuch as there is *no means of determining whether or not the actual standard conforms to the theoretical one.*" [176] This statement reveals that by the turn of the century the concept of a monetary standard, which had been abundantly clear to the classicists, was becoming as fuzzy as its application.

Classical authorities had assumed that price-level stability was unattainable. They had been willing to accept the nearest approach to it that seemed realizable, through the selection of the commodity most stable in value (gold or silver) as the standard of value.[177] Dissatisfaction with this degree of price-level stability led to monetary innovations. Such intellectual and institutional experimentation was not bad, per se, but attempts to carry them forward within an uncongenial classical conceptual framework resulted in inescapable inconsistencies. Neoclassical and modern writers could not resolve the discrepancy between their

32

classical interpretation of the monetary standard as a commodity standard of value, on the one hand, and their acceptance, if not recommendation, of the anticlassical notion of an abstract standard, on the other hand. Thus, alleged abstract standards—such as paper,[178] tabular, price index, or multiple [179]—could not, despite valiant efforts, be brought within the scope of the received conception of the monetary standard. Nor could these alleged standards be clearly distinguished. The result was distinctions without differences and differences without distinctions.

Reductio ad absurdum. Finally, this conception of a monetary standard reduces to an absurdity: [180] The monetary standard is the material constituting the standard of value (major premise). But money is the standard of value (minor premise). Therefore, the monetary standard is, simply, money (conclusion). If the monetary standard is merely money, there has been a lot of shouting to no purpose. The critical step in the above syllogism is the minor premise. That an impressive number of authorities believe it to be true cannot be denied. Some have said so in terms that cannot be misunderstood.[181] The unmistakable implication permeates neoclassical and modern literature.[182]

Is there no escape from this absurdity? Yes, there is a way out—by maintaining that only standard money can serve as the standard of value.[183] But this escape route is not open to anyone who distinguishes the standard of value from standard money.[184] It is available only to those who identify standard money and the standard of value. These authors and this means of salvaging the classical concept of the monetary standard will be considered in the next section.

THE MATERIAL CONSTITUTING BOTH STANDARD MONEY AND THE STANDARD OF VALUE

The received concepts of the monetary standard as the physical substance of *either*

33

standard money or the standard of value imply the possibility of a third concept in the form of a combination of the two. However, neither of the first two necessarily implies the third. Differences between the former have been pointed out.[185] This third possibility would narrow the generic concept and reduce the variety of its species because, as already demonstrated, some monetary systems embrace no specific standard of value and others contain no standard money.[186] Since most people interested in the subject have focused primarily on one of the aspects, the double-barreled conception of the monetary standard has not inspired as many supporters as its alternatives.

Evidence of this interpretation. In view of the mechanically oriented "standard-money" feature, it is not surprising to find authoritative preclassical support for this interpretation of the monetary standard.[187] For the same reason, the standard battles of the nineteenth century furnished little evidence of this view.[188] The "combined operation" approach to the monetary standard did not really get started until the conclusion of the bimetallic controversy. Thereafter, statements clearly implying this position are discernible.[189] Moreover, authors who sometimes imply that the monetary standard is the material constituting standard money and at other times imply that it is the thing used as the standard of value [190] may mean that the monetary standard is that which is both.[191] However, "proof" is not limited to such conjecture. Recent literature has furnished an explicit statement of the concept: "The *concept of a 'monetary standard' implies* that there is some form of *standard money* into which all other types of money are convertible and, being freely convertible, are thereby kept at par with the standard money. The concept *also implies that people evaluate the exchange value of goods and services in terms of the standard money;* they 'look behind' the convertible money which is being used to effect exchanges to the intrinsic worth of the standard money commodity or commodities." [192]

Escape from the reductio ad absurdum? The concept of a monetary standard as the material constituting both standard money and the standard

34

of value appears to circumvent the reduction to absurdity. It would seem possible to infer from this concept that performance of the standard-of-value function of money is limited to standard money. The inference, usually combined with a corollary proposition that only the medium-of-exchange function is performed by all kinds of money, has been more popular among neoclassical monetary experts than its supporting premise.[193] If the standard-of-value function is not discharged by all forms of money, the dual conception of a monetary standard does not reduce to the absurdity that the monetary standard is money. But, is the alleged distinction between standard and nonstandard money real enough to permit this evasion of the absurdity? Serious doubts immediately arise.

First, the distinction between "standard" and "nonstandard" money is absolutely meaningless—in fact, nonexistent—in either a pure commodity money system or a paper standard.[194] Although the former is confined to primitive societies, some form of the latter has become typical of "developing" as well as "developed" economies. Consequently, application of the distinction is severely limited in the world of today.

Second, even if applicable conditions can be found in the contemporary scene, the importance of the difference between "standard" and "credit" money is questionable. Much has been made of the parity of the various forms of a nation's money, on the apparent assumption that the causal sequence relative to value runs from standard to credit money. The assumption is irrelevant to the value of each type of money in terms of the other because that is a definitional identity. And, relative to the goods value of money, the assumed order of value causation is questionable. Without any modification of standard money, the goods value of even the unrestricted nineteenth-century gold standard of value could be changed by a variety of causes,[195] namely, variations in the: (1) nonmonetary demand for standard metal,[196] (2) foreign monetary demand for standard metal (caused by adoption or abandonment of the same standard by other countries),[197] (3) supply of standard metal (due to such changes in foreign monetary standards),[198]

35

(4) domestic demand for standard metal,[199] (5) demand for money for spending or holding,[200] (6) quantity of nonstandard money,[201] and (7) central bank and treasury policies.[202] In short, while the value of nonstandard money in terms of standard money is a definitional identity under a metallic standard, the value of standard money (i.e., standard metal) became a relatively insignificant element in determining the goods value of money even before the traditional gold standard was abandoned. Since the classical period there has been a subtle, surreptitious (though unplanned) shift in the significance of the parity of standard and nonstandard money, on the one hand, and in the relationship between standard money and the standard of value, on the other hand. Classicists conceived parity as an actual equality because nonstandard media of exchange were viewed as mere circulating substitutes for standard money.[203] Accordingly, they regarded standard money and the standard of value as such an obvious identity that they would have looked upon this third definition of a monetary standard as a redundancy. Neoclassical writers, on the other hand, came to treat nonstandard media as a *supplement* to, instead of a substitute for, standard money.[204] Parity then ceased to prevent nonstandard money from affecting the goods value of money. It became a matter of form, not substance, maintained by the right of convertibility—a right that was exercisable only so long as it was not generally exercised.[205] These developments obscured the "real" nature of the standard of value and its relationship, if any, to standard money.[206]

Standard money can therefore be changed without changing the value of the standard of value in terms of goods.[207] Both the compensated money plan for stabilization and the devaluation route to recovery imply that the standard money and the standard of value are not identical. Criticism of these plans—and criticism has been practically unanimous in orthodox circles—is based on the proposition that standard money and the value of the standard of value are not even directly related.[208] Its original significance can logically be attached to the notion of parity today by only those who purport to explain the short-run

36

as well as the long-run value of money by the so-called commodity theory. George F. Warren and Frank A. Pearson were probably the last (and possibly they were also the first) to make this claim.[209]

However, notwithstanding the facts they themselves described and the quantity theory they espoused, some orthodox money doctors kept the domestic parity dogma alive by artificial respiration.[210] This was apparently supposed to preserve the prestige of the gold standard.[211] "The successful utilization of gold as the gold standard requires that provision be made for the unquestioned maintenance of the value of all kinds of money in circulation, other than standard money, at parity with the standard. . . . The most effective expedient . . . for guaranteeing parity between standard money and other kinds is to make all forms of money redeemable in standard money." [212] But "the promise to redeem all money in gold on demand became more and more difficult to keep as the money supply became a larger and larger multiple of the available gold supply. A growing recognition of this was one reason for limiting the redemption of money in gold." [213] The practical irrelevance of domestic parity in the modern world is illustrated by the present domestic convertibility of nonstandard moneys into other nonstandard moneys instead of specie.[214]

Domestic parity is not merely irrelevant today; it is ironic. Acceptance of the monetary facts of modern life leads inexorably to the inference that the causal order of value involved in the concept of parity is the reverse of the heretofore orthodox presumption.[215] Standard money is equated to nonstandard money, rather than the reverse. Whether or not it ever did, the goods value of standard money no longer determines the goods value of nonstandard media. It is the latter that determines the former. The value of standard money is now the result, rather than the cause, of the value of money in general.[216] This is the irony of parity.

Consequently, the "standard-of-value" function is not limited to standard

37

money.[217] Thus, the distinction between standard and non-standard money offers no escape from the *reductio ad absurdum* in the concept of a monetary standard as the material comprising the standard of value. Therefore, interpreting the monetary standard as the material constituting both standard money and the standard of value reduces to the same absurdity: The monetary standard is money.

Furthermore, the limitations of the first two concepts of the monetary standard are not overcome by combination. They are not of the type that cancel out. On the contrary, construing the monetary standard as the material comprising both standard money and the standard of value compounds the inconsistencies in each of the other interpretations.

Not the basis of classification actually used. Because this is a minority concept, its general use as the basis for classifying monetary standards could not be expected. But use by its advocates should be expected. The expectation, however, is due for the same disappointment as that experienced in the previous cases. No one attempted to reduce the variety of specific standards to fit this classificatory concept. As a result, the species have often been inconsistent with the genus. Besides the anachronism of a paper standard, other species without any ascertainable standard money have allegedly been identified.[218] In addition, the term "standard of value" has been used occasionally in relation to moneys instead of goods, a use which implied the first concept of a monetary standard, rather than this one.[219] In short, those who implied that the monetary standard is whatever is used as both standard money and the standard of value generally failed to follow their own implications.

Indeed, the exceptional author who explicitly defined the idea of a monetary standard in these terms implicitly conceded that it has little relevance to modern conditions. He branded the notion of a commodity standard of value as "unrealistic." [220] Whereupon, he distinguished between the legal (commodity, i.e., gold) and the actual (abstract) standards of value.[221] The latter reduced the two elements in his definition of a monetary

38

standard to the same thing, an abstraction. He then maintained that the abstraction, sometimes called a "paper standard," cannot be a standard of value in any normal sense of the term: "The so-called paper standard involves as many standards [of value] as there are individuals dealing in the markets." [222] Thus, this conception of a monetary standard is, in effect, admitted by its own expositor to have no actual application to contemporary monetary affairs.

CONCLUSION

Three concepts of a monetary standard are implicit in preclassical, classical, and neoclassical literature: (1) the material comprising standard money, (2) the material constituting the standard of value, and (3) the material serving as both standard money and the standard of value. The first originated in a period when different materials competed for coinage on the basis of technical feasibility and mechanical convenience. It was generally abandoned with the termination of this phase of the coinage competition. Modern monetary developments then reduced the mechanical concept of the standard to a legalism. The second conception of a monetary standard flourished with the interest in more substantive issues that began with the English bullion controversy. The substance of this concept, however, ultimately evaporated. A changing institutional and conceptual environment reduced it to the absurdity that the monetary standard is money. As substantive monetary issues mushroomed and instability worsened, some neoclassical and modern authorities reverted to the fictional stability of the preclassical mechanical view of the monetary standard. Others sought to capture the best of both the mechanical and substantive worlds by combining the previous concepts of a monetary standard. But this proved to be a redundancy that reduced to the same absurdity as the second version.

A basic limitation, common to all three meanings of a monetary standard, was

39

the inapplicability to modern conditions covered (i.e., obscured) by such euphemisms as the "tabular," "multiple," or "paper" standard. The conventional constructions of the standard concept were appropriate to the "hard money" era, but not to the present age of abstract money. Some authorities expressly limited the concept to a specific commodity.[223] Attempts to fit the so-called "paper standard" into the commodity standard mold were feeble—almost farcical—and certainly futile.[224]

The persistence of thinking pertinent to the prehistoric commodity origin of money, in the modern world of abstract money, is nothing short of phenomenal. The propensity to reason about the abstruse phenomenon of money in the complex pecuniary societies of advanced industrialized nations from the behavior of aboriginal savages is, to say the least, a curiosity. Although the substance of modern money is "immaterial," the very concept is still confused with its ancient commodity origin.[225] Money continues to be interpreted as a commodity.[226] The ritualistic regurgitation of the requisites of the *commodity* to be used as money,[227] still required of unsuspecting students by modern monetary medicine men, further demonstrates the powerful influence of money's commodity origin on contemporary "thought." [228] Recent efforts to break loose from the fetters of commodity cogitation about money, though valiant, have not entirely succeeded.[229] How long will monetary analysis continue to be dominated by atavistic anthropological antiquarianism? How did we get into this mess, anyhow?

III

SOURCE OF THE DIFFICULTY: PRESERVATION OF CLASSICAL TERMS INCOMPATIBLE WITH MODERN VALUE THEORY

Some years ago, Lester V. Chandler warned that understanding of the integrated subjects of money, credit, and banking requires cognizance of the dynamic nature of the subject matter and the static nature of the terminology: "Though we must, for economy's sake, use names for things, these names have an unfortunate tendency to remain fixed while the things to which they apply undergo marked changes. The unwary may thus make the mistake of assuming that a generalization that is valid for things called by a certain name at one time is equally valid for the thing answering to the same name at another time . . . Static names must not be allowed to impede our analysis of a constantly, though sometimes slowly, changing mone-

41

tary system." [1] Although the warning was long overdue, there is little evidence that it has been heeded. What Chandler cautioned us against was precisely the source of the growing difficulty with the concept of a monetary standard. Neoclassical and modern economists continued to use classical monetary terms incompatible with modern facts and theories. And loyalty to an outmoded terminology helped to preserve concepts that are no longer operational.

THE LOGIC AND APPLICABILITY OF CLASSICAL TERMINOLOGY

Classical monetary literature was not plagued with these anomalies because the classical lexicon was designed to describe existing conditions within the contemporary theoretical frame of reference. Classical terms were labels for contemporaneously operational concepts.

Classical "monetary standard" consistent with classical premises. Classical economists worked strictly within their own terms of reference. Consequently, their conception of the "monetary standard" was consistent with their premises. It meant the "standard of value," [2] which classicists translated into the "universal equivalent" in intrinsic value.[3] But the classical "monetary standard" did not reduce to the previously noted absurdity because classicists normally recognized only intrinsically valuable metallic media of exchange as money. In short, they limited money to what has since become known as metallic standard money.[4] To classicists, the phrase "standard money" would have distinguished the money of account from another circulating medium of exchange generally accepted at the market value of its commodity content. Where this situation did not prevail, the word "standard," with reference to money, would have appeared redundant.[5]

Paper media were regarded by the classical school merely as "substitutes for

42

money." [6] The total "circulation" was therefore considered to be unaffected by convertible paper.[7] Inconvertibility, conceived by classicists only as a temporary, pathological currency condition, was conceded to affect the "circulation," but not the standard.[8] The latter continued to be gold and/or silver during periods of inconvertibility.[9] Bank deposits were not included in the classical concept of "currency," but interpreted simply as another form of nonmonetary, commercial credit.[10] In short, the classical concept of money embraced only commodities. The commodity used as money was referred to as the "standard of value."

That the monetary standard was money, in the classical schematism, was not an absurdity, but simply an identity. Consequently, the phrase "monetary standard," which would have seemed as redundant as the expression "standard money," was seldom used. The relevant generic term was "standard of value." Classical economists accordingly recognized such species of the standard as the gold standard (if gold was the money of account), silver standard (if silver was the money of account), or bimetallism (if either gold or silver, in a fixed ratio, was the money of account). The notion of a "paper standard" (of value) was rejected as a contradiction of terms.[11] The rare appearances of the term "monetary standard" in classical literature referred merely to the material by which money was made, or to the monetary, as distinct from the nonmonetary, application of the word standard. In the contemporary institutional and theoretical environment, the classical view of the monetary standard was reasonable and the terms were both consistent and appropriate.

Classical monetary concepts applicable to the classical period, but not to the present. On the other hand, modern conditions are not those that classical monetary terms were designed to describe. The classical period was generally characterized by commodity money and metallic standards, whereas the present is epitomized by abstract money and domestically inconvertible "paper" standards.[12] The rationale of the classical doctrine on money was gradually subverted as credit money became a

43

supplement to, instead of a substitute for, standard money.[13] The classical proposition that credit media could replace, but not augment, money had validity only so long as note issue was confined to one country. The doctrine was invalidated by the fact of simultaneous substitution of "soft" for "hard" money by several countries. Neoclassical attempts to rationalize the facts with the received tenets mistook the *growth* of credit media for the mere replacement of standard money to suit personal convenience.[14]

Failure of neoclassical and modern attempts to embrace abstract money with classical concepts. The neoclassical rationalization obscured the growing discrepancy between fact and fancy. Economists persisted in the attempt to handle the increasingly abstract phenomenon of money with classical tools designed for different materials.[15] Insistence that money must have inherent value or be freely convertible into a valuable material continued while the memory of full-bodied money faded [16] and convertibility was abandoned.[17] The "paper standard" was first implicitly declared an impossibility,[18] then successively conceded to be a possibility,[19] recognized as a universal but temporary fact,[20] and finally accepted as a permanent condition.[21] But no one described that fact or condition in positive terms. The "inconvertible (paper) standard" remained a negative conception, implying merely the absence of certain attributes.[22]

FAILURE OF MONETARY TERMINOLOGY TO REFLECT POSTCLASSICAL MODIFICATION OF VALUE THEORY

The absence of positive description of the (a?) "paper standard" in neoclassical and modern literature has not been a mere oversight. The received monetary terms were literally incapable of such application.[23] The modern concept of a paper standard was developed by writers who spoke a different language relative to value, but paradoxically retained the monetary terminology of the classicists.

44

Classical "standard of value" antedated modern value theory. According to classical theory, value was considered an objective, intrinsic quality of a good. The subjective connotation of "value in use" was lost in the objectivication of "exchange value." Classical economists addressed themselves to the latter, which they specifically characterized as "objective value," determined by impersonal market forces.[24] Exchange value was explained by the Ricardian school in terms of "embodied labor." Whatever the interpretation of the classical "labor theory of value," it embraced the notion of intrinsic value.[25] Classical value, therefore, was an objective, intrinsic attribute of things. This view was substantially modified by the principle of marginal utility.

According to modern thought, value is not an objective property of *a* thing, but a subjective idea about the relative desirability of *different* things.[26] Consequently, the value of one thing alone cannot be calculated—cannot even be conceived. Value is a ratio,[27] and the value of one commodity in terms of others will change with its quantity, *ceteris paribus,* even though its intrinsic qualities remain the same.[28]

"Standard-of-value" *concept eliminated by modern value theory.* Thus, the principle of marginal utility eliminated the possibility of a "standard of value." Since value is not inherent in anything, but a relation between things established by subjective preferences of people, the value of *any* given good is incapable of measurement without reference to other goods. Attention to the analytical distinction between, in contrast to the common confusion of, the terms "standard" and "measure" will help to make this clear. "Standard" has been used by economists sometimes as a synonym for, and other times as a modifier of, "measure." This is due to the ambiguity of the term "measure," which may mean either a "unit" or a "standard" of measurement. And these are *not* the same. "It is essential that there be established and kept in mind the distinction between the terms 'units' and 'standards.' "[29] The National Bureau of Standards distinguishes them in the following manner:

45

A *unit* is a value, quantity, or magnitude in terms of which other values, quantities, or magnitudes are expressed. In general, a unit is fixed by definition and is independent of such physical conditions as temperature. Examples: the yard, the pound, the gallon, the meter, the liter, the gram.

A *standard* is a physical embodiment of a unit. In general it is not independent of physical conditions, and it is a true embodiment of the unit only under specified conditions. For example, a yard standard has a length of one yard when at some definite temperature and supported in a certain manner.[30]

In short, the "unit" is abstract, whereas the "standard" is the physical embodiment of the unit in the quality to be measured.[31] A standard of length must possess length; [32] a standard of weight must possess weight.[33] Likewise, a *standard of value must possess value.*[34] Applying these terms to the measurement of value, we have the abstract monetary unit (the dollar, pound, franc, mark, yen, etc.) as the "unit of value" and, for example, the number of grains of gold and/or silver in the monetary unit as the "standard of value." [35]

As long as value was thought to be an attribute intrinsic in a given economic good, a "standard of value" was conceivable. But the denial of intrinsic value implicit in the generally accepted marginal-utility doctrine precludes the concept of a standard of value. A standard of any measurement must embody the property it presumes to measure.[36] If nothing intrinsically possesses a specific amount of value, there can be no standard measure of value.[37] Thus, the familiar analogy of the yardstick is invalidated.[38] There is no standard of value analogous to standards of physical measurement.[39] Hence money—standard or otherwise—is neither "the" nor "a" standard of value.

Money a "unit of account," not "standard of value." Money provides us with a "unit of account," or "common denominator of value," not a "standard of value." The distinction is of utmost importance to the understanding of money. A "unit" and a "common denominator" are abstractions. A "standard" unit of measure is concrete. Walker attempted to correct the allegedly erroneous impression conveyed by Jevons' synonymous treatment of

46

the "common measure" and "common denominator" of value by substituting the latter for the former as the name for this function of money.[40] Jevons' use of the phrase, "measure of value" to identify money's function as a means of making *simultaneous* comparisons of value did not necessarily violate the abstract denotation of the word "measure." But what bothered Walker was that "measure of value" in common usage connoted a concrete standard measure of value.[41] He attributed the confusion to the contemporary monetary application of the "measure of value" in the classical theory of the relative values of goods. Use of the same term in these different senses, Walker argued, led to the false inference that only a commodity of intrinsic value could be money because it must be a universal equivalent.[42] He feared that Jevons' monetary terminology would serve to preserve instead of remove this error. Walker argued that his predecessors' delineation of this function of money proved only the necessity for a "common denominator" of value (a term he attributed to Jevons), or a "unit of calculation" (a term he attributed to John Stuart Mill).[43]

Few economists have since disagreed with Walker's argument, which was reinforced by the general abandonment of the labor theory of value. But the revision of monetary terminology, begun by Jevons and carried one step further by Walker, was not continued until it was brought into conformity with its modern institutional and theoretical setting. It is time to finish the job.

Relative values are *not measured by* money.[44] Being relative, values are *expressed in terms of* the common denominator of the monetary unit.[45] Like any common denominator, it is an abstraction, not a concrete standard. Paradoxically, however, even those who espouse these propositions cannot rid themselves of the term "standard of value" and the concept for which it stands. Reversion to this atavism is common, despite interpretation of value as a subjectively influenced, if not determined, ratio.[46] Common also is the confusion of the "unit of account," or "common denominator of value," and "standard of value"— concepts from different planes of thought, one abstract and

47

one concrete.[47] The conventional textbook procedure of calling money alternatively a "standard of value" (concrete concept), "unit of account" and "common denominator of value" (abstract concepts), as well as a "unit of value" and "measure of value" (ambivalent concepts which shuttle between the two levels of thought) is symptomatic of the confusion prevailing at the very roots of monetary economics.[48]

The classical school was not guilty of this confusion. Its members clearly distinguished between the monetary unit (of account) and the standard of value, interpreting the former as the pound sterling and the latter as a specified quantity of gold. The two were not considered identical. Gold was regarded as the standard of value even when the pound was inconvertible and the price of gold fluctuating.[49] Moreover, the "ideal money" advocated by antibullionists was viewed by classicists as a monetary unit without a standard.[50]

Ordinarily, "measure of value" was an elliptical expression for "standard measure of value," meaning "standard of value." [51] Where a distinction between the "standard" and "measure" of value was implied, the standard was considered the physical embodiment of the monetary unit or measure of value. The standard gave substance and meaning to the abstract unit.[52] And for the classicists standard of value meant a *standard,* not just a unit in terms of which values were expressed. After selecting as the standard of value the commodity believed to be least variable in value, they abstracted from its variable exchange value as a commodity and assumed its invariability as a standard of value. This they correctly understood to be the procedure required by the logic of their language.[53] To Ricardo, the antibullionist criticism of the gold standard as a variable standard of value was a contradiction of terms. He knew that a standard is invariable or it is not a standard. This was why he insisted, during the inconvertibility of the pound, on measuring the depreciation of the currency by the premium on gold rather than by the prices of other goods, as some of his opponents sought to do.[54] He insisted that changes in the value of money could be measured only against the standard of value.[55] Given the classical premises and the existence of a standard of value, this position was logically unassailable.

The general confusion of the "standard of value" and "unit of account" began in the postclassical period,[56] when even the neoclassicists began thinking of money primarily in terms of *its own* exchange value *relative to goods* instead of as the standard for measuring the *relative values of goods*.[57] The reorientation spread as people ceased being content with the degree of price-level stability obtained by the stabilization of the monetary unit in terms of gold and began desiderating the stabilization of the monetary unit in terms of goods in general.[58] In short, the classical standard of value was turned upside down: Goods became the standard for the valuation of money. Thus, the abandonment of the classical standard of value and its replacement by the abstract unit of account, which had been the goal of the contemporary opponents of the classical school,[59] was finally accomplished by—of all people—the supposed stewards of the classical tradition! [60]

Persistence of classical terminology. However, postclassical writers preserved the classical term "standard of value." Those who remained unimpressed by subjective value theory quite logically retained the concept of a standard of value.[61] But even those who recognized that value is not an intrinsic property of anything continued to use the term.[62] This represented a misuse of "standard of value" as a synonym for "unit of account," involving varying degrees of conceptual confusion.[63]

CONCLUSION

Classical interpretation of the monetary standard as the material constituting the standard of value was logical and practical. The concept of a standard of value was consistent with classical premises, and it furnished the genus which permitted identification of all species of standards allowed by classical doctrine. Moreover,

49

the concept and its premises were consistent with their institutional environment.

However, the standard-of-value image was gradually obscured by changes in institutions, objectives, and theory. Recognition that credit media supplemented instead of merely replaced standard money transferred the "standard of value" from specie to money, per se, whatever its form.

With the growing concern for the purchasing power of money and the rising antagonism to declining or fluctuating price levels, the classical view of the standard of value was unwittingly abandoned. Instead of thinking of money as a neutral standard for measuring the relative values of goods, people became concerned with the exchange value of money. That is, concern shifted from the relative exchange values of goods to the exchange value of money (in terms of goods). In short, instead of money being the standard for the valuation of goods, the latter became the standard for the valuation of money. (What happened to the value of gold is something the experts are still trying to figure out.) This change in attitude introduced the anomaly of a varying standard of value, a notion that had been viewed by classicists as a contradiction of terms. It also led to the contradictory desire to stabilize the monetary unit in terms of both one commodity (gold) and all goods simultaneously. All this amounted to a revival of the antibullionist fallacy of confusing the concrete standard of value and the abstract unit of account. The confusion has been abetted by the fact that the growing use of credit media, particularly bank demand deposits, has "converted" money to abstract debts incompatible with the idea of a standard of value.

While the classical concept of the standard of value was thus being implicitly abandoned in practice, the discovery of the principle of marginal utility removed its theoretical foundation. Intrinsic value being disproven, a standard of value became an impossibility. Yet the monetary standard continued to be interpreted as the material comprising the standard of value. How can this paradox be resolved?

50

IV

REASON FOR PERSISTENCE OF CLASSICAL MONETARY TERMINOLOGY: NEOCLASSICAL SEPARATION OF VALUE THEORY AND MONETARY THEORY

The basic reason for the persistence of classical monetary terminology was the failure to realize that abandonment of the cost-of-production theory of value required revision of monetary theory.[1] Explaining the relative values of goods by their respective production costs implied that value is an intrinsic property of things. The implication and its inferential concept of a standard of value fell with the value theory that comprised their common premise.[2] However, the term "standard of value" lived on in the field of monetary economics, which had become immunized against the effects of changes in value theory. How was this immunity acquired? The present chapter is addressed to this question.

51

Discovery of the marginal-utility principle, development of the Austrian utility theory of value, and the Marshallian compromise between the cost and utility doctrines had no apparent effect on monetary theory. The reader who has been well indoctrinated with *post-classical* orthodoxy (whether neoclassical or Keynesian) will ask why *should* monetary theory have been affected? By the time these developments in value theory were incorporated into the literature, it was generally supposed that the quantity theory represented the sum and substance of classical monetary theory. It was assumed that the quantity theory of the value of money, on the one hand, and the labor or utility theory of the value of goods, on the other hand, were unrelated doctrines, applicable to different areas of analysis. It has since become commonplace to complain of the lack of correlation between monetary theory and value theory.[3] Actually, this traditional view of the alleged independent development of monetary and value theories stems from neoclassical misinterpretations of classical thought. The classical school was not guilty of the doctrinal dualism attributed to it. Classical monetary theory was merely an application of classical value theory to money. Consequently, the postclassical changes in value theory *should* have been reflected in monetary theory, concepts, and terminology. This will, it is hoped, be made clear by a brief reconsideration of classical theory and attention to the neoclassical removal of the monetary component from classical value theory.[4]

COMPATIBILITY OF CLASSICAL VALUE AND MONETARY DOCTRINES

Due to pseudoclassical oversimplification, it became generally believed by unsophisticated students of classical thought and sophisticated students of Marx that the classical labor theory of value was supposed to be an explanation of the *cause* of value. Such was not the case.

52

Classical value theory.
The classical school regarded labor as the *measure* of value, not as the cause of value. Demand was explicitly recognized as the cause of value.[5] The classical viewpoint was that by incurring additional labor cost, producers tended to overcome scarcity and limit the value of the product caused by demand.[6] Classical economists sought to explain only the value of reproducible goods in competitive markets,[7] where additional labor would be hired as long—and only as long—as such costs were covered by income from the sale of the products produced. Consequently, cost of production, which classicists viewed as ultimately reducible (substantially, if not completely) to labor cost, was thought to be the long-run upper—not lower—limit to the value of a good. Thus, the classical school maintained, exchange values tended in the long run to be proportionate to labor cost.[8] Any long-run tendency to exchange reproducible goods in competitive markets at a ratio other than that of their respective costs would have appeared irrational to the classical school and, therefore, beyond the scope of their analysis. Labor was thought of as "determining" value only as a regulator, not as the—or even a—cause. John Stuart Mill compared labor to the pendulum rather than the spring or weights of a clock.[9] When classicists said that labor "caused" the value of a product to be what it was, they were *not* using "cause" in the sense of "source." They did not mean that labor caused the value to be *as much as* it was; they meant that labor caused the value to be *no more than* it was. In short, the classical labor theory of value did not purport to be a philosophical explanation of the *origin* of value. The classical schoolmasters merely meant that labor was the ultimate, long-run *measure* of economic values.

But labor was not a practicable measure of value. Though a "real" measure in the technical sense of theoretical economics,[10] it was not an operational measure in the "real world." An "hour of unskilled labor" as a labor unit has some usefulness for theoretical or philosophical purposes,[11] but none for the practical purposes of the marketplace because even unskilled labor lacks homogeneity. Comparison of actual market values requires a unit of measure more capable of standardization than labor. At the same time, classical economists thought it desirable that the nominal measure of value approximate the real measure (labor) as closely as possible. Corn qualified in this respect for comparisons over decades of time.[12] For shorter periods commensurate with the completion of most market transactions, however, the production of a given amount of precious metals was thought to represent less variation in labor cost.[13] Classical authorities, therefore, recommended a specified quantity of gold or silver as the nominal standard measure of value which would most closely approximate the real measure, labor.[14]

The classical rationale of the gold standard implied the desideratum of a relatively stable money-wage level and a price level that fell with production costs as the productivity of labor improved through technological progress. The classical conception of the gold standard (of value) was a casualty of the opposition to the secular deflation of the latter nineteenth century, which was aggravated in the United States by the resumption of specie payments on the prewar basis. Classical monetary theory, in general, and the classical rationale of the gold standard, in particular, were lost in the policy polemics of the bimetallic controversy. The few exceptional echoes of the *classical* defense of the gold standard[15] were drowned in the partisan uproar. By the time fortuitous discoveries of new gold fields permitted an armistice in this battle of standards, the memory of the classical rationale of the gold standard (i.e., the classical concept of the gold standard) had completely disappeared. Subsequently, attempts were made to accomplish the impossibility of stabilizing the monetary unit at once in terms of both one commodity (gold) and many commodities. Theorists were not wanting who, while professing to follow in the classical tradition, thought that this dual stabilization was possible.[16] Allusion has already been made to this ultimate (but unrecognized) triumph of anticlassicism.[17]

The failure to recognize the abandonment of the classical concept of the gold

54

standard by its professed defenders may be explained by what the neoclassical custodians had meanwhile done to classical monetary theory. The above discussion has shown that the concept of a "measure of value" constituted the link between classical theories of the relative values of goods and of the goods value of money. The inadvertent breaking of this link was facilitated by the equally unconscious neoclassical removal of classical monetary theory from its value-theory mold. A brief reconstruction of the anatomy of classical monetary theory is necessary before the nature and significance of the neoclassical "doctrinectomy" can be appreciated.[18]

Classical monetary theory. Contrary to the present generally accepted view, classical monetary theory did not develop independently of classical value theory. In classical analysis monetary theory was merely a particular aspect or application of value theory. Since classicists defined money as specie, they explained its value exactly as they did any commodity—in the short run by the supply of and demand for it (gold or silver) and in the long run by the cost of producing or obtaining it.[19] The classical quantity theory was merely an application of market supply-demand analysis to the commodity (gold or silver) used as money.[20] As in the case of any commodity or service not artificially restricted in supply, while the value of money could neither exceed nor fall short of its cost of acquisition in the long run, the short-run value of money was explained by the peculiarities of, and changes in, its supply and demand. Because of classical assumptions familiar to students of economics, the classical demand function for money demonstrated, in modern terms, a unitary elasticity. The classical money supply function, on the other hand, had only a very slight elasticity because it was explained exclusively by the alternative uses for the precious metals as money or plate.[21] Marginal gold producers were not considered capable of affecting the market supply of gold significantly because the durability of gold made the accumulation of centuries continuously available for use. Changes in a country's money supply (in modern parlance, shifts in the money supply curve)

55

were attributed primarily to a redistribution of the worldwide accumulation of precious metals through international bullion movements in response to changes in the cost of producing things other than the precious metals.[22] Such bullion movements in conjunction with the quantity theory tended in the long run to equate the value of money everywhere to the cost of obtaining it. Thus, instead of a dichotomy, classical analysis demonstrated a complete harmony of doctrine in its real and monetary sectors. The quantity theory of the value of money was an integral part of classical value theory.

NEOCLASSICAL REMOVAL OF THE QUANTITY THEORY FROM ITS CLASSICAL VALUE-THEORY CONTEXT

By misinterpreting classical doctrine and failing to keep their concepts in step with changing institutions and practices, early neoclassical economists inadvertently removed the quantity theory from its classical value-theory context.[23]

Downgrading of the cost of money. Nineteenth-century neoclassical monetary theorists eliminated the classical cost doctrine from monetary theory. Francis Walker effected this quite unconsciously through mere semantics. By substituting the term "price" for "cost," Walker switched the classical explanation of the quantity of money by its cost to an explanation of the value of money by its quantity.[24] J. Shield Nicholson accomplished the same result by claiming that the classical school overemphasized the significance of the cost of producing specie through neglect of the durability of the precious metals.[25] Nicholson argued that changes in the cost of producing gold could have little effect on the supply of gold in the short run because the gold supply at any time represented the accumulation of the ages.[26] From the classical premise that "cost of production can only affect the value of any article through supply," [27] it was then deduced that the significance of the

56

quantity theory was substantially limited to the long run (in either the analytical or historical sense of the term, or both).[28] This at once obliterated the classical distinction between the long run and short run, and reduced the classical cost doctrine to insignificance in monetary analysis. Apparently, Nicholson mistakenly applied the classical cost theory of value to (in modern terms) the elasticity, instead of shifts, of the money supply function. And he neglected the fact that classicists equated the cost of "producing" to the cost of "obtaining" specie in exchange for an export surplus.[29] Thus, the early neoclassical interpretations of classical monetary theory substituted the quantity for the cost of money as the explanation of its "long-run" value.

Restriction of the quantity theory to the "long run." [30] After the quantity theory had been distended to encompass the "long run," later neoclassical monetary theorists lopped off its short-run application and restricted the doctrine to the "long run." This was the inevitable result of their unwillingness to include bank demand deposits in their concept of money, despite acknowledgment that most domestic exchanges were effected by this medium. The primary impact of "money" (as neoclassicists defined the term) fell on bank reserves. It took time for the full effect of the alteration in reserves to be reflected in bank deposits and their circulation. Consequently, neoclassical authorities concluded that the proportionate relationship between "money" and prices envisaged by the quantity theory, actually prevailed only "in the long run." [31] Transitional periods between "long-run" equilibria were specifically exempted from the operation of the quantity theory.[32]

Thus, the short-run classical quantity theory was transposed into a "long-run" doctrine. Therefore, in neoclassical analysis, the "long-run" value of money appeared to be explained quite differently from the long-run value of goods. Thence arose the erroneous tradition that monetary theory originated and developed independently of value theory.[33] It was this unconscious removal of the quantity theory from its classical value-theory frame of reference that made the developments in value theory which subverted the notion of intrinsic value appear to be irrelevant to monetary theory. Hence, it was not recognized that the principle of marginal utility and the psychological approach to value destroyed the concept of a standard of value. Accordingly, although the notion of intrinsic value was purged from value theory, it persisted in the field of money.[34] Consequently, the term "standard of value" survived as the label for a concept that became progressively unworkable in its hostile postclassical theoretical and institutional environment.[35]

THE JEVONSONIAN PARADOX

In view of W. Stanley Jevons' pioneer work in marginal utility and his denial of intrinsic value,[36] his adherence to classical orthodoxy in monetary matters seems to suggest a paradox. His interpretation of the monetary standard as the standard of value and his insistence that the standard of value must be a commodity possessing value appear to have been strictly in the classical tradition.[37]

Jevons' interpretation of the "standard of value." However, his monetary orthodoxy was not as classical as his terminology seems to imply. His interpretation of the standard of value was more neoclassical than classical. Ignoring the classical abstraction from the variability in the value of the standard of value relative to goods, he viewed such instability as a problem requiring attention.[38] This unclassical attitude was reflected in his terminological innovation, splitting the classical "standard of value" function of money into the "measure of value" and "standard of value" functions.[39] His "standard of value" was what Walker renamed the "standard of deferred payments," [40] a concept focusing attention on the goods value of money, rather than the relative values of goods.[41] It was this shift from the classical to the neoclassical conception of the standard of value that permitted accommodation to the notion of

58

a variable standard of value, with its implicit corollary of variable intrinsic value.[42] Jevons, however, stopped short of completing this transition. Though he regarded the variable value of the gold standard of value as a problem, he argued that the solution lay in adjustment *to* the standard, not adjustment *of* the standard.[43] Thus, despite his modification of terms for the functions of money, he never completely abandoned the classical construction of the standard of value.[44] In fact, he reverted to it with sufficient vigor explicitly to deny that value is a psychological phenomenon and to argue that it is analogous to a physically measurable quantity.[45] Consequently, despite his innovations in value theory, Jevons conveyed the impression of his adherence to the classical standard-of-value conception of the monetary standard. Hence, the irrelevance of value theory to monetary theory appeared to be confirmed. So, the notion of a fixed, concrete standard measure of value survived the apparent destruction of the cost-of-production theory of value.

Resolution: Jevons' value theory not anticlassical. The paradox is resolved by the fact—as opposed to the currently received opinion—that Jevons' analysis was not anticlassical.[46] He intended, effected, and claimed only an improvement, not a refutation, of classical *value theory.*[47] Unlike the "Austrians," Jevons did not attempt to explain the ultimate cause of value.[48] Such philosophical speculation had no interest for him. Like his classical predecessors, he sought only to explain the *regulation* of value.[49]

Jevons' contribution to value theory was an explanation of what the classical school had heretofore assumed—the basis of value in a combination of utility and scarcity.[50] He, himself, characterized his utility theory as merely filling in the missing details of the classical "laws" of supply and demand: "This law of [diminishing final degree of] utility has, in fact, *always been assumed by political economists under the more complex form and name of the Law of Supply and Demand. But once fairly stated in its simple form, it opens up the whole of the subject. Most of the conclusions are, of course, the old ones*

59

stated in a consistent form . . ." [51] As this statement indicates, his innovation in value theory applied only to the short run. Consequently, in the final section of his chapter on the "Theory of Exchange" Jevons characterized his exposition as strictly in the classical tradition.[52] His utility and disutility functions supplied the missing explanations of the classical market demand and supply functions.[53]

It seems to have been forgotten that Jevons' criticism of the labor theory of value was made in the context of his theory of *market* exchange value.[54] It was directed not at the theory, per se, but at its misapplication to market, instead of normal, values.[55] Jevons, like most innovators, overemphasized his innovation in the analysis of demand; his justification was its underemphasis in classical literature.[56] However, his emphasis no doubt contributed to the misinterpretation of his *Theory of Political Economy* as a general critique of classicism.[57]

But this was neither the intention nor effect of any of Jevons' works. He did not question the classical cost-of-production explanation of long-run values. In fact, he explicitly reaffirmed it. For instance, although his *Theory of Political Economy* was addressed primarily to explaining short-run values, it included a section rationalizing his theory of market exchange values with the labor theory of normal values, stating, in part: "It may tend to give the reader confidence in the preceding theories when he finds that they *lead directly to the well known and almost self-evident law, that articles which can be produced in greater or less quantity exchange in proportion to their cost of production.* The ratio of exchange of commodities will, as a fact, conform *in the long run* to the ratio of production." [58] Moreover, since Jevons accepted, without qualification, the classical interpretation of money as a commodity,[59] for which credit media were merely circulating substitutes,[60] he reiterated the classical dictum that the value of money is explained no differently than the value of any other commodity.[61] Accordingly, he specifically explained the long-run value of money (i.e., gold or silver) by its cost of production: "Looking at the question, in the first place, as a *chronic* one,

60

that is, as regarding the constitution of monetary systems during centuries, it is indispensable to remember the fact, too much overlooked by disputants, that *the values of gold and silver are ultimately governed, like those of other commodities, by cost of production.* Unless clear reasons, then, can be shown why silver should be more constant in its circumstances of production than gold, there is no ground for thinking that a bimetallic gold and silver money will afford a more steady *standard of value* than gold alone." [62] Jevons' adherence to classical value theory is as demonstrable as his identification with classical monetary theory.

Classification of Jevons as a member of the utility school in opposition to the classical cost school of long-run value theory was the result of attending to some of his isolated exaggerations instead of to the substance of his entire analysis.[63] His English contemporaries were less prone to this mistake. They more generally recognized Jevons' exaggerations for what they were; consequently, instead of exiling him to a foreign school, they downgraded his innovations *on* classical theory.[64] Alfred Marshall's original reaction was unenthusiastic. He found Jevons' *Theory* to be neither a departure from, nor a significant improvement on, classical analysis.[65] Marshall's attitude toward Jevons improved as he came to see more significance in his contribution to the rounding out of classical thought.[66] Finally, he ranked Jevons among the greatest in the classical tradition.[67] Notwithstanding the stereotype of the "English Austrian," competent contemporary Englishmen knew better. Jevons' classicism in the monetary field was, therefore, a demonstration of his consistency, not inconsistency.

His allegiance to the classical conception of the monetary standard followed as a logical consequence. The orthodox notion of a concrete "standard of value" did not appear to Jevons inconsistent with his principle of diminishing utility because the two concepts belonged to different areas of analysis—the long run and short run, respectively.[68] Diminishing utility, a phenomenon abstracting from time, must have appeared irrelevant to the "standard of value," which Jevons distinguished from the

61

"measure of value" and explicitly applied to the passage of time.[69] Jevons' explanation of long-run value in terms of embodied production costs was consistent with his view of the standard of value. He was a classicist, not a subjective-value theorist.[70] His value theory required no modification of classical monetary theory or terminology.

Therefore, he could not have been expected to see the necessity for completing the elimination of the concept of a "standard measure of value" which he began.[71] This could not have been expected until the concept of intrinsic long-run value was eliminated by abandonment of the notion of "embodied cost." Unfortunately, by the time the continental psychological school had shown the way, appropriate action in the field of money was obstructed by the neoclassical separation of value and monetary theory. This legacy of the historical school—preserved by the Austrians, reinforced by the growing propensity to specialize, and reflected in the traditional limitation of "economic theory" to value and distribution theory—has become formalized in college catalogue course descriptions and in the American Economic Association's classification of the branches of economics. Apparently, the Association has not even yet officially recognized the recent belated attempts to reconcile the two kinds of value—relative and monetary. "Money and banking" remains in the category of institutional economics, outside of the primary interest of most theorists.[72] Thus, economists need look no further than their own doctrinal dichotomy for an illustration of the unproductiveness of overspecialization.

CONCLUSION

Postclassical distortions of classical monetary doctrine introduced the separation of monetary from value theory which appeared to render developments in value theory irrelevant to monetary theory. The need for a revision of monetary theory and terminology after the development of the concept of marginal utility was, therefore, not recognized. Moreover, the erroneous assumption that Jevons used the term "standard of value" in the classical sense and the general interpretation of his value theory as modern, instead of classical, apparently led to the conclusion that the classical concept of a "standard measure of value" is compatible with modern value theory. Thus, the notion of an intrinsic "standard of value" lives on despite general denial of intrinsic value.

V

RESULT OF THE
CONFUSION:
SHIFT IN APPROACH
AGGRAVATING
THE PROBLEM

Though classical monetary terminology persisted, the concepts represented by the terms have been variously distorted in attempts to use them in an unclassical institutional and theoretical environment. Previous chapters have dealt with the received concepts of a monetary standard, the resulting confusion, the source of the difficulty, and the basic reason for our failure to diagnose the malady. This chapter will describe the consequent disintegration and virtual disappearance of the idea of a monetary standard.

CONCEPT OF A MONETARY STANDARD
AS A MONETARY SYSTEM

Recent writers have broadened the coverage of the term "monetary standard" so as to make it a synonym for the "monetary system." Some have done this explicitly in an attempt to reduce the prevailing confusion. J. Whitney Hanks and Roland Stucki, for example, observe that "when associated with money," the dictionary definition of the word *"standard . . .* obviously refers to the 'measure of value characteristic.' " [1] "But," they add, "the expression *monetary standard* has come to mean more than a standard for fixing values. Common usage views the expression as encompassing an *entire monetary system* founded upon a particular standard or unit of measurement." [2] Raymond P. Kent is equally explicit: "Although the terms *monetary standard* and *standard of value* are so closely related as at times to appear identical, in usage the former is much more comprehensive than the latter. A standard of value is a monetary unit—such as the gold dollar, a paper pound, or a silver yuan—with which economic values are measured, while a monetary standard comprehends an entire monetary system having for its foundation a particular standard of value . . . A monetary standard, therefore, may be defined as *a monetary system built upon a specific standard of value."* [3] On the other hand, implicit—rather than explicit —identification of the concepts of the monetary standard and the monetary system have been more the result of the existing terminological and conceptual confusion than an effort to remedy it. In Charles A. Conant's chapter entitled "Types of Currency *Systems,"* several of the specific types of systems are called "standards," and later referred to as "systems." [4] Likewise, Karl Helfferich distinguished specific "monetary standards" in his chapter on the "Development of Monetary Systems." [5] Although he recognized several nominal uses of the term "currency standard," he held that the concept represented by this label included the "monetary system in its entirety." [6] Helfferich's classification of "currency systems," therefore, consisted of a list of the various monetary "standards." [7] This view of the monetary standard, which increased in popularity after the financial debacle of the 'thirties,[8] added ambiguity to the already existing confusion.

Few people other than those mentioned above addressed themselves to the generic

65

concept of a monetary standard. Most discussions of the standard question have been conducted in terms of specific standards.[9] But characterization of the monetary standard as a "system" is implied in a number of ways: The literature is littered with the term "gold-standard system."[10] The terms "specie régime" and "paper régime" have the same amorphous connotation.[11] The various monetary standards are often referred to as "systems"[12] or, what amounts to the same thing, as "plans,"[13] "mechanisms,"[14] etc. References to the "working" or "operation" of the monetary standard imply that the latter includes more than merely the material constituting standard money or the standard of value,[15] for that material, like any standard, does not "operate." A standard either exists or it does not. If it does, it is either used or neglected. The once popular term "automatic gold standard"[16] connotes a mechanism insuring automatic *use* of the gold standard. Would anyone claim there is such a thing as an "automatic yardstick"? Even if such an expression were used, it could be interpreted only as an elliptical expression for an automatic mechanism that employed the standard in measuring lengths of material. The standard measure itself would be in no way affected by the manner of its application. "Management" of the monetary standard really means management of the monetary system, with the management being related in some manner to the standard.[17] A managed (i.e., manipulated) standard is a contradiction of terms—given meaning only by short-weight vendors. Finally, interpretation of the "monetary standard" as the "monetary system" is indicated by widespread synonymous use of the terms.[18]

Confusion of "standards" and "policies." The "monetary system" is a rather nebulous concept. Over the years, it has changed as much, if not more, than the concept of money. Moreover, at any one time, including the present, a consensus—even agreement between any two experts—on what is included in the monetary system cannot be expected. Nevertheless, although informed opinions may differ as to what is "monetary" and what is not, the monetary policies carried out by and through monetary institutions (however "monetary" may be defined) are

66

generally included in the "monetary system."[19] Broadening the concept of the monetary standard to embrace the whole monetary system, therefore, adds not only ambiguity, but also another confusion—the confusion of the monetary standard with monetary policies.

Although a given monetary standard requires for its implementation certain monetary policies, identification of standards and policies represents a confounding of substance and mechanism, of ends and means. D. H. Robertson defined "a gold standard" as "a *policy* of keeping this value [of the monetary unit] at an equality with that of a defined weight of gold . . ."[20] Others have been almost as explicit in referring to the standard as *a* policy.[21] Still others identify the monetary standard as a *set* of policies. In most cases the policies are called "characteristics," "requirements," or "practices" of the particular standard under consideration.[22] In the case of a metallic standard, the list of requisites invariably includes the definition of the monetary unit as a fixed weight of metal of a specified fineness, as well as the usual "practices" of unlimited government purchase and sale of the standard metal at the fixed mint price, unlimited convertibility of all forms of money ultimately into the standard metal, and unlimited exportation and importation of bullion.[23] Since many of these same writers imply elsewhere that the monetary standard is the material constituting either standard money[24] or the standard of value,[25] their description of specific standards fails to distinguish between the legal definition of the standard money or standard of value (i.e., the monetary standard) and the policies necessary to establish and maintain that standard.[26] Identification of the monetary standard with its policies obscured the guide to policy that the standard was supposed to supply.[27]

Not the basis of classification actually used. The inherent confusion of standards and policies in the concept of the monetary standard as a monetary system makes classification of standards practically impossible. The concept confronts us with an unlimited variety of monetary policies and provides no precise criterion of classification. As a result, alternative standards cannot be

67

clearly differentiated,[28] and attempted classifications contain overlapping categories,[29] with perhaps as many differences within as among the classes.[30] Moreover, even the limited usefulness of this generic concept of a monetary standard is restricted to species of commodity standards, which may be respectively identified with particular positive policies. The paper standard, being essentially a negative concept—as indicated by its alternative label "inconvertible paper standard" [31] —cannot be positively identified by listing its policies.[32] Such a list would be limited only by the imagination of the author. Consequently, even those who explicitly define the concept of a monetary standard as a system and differentiate the species by their respective policies do not extend this system of classification to include "inconvertible or managed paper standards." [33] It is this conceptual confusion of standard and policy that accounts for such apparent contradictions as the "managed inconvertible gold bullion standard." [34]

AMBIGUITY OF SPECIFIC STANDARDS

As a result of the mixture of standards and policies implicit in the equation of standards and systems, specific monetary standards are no longer specific, but ambiguous in the extreme. Like viruses, they are difficult to identify and impossible to isolate.

Paper standard. The term "paper standard" means anything the user wishes it to mean.[35] To those sympathetic to the concept it is presumed to represent, "paper standard" means "managed currency," connoting probity as well as rationality.[36] Those of the opposite persuasion translate the term as "mismanaged currency," which they generally brand as "fiat," "forced," or "depreciated"—all regarded as synonymous terms of opprobrium.[37] If it is not indicted by its opponents as a fraud, per se, the so-called "paper standard" has, at least, been identified with deceit and "public dishonesty." [38] Obviously, diametrically opposed conceptions are presently designated by the same label.

But is it the label for a genus or species? And should one refer to "the" paper standard or "a" paper standard? The Preparatory Committee for the World Economic Conference of 1933 seemed as unable to agree on this as on anything else.[39] Traditionally, when it was viewed simply as the absence (usually considered temporary) of a metallic standard of value, the "paper standard" was construed as a species—and one that had not been positively identified. The term had no positive meaning.[40] As the concept of a monetary standard grew to envelope the monetary system and as the recognized variety of monetary policies under inconvertibility multiplied, "paper standard" came to mean almost anything. The term became the name of a genus,[41] none of whose manifold species had ever been precisely identified. Not being sure of exactly what it is that they are referring to, modern authors vacillate between references to "the" paper standard and "a" paper standard.[42] Today, "paper standard" means anything other than domestic convertibility; therefore it means nothing in particular.

Gold standard. The "gold standard," on the other hand, denotes the presence, rather than the absence, of something. But what are the elements whose presence is both necessary and sufficient to affirm the existence of the gold standard? Agreement has been reduced instead of broadened by modern attempts to describe the mechanism and operation of the "gold standard system." "The gold standard" has been so variously interpreted that its proponents have appeared to confuse it with division of labor,[43] economic progress,[44] honesty, and virtue in general,[45] while its opponents have blamed it for practically all the economic ills that have beset modern societies.[46] Truly, the "gold standard means many things to many people." [47]

The general abrogation of the gold standard in the early 'thirties was followed by repeated affirmations of *the* gold standard and the desirability of *its* reinstatement. But the supporting arguments often obscured, rather than clarified, what was really wanted. "Indeed, the many conditions and qualifications with which a declaration in favour of a restoration of the gold standard

69

is usually accompanied, render it more of an epitaph than a confession of faith."[48] Recently, reinterpretation of the gold standard has replaced restoration in popularity.[49] We appear to be in the process of reestablishing the gold standard by the painless process of redefinition. Some of the restatements have broadened the gold standard into such an amorphous notion that it is impervious to any attack short of a denial that gold has value.[50] Some years ago Chandler wrote, "It is almost meaningless to speak of *the* gold standard . . ."[51] Today, "almost" can safely be dropped from the statement.

It would seem extremely doubtful that we can any longer speak meaningfully of even *a* gold standard. The recent tendency to interpret *any* monetary use of gold—however indirect or variable its relation to money—as a gold standard[52] obliterates the distinction between gold and paper standards. Anything as universally desired and as comparatively stable in value as gold will be related in *some* way to *any* monetary system, at least insofar as foreign transactions are concerned.[53] Moreover, some "standard" other than gold is implicit in any so-called "gold standard" that involves the manipulation of the price of gold.[54] The concept of a "gold standard" has disintegrated as its label was emptied of any substantive content by broadening its coverage to include any monetary system that makes use of gold in any way.[55]

The term "gold standard" should, therefore, either be dropped as a meaningless source of confusion or be restored to usefulness by a substantive transfusion. Any attempt to accomplish the latter raises several troublesome questions, viz.: (1) Is it *the* gold standard or *a* gold standard? (2) What is the distinction between the "pure" and "limited" ("modified," "restricted," etc.) forms of the gold standard? (3) What is the difference between modification and abandonment of the (a?) gold standard? The remainder of this chapter will be devoted to a consideration of these questions. It will be shown that with present monetary concepts only the first of the three questions can be answered.

70

Which is the appropriate article modifier for the term "gold standard"? Some authors use "the";[56] others use "a";[57] still others employ both interchangeably.[58] In some cases, resort to both articles appears to be explained by a distinction between *the* genus gold standard and *a* species of that genus, such as a gold-coin standard, gold-bullion standard, etc.[59] However, the identified species may not be standards at all, but merely gold policies considered appropriate to different conceptions of *the* gold standard which have varied from the classical school's substantive identification of the value of money with that of gold,[60] to the more recent purely formal and nominal equation of these values by methods which mean that the goods value of gold varies with that of money, instead of the goods value of money varying with that of gold.[61] In other words, the different alleged gold standards may actually be different monetary systems (i.e., sets of policies relative to gold and related matters) based on different views of *the* gold standard.[62] This would imply that the term "gold standard" is the name of a species, not a genus, which would, in turn, indicate that there is only one gold standard, not many. Though this conceptual construction would permit differences of opinion as to the meaning of *the* "gold standard," and as to the policies appropriate thereto, it precludes the possibility of multiple gold standards. Moreover, this interpretation does less violence to language than one which includes many different gold standards. As gold is a single element,[63] the plural form "gold standards" smacks of a contradiction of terms. Since gold is *one* thing, it does not appear to be logically possible for there to be more than one gold standard. In short, though there may be different interpretations of *the* gold standard, logic precludes the possibility of a variety of gold standards. Therefore, it appears that the various alleged "gold standards" actually refer to different sets of policies deemed by different people to be necessary to implement their respective concepts of *the* "gold standard."

Nevertheless, protracted discourses on "modified" versus "pure" forms of the gold standard have filled the pages of popular and professional publications.[64] Such discussions naturally raise the question, what is the difference between the "pure" ("full," "free," etc.) gold standard [65] and the "modified" ("limited," "restricted," etc.) variants? [66] Authorities offer varying explanations of the difference, namely: (1) a constant versus variable "gold-money ratio," [67] (2) absence versus presence of management of the monetary system,[68] and (3) freedom versus control of the supply of and demand for gold,[69] including exportation and importation [70] as well as acquisition of gold "from the monetary authorities." [71] However, it has been doubted that a "pure gold standard" in any sense of the term ever existed anywhere.[72] "Modern gold standards have differed in degrees of impurity rather than in differences in kind . . ." [73] F. A. von Hayek acknowledged this by calling the "traditional gold standard" a " 'mixed' system." [74] Thus, the distinction between the so-called "pure" and "modified" gold standards reduces to one of mechanics rather than substance; and the mechanics relate more to monetary systems than to standards.[75] Consequently, the supposed differentiation appears to be merely another form of the confusion springing from the failure to distinguish between monetary standards and policies.

The term "restricted gold bullion standard" [76] suggests the question, how much can the gold standard be restricted and still remain the gold standard? In other words, what is the difference between modification and abandonment of the gold standard? It was once thought that convertibility made the difference, but in the modern age of quasi-convertibility, the question persists in the following form: How much restriction on domestic convertibility can the gold standard sustain? Before this question was answered, convertibility came to be interpreted as primarily an external instead of internal phenomenon.[77] This transition coincided with the virtual elimination of internal convertibility, and, in effect, the reinterpretation eliminated convertibility as a criterion for the distinction between restriction and rejection of the gold standard in any substantive sense. Paper-standard currencies have generally been externally convertible in the modern sense of the term.[78] Neither is "management" any longer believed to distinguish the paper standard from the gold standard.[79] "All monetary standards, metallic as well as inconvertible, are now highly managed, and their success depends largely on the quality of their management." [80] Even the one-time "money doctor" who specialized in the gold-standard cure for monetary ills said, "A highly managed paper money currency [neither convertible nor defined in terms of gold] might conceivably be on a gold standard." [81] Respecting monetary management "to insulate the domestic income flow from the vagaries of international commerce [gold flows]," Shaw remarked, "The policy condition of equilibrium is violated to satisfy the payments condition of equilibrium in the balance of payments. This is a deviation from gold-standard practice and constitutes going off gold when it is pushed to extremes." [82] But when are the "extremes" reached? What are the criteria of the gold standard's extremity? The answer is not to be found in current literature. R. A. Lehfeldt maintained, moreover, that Fisher's "compensated dollar plan" and government control of gold production to stabilize the price level represented no more of a departure from the gold standard than did vigorous central-bank policy for the same purpose.[83] In the absence of a boundary line between limitation and abrogation of the gold standard,[84] it is understandable—indeed, it was inevitable—that the present monetary standard of the United States is alternatively interpreted as gold,[85] paper,[86] a compromise between the two,[87] or a combination of both (gold externally and paper internally).[88] From the never-never land created by obliteration of the boundary between gold and paper standards has come the paradoxical term "variable gold standard" [89] and the enigmatic characterization of the post-1934 standard in the United States as an "inconvertible paper money gold standard," [90] an "inconvertible managed gold standard," [91] or a "managed inconvertible gold standard." [92] It is significant to note that the irony implicit in these labels [93] is no longer recognized.[94] "Finally, the battle of the standards in the future . . . will be . . . between *some form of gold standard* and *managed credit systems*." [95] Un-

73

fortunately, since we cannot tell the difference, we cannot predict the outcome.

CONCLUSION

Enlargement of the concept of a monetary standard to embrace the entire monetary system not only aggravated the ambiguity of the concept, but also added another conceptual confusion. This construction of the monetary standard confused it with monetary policies. Specific standards, therefore, became so ambiguous that differentiation of species was impossible. Even the line of demarkation between such supposed opposites as the gold standard and the paper standard was destroyed. Terms for alleged standards have come to mean everything; therefore they mean nothing. Substantive issues have been sucked into the quicksand of a spreading terminological swamp. The swamp must be drained. To restore sufficient communicability among economists to give promise of resolving the "real" monetary issues of our time, two courses of action are open: One alternative is to drop the term "standard" from the field of money, thus enabling economists to concentrate on monetary objectives and policies unencumbered by the emotional overtones of a vague and possibly obsolete term. Modern monetary literature is moving in this direction. The other alternative is to formulate a workable generic concept of a monetary standard for modern conditions. The next chapter will explore the latter possibility.

VI

TOWARD A
WORKABLE CONCEPT
OF A MONETARY
STANDARD

The monetary standard was once a distinct and useful concept. Modern confusion of the standard with policies and objectives has led to neglect of the idea of a monetary standard. If it no longer serves any useful purpose, the term should be abandoned along with the idea. Before this logical consequence of the present tendency comes to fruition, however, it would seem advisable to consider the possibility of restoring the usefulness of the concept by a reconstruction compatible with modern economic institutions and theory. This chapter will consider a reinterpretation that is found in current literature and offer an alternative.[1]

75

THE PRINCIPLE BY WHICH THE SUPPLY OF MONEY IS LIMITED

Some modern authorities appear to conceive of the monetary standard as the principle by which the supply of money is limited.[2] This view, with its shift in emphasis from the cost to the quantity of money, represents a clear break with classical metallism and the commodity theory of the long-run value of money. Accordingly, its advocates include some of the more emancipated of monetary economists. A few of them expressly address themselves to elucidating the generic idea of a monetary standard. E. M. Bernstein furnished an exceptional consideration of "The Meaning of the Standard" as an introduction to his chapter on "Gold and Other Monetary Standards."[3] "For simplicity,"[4] he explained, "the *monetary standard* is hereafter regarded as the *basis* by which the *supply of money and its value* in a country are *ultimately limited.*"[5] A few years later, George N. Halm said, "Different monetary standards are fundamentally nothing else but different *methods of limiting the total quantity of money.*"[6] It should be noted that Halm substituted "methods" for Bernstein's "basis" and dropped the "value" of money from the concept of the standard. The elimination of "value" represented a step forward in clarifying the concept, whereas the substitution of "methods" marked a step backward. Since the relationship between the quantity and value of money was—and still is—a disputed issue in monetary theory, no generally applicable concept of a monetary standard can—at least for the present—include a direct connection between the quantity and value of money.[7] In freeing the concept from the dualism in Bernstein's statement, Halm contributed to its clarification. On the other hand, however, in substituting "methods" for "basis" Halm injected the confusion of standards and policies that is characteristic of the alternative concept of the monetary standard as a monetary system.[8] Edward S. Shaw's treatment of the subject does not appear to be quite so encumbered with these traditional difficulties. His definition of "the monetary standard" as "an optional instrument of monetary control" seems to mean the *principle* limiting the quantity of money.[9]

This concept of a monetary standard is occasionally implied by modern discussions of specific standards. Paradoxically, the implication is found in the writings of the most conservative as well as the most liberal monetary thinkers. An example of the former is the orthodox defense of the traditional gold-coin standard on the ground that it leaves control of the quantity of money in the hands of the people, who can, therefore, protect their property from indirect confiscation through the fiscal irresponsibility of politicians.[10] Though his emphasis relative to mechanics is quite different, Sir Dennis H. Robertson's more liberal view of the gold standard implies the same concept of a monetary standard:

> In this book, then, the phrase "a gold standard" will be used to denote a state of affairs in which a country keeps the value of its monetary unit and the value of a defined weight of gold at an equality with one another. The reader is invited to pay particular attention to this definition, which as he will appreciate later is framed with a certain low cunning.
>
> Since the value of money depends among other things on the quantity of it in existence, a policy of keeping this value at an equality with that of a defined weight of gold involves the *regulation of the supply of money,* and demands therefore from the central monetary authority (whether this be the Government or a Central Bank or a combination of the two) a certain measure of continuous and conscious activity.[11]

Irrespective of viewpoint, therefore, the conception of a monetary standard as the principle by which the money supply is regulated—or, at least, limited—appears to be implicit in many modern discussions of money.[12]

Not necessarily implicit in discussions of metallic standards. Nevertheless, the rationale of a metallic standard does not necessarily imply this concept of a monetary standard. Insofar as any particular defense of a metallic standard may imply this interpretation of the genus monetary standard, the latter can refer today only to the ultimate limitation, not the regulation, of the

77

money supply. Particularly since nonstandard money has been a multiple of standard money, the cyclical oscillations of the money supply short of the maximum limit permitted by the standard have often been regulated by things other than the reserve of standard metal.[13] And viewing a monetary standard as the principle limiting the quantity of money is precluded by a number of beliefs widely held by defenders of the gold standard in the past and/or present. First, neoclassical and modern recognition that credit media are designed to supplement, not merely replace, standard money implicitly acknowledges a conscious and successful effort to circumvent the supposed standard limitation on the currency.[14] Second, this concept of the standard, with its long-run quantity-theory orientation, is antithetical to the commodity theory of money, on which the nineteenth-century defense of the gold standard was based.[15] Third, the "real bills" doctrine (otherwise known as the "banking principle" of note issue and later as the "commercial loan theory of banking"), another premise of the monometallist argument against bimetallism,[16] denied that the volume of currency was limited by gold reserves.[17] Fourth, the gold limitation on the currency—such as was presumed under the gold-coin standard [18]—was precisely what was supposed to be eluded by the gold-bullion [19] and gold-exchange standards.[20] And fifth, acknowledgment that the money supply was managed under the various forms of the gold standard constitutes an admission that the gold standard did not necessarily mean the regulation or limitation of the quantity of money by the quantity of gold reserves.[21] Generally, therefore, in modern literature, control of the money supply under metallic as well as paper standards has been a problem rather than a matter of principle.[22]

Although interpretation of the monetary standard as the principle limiting the money supply appears to be consistent with the classical view of the monetary standard as the material comprising the standard of value,[23] the two concepts are not identical. They are different in orientation and emphasis. The modern concept of the standard is oriented to the quantity theory and the goods value of money, whereas the classical concept was

78

oriented to the commodity theory of the long-run value of money [24] and to the relative values of goods.[25] The dissimilarity in emphasis is equally significant. While the modern concept regards the "long-run" value of money as incidental to its quantity, classical thought viewed the quantity of money as incidental to its long-run value (relative real cost).[26] In fact, Ricardo looked upon his bullion standard proposal as an "expedient" for temporarily relieving the quantity of currency from the limitation of the bullion reserve in order to moderate short-run deviations of the value of money from its cost of acquisition.[27] It appears, therefore, that neither classical nor modern thought is consistent with the concept of a monetary standard as the principle by which the supply of money (in classical parlance, "currency"[28]) is limited.

Limited relevance of this concept. Moreover, the relevance of this concept of a monetary standard to modern conditions is severely limited. Any really effective limitation on the money supply in recession or depression will be promptly removed in order to eliminate an aggravation of contraction and/or an obstacle to recovery. The very authorities who appear to support this view of a monetary standard recognize its irrelevance to cyclical fluctuations.[29] It has more relevance to the long run, but not a great deal more. In the analytical long run, the limitation on the quantity of money is of no consequence. Commodities and services would merely exchange at higher or lower prices, with no necessary effect on real incomes.[30] In the historical long run, on the other hand, some distributive effects must be acknowledged, particularly between debtors and creditors.[31] Under either interpretation of the "long run," however, the aggregative consequences are presently considered by many as less important than other considerations, such as employment and growth.

Even in the "long run," whatever the interpretation of the term, monetary standards have not, in fact, afforded a precise—or even an ascertainable—limit to the money supply. Under the supposedly "automatic" metallic standards of the nineteenth century,

79

credit media of exchange mushroomed more or less independently of gold and silver reserves as long as such "currency" was not recognized as "money."[32] After bank deposits, as well as notes, were included in the concept of money, the limitation imposed upon the money supply by metallic reserves was evaded through efforts to "economize" the standard metal.[33] Furthermore, the maintenance of excess reserves by some reserve countries, such as the United States, tended to insulate their domestic currencies from variations in reserves. Modern societies appear to be unwilling to abide any physical limitation to the money supply.[34] The so-called "paper standard" constitutes *de jure* recognition of this fact.[35]

Not used as the basis of classification. The various monetary standards have not been generally distinguished by different principles for limiting the quantity of exchange media. By the time the connection between gold and bank deposits as well as bank notes was acknowledged, the role of gold as the exclusive—or even primary—determinant of the money supply was denied by even most advocates of the gold standard.[36] Public officials and private authorities emphasize many other factors affecting the money supply directly, as well as indirectly through their impact on the decisions of the monetary authorities.

Even those who conceive of a monetary standard as the principle by which the supply of money is limited do not use this concept as the basis for classifying specific standards. They explicitly acknowledge species that are inconsistent with their expressed interpretation of the generic concept. The latter, for example, is contradicted by the use of the term "tabular standard" or "multiple standard" to mean a standard for adjustment of contractual payments to eliminate inequities arising from changes in the quantity and value of money.[37] The "limping standard"[38] and the "paper standard"[39] are also not species of the claimed genus. Nor is the "managed gold standard" when it is managed for any purpose other than maintaining a direct linkage between the volume of money and gold reserves.[40] A concept that is not used by its own authors can

80

hardly be taken seriously by others.[41] Neglect of the concept has not been a mere accidental oversight, either. "Changes in the structure of the monetary system have brought about a situation in which there is no real method [i.e., principle] of regulation [of the money supply] and therefore no real standard."[42]

THE CRITERION OF MONETARY POLICY

The concept of a monetary standard considered in the preceding section of this chapter represents an incomplete break with traditional views in the quest for relevance and workability in the modern institutional and theoretical setting. The transition from historical to modern relevance and usefulness may be completed by conceiving a monetary standard as the criterion, or referent, of monetary policy.[43] This interpretation is free from the logical and theoretical difficulties inherent in the alternative concepts of a monetary standard. It involves no internal inconsistency,[44] and it is consistent with abstract money and modern value theory, as well as with commodity money and classical value theory.[45] All species of this genus can be identified without difficulty. Whatever is, in fact, used as the criterion of monetary policy constitutes the monetary standard. Conversely, this concept enables us to recognize the absence of a standard. If policy decisions are made without any ascertainable criterion for the choices among alternatives, then there is no monetary standard. The latter condition may or may not be desirable, but concepts and terms which reveal facts, rather than obscure them, are desirable.

What are the specific standards embraced by this generic concept? On the assumption of the primacy of the national approach to social goals, a list of possible *national* monetary standards (criteria of monetary policy) would include: gold, silver, bimetallism, symmetallism, commodity-reserve, goods, labor, and employment. In contrast, assuming the priority of the international ap-

81

proach to our objectives, we should characterize the first five criteria in the above list as *international* standards and replace the last three by a balance-of-payments standard. Notice that all except the last in each list (national and international) purport to stabilize the internal value of money in terms of some thing or things. The stable exchange rates between metallic standard currencies is explained by the fact that things equal to the same thing are equal to each other. The last standard in each group is more abstract (and, therefore, more in keeping with the abstract nature of modern money?). Other standards may be added as the list of possible criteria is supplemented by further knowledge.[46] Meanwhile, we should recognize that the so-called "managed" (plus whatever other qualifying adjectives may be used) "gold standard" which is managed on the basis of criteria other than gold (whether business conditions, price level, employment, or what not) is *not* a *gold* standard.

Clarification of the significance and relationship of monetary objectives, policies, and standards. Interpreting the monetary standard as the referent of monetary policy facilitates comprehension of monetary objectives and monetary policies and of the distinctions as well as the interrelationship among all three concepts. Monetary objectives are goals that are attainable primarily (though not necessarily exclusively) by monetary means. Monetary policies are alternative courses of action relative to monetary phenomena.[47] More specifically, a monetary policy may be defined as an alternative course of action designed to affect the effective quantity of money in some particular way.[48] Monetary objectives are the ends of the monetary system, and monetary policies are the means to those ends.[49] But, as in other areas of human endeavor, there are many means to achieve a given end. If the selection is a rational one, it is based on some criterion. The criterion guiding the choices of policy makers among alternative monetary policies is the monetary standard.

The analogy of a mountain climber's approach to a strange mountain might be illustrative. His objective is to reach the top of the mountain.

82

There are many ways to get there. If he begins the ascent from the nearest bus stop and merely "follows his nose," he will likely lose his way or his life. No rational man would proceed in this manner. He would select the most expeditious of the alternative routes to his goal by referring to a map or a professional guide. Either referent would indicate the best route and means of getting to his destination. Use of a burro for transporting supplies might be suggested. If the would-be mountain climber failed to distinguish the peak from either the burro or guide, he might mount the latter, thinking he had accomplished his objective. In such an eventuality, his friends would lose no time in referring him to the nearest psychiatrist.

Such mistakes are not made by normal people in the trivial aspects of day-to-day living. It is only in important matters like the operation of the monetary system that such confusion has become common. Here ends and means are often confused. "Full employment," for example, is alternatively referred to as a "policy" and as an "aim" of policy.[50] The same ambivalence characterizes modern usage relative to "price-level stabilization." [51] Similarly, the goals and guides (i.e., standards) of monetary policy are frequently confounded.[52] "Price (level) stability" reappears as, alternatively, a monetary objective and a monetary standard.[53] What were formerly designated as changes in the monetary standard are now called shifts in the objectives of monetary policy.[54] However, the alleged mutations actually appear to be modifications of the criteria for the perennially desiderated stabilization.[55]

The distinction between guides (standards) and means (policies) is also obliterated in traditional treatments of the subject.[56] The customary description of the unrestricted gold standard, for example, confuses the standard with policies appropriate to it. Only the first of the traditional requisites—definition of the monetary unit in terms of a specific quantity of gold—is substantive. All the other requirements are the mechanical means of implementing the first; that is, they are the policies required to maintain the gold standard. Only a few modern writers have recognized this crucial distinction between the monetary stand-

83

ard and monetary policies.[57] In short, some modern writers have confused the objectives of monetary policy with the policies designed to achieve the objectives; others have confounded monetary objectives with monetary standards; still others have failed to discriminate between the monetary standard and the policies necessary for its implementation. Finally, and even more regretfully, it must be observed that modern economic literature appears at times to demonstrate a combination of all these confusions, seeming to fuse monetary objectives, policies, and standards into one amorphous mess.[58] Such conceptual anarchy would be precluded by interpreting the monetary standard to be the criterion for the selection of the monetary policies most efficacious in achieving the society's objectives.

Resolution of the "rules-versus-authorities" issue. The twentieth-century controversy between the advocates of the gold standard and the proponents of a managed currency has been traditionally cast in terms of a choice between a monetary standard operating automatically according to objective rules, on the one hand, and monetary management in accordance with the subjective discretion of authorities, on the other hand.[59] "Shall the Quantity of Gold Subject to World Influences of Supply and Demand or the Deliberate and Conscious Administration of Men Determine the General Level of Prices?" [60] If a choice between such clear-cut opposites was ever actually available, it is not now, and it has not been so for a long time. Management of the monetary system is inescapable. As Walter Bagehot observed, "Money will not manage itself . . ." [61] Provision of money long ago became one of the responsibilities of government. In modern times, management of money has been largely delegated to the central bank,[62] which "has a great deal of money to manage." [63] The volume of money to be managed has not diminished since Bagehot's time. "For effective monetary policy, adequate power must have been delegated to the monetary-fiscal authority . . . This is true whether the basic plan is for a discretionary authority or a 'rule,' since *even under the rule the problem of implementation remains to be handled on at least a semi-discretionary*

84

basis." [64] Good, bad, or indifferent, management of money is a fact.[65]

The monetary *system* was managed even when gold was—in its traditional, nineteenth-century, unrestricted sense—the monetary *standard*.[66] The claimed "automatic operation" of the gold standard [67] represented a confusion of the monetary standard with the monetary system [68] and, therefore, a confounding of the standard and its implementing policies.[69] Although some policies were specified by law under the gold standard,[70] all were not; [71] consequently the operation of the monetary system was not automatic.[72] Bagehot's classic, *Lombard Street,* is a description of monetary management under the traditional gold standard.

Currency management has increased perforce with the growth of credit media as a supplement to, instead of a mere substitute for, standard money.[73] Augmentation of "pure Commodity Money" by credit money converted the monetary structure into what John Maynard Keynes called a "mixed Managed System." [74] The British Bank Act of 1844 constituted explicit acknowledgment that additional legislation was required to insure that the "mixed currency" system would be managed consistently with the gold standard.[75] However, since bank deposits were not included in the "gold cover" requirement of this act, the Bank of England enjoyed an ever-widening latitude in its monetary management as the deposit component of the circulation expanded relative to the note component.[76] Neglect of the monetary significance of deposits would have been fatal to the gold standard had not the central bank discovered how to manage the aggregate of bank credit by manipulating the "bank-rate." [77] Thus, the development of credit money made monetary management mandatory even under the "gold-coin standard." [78]

In the nineteenth century the central bank managed the monetary system with two often-conflicting purposes in mind,[79] namely, preservation of the gold standard [80] and prevention of the economic collapse that rigid adherence to the gold standard would cause in the

85

event of a scramble for liquidity that could not be satisfied by the limited gold reserves relative to the claims against them.[81] The former objective normally took precedence over the latter, which was typically dealt with primarily as an emergency. "The ostensible duty of a central bank," wrote R. G. Hawtrey, "is *to maintain the monetary standard* of the country. That is what *limits its powers as a lender of last resort.* And nineteenth-century doctrine accepted the maintenance of a prescribed metallic standard as affording the central bank complete guidance. The art of central banking comprised simply the technical apparatus by which this end was to be secured." [82] Such was the classical bullionist position, which Hawtrey updated by pointing out that there is no gold reserve ratio that will automatically maintain the gold standard, much less the stability of the economy:

> Even if the central bank covered the whole of its obligations with gold, that would still not be enough. The depositors of commercial banks would draw out gold, and when the commercial banks had exhausted their reserve deposits at the central bank and the demands of their depositors still persisted, they would have either to stop payment or to borrow from the central bank. To save the entire banking system from breaking down, the central bank would be compelled to fulfil its essential function of the lender of last resort, and would thereby create new obligations uncovered by gold for the express purpose of enabling panic-stricken depositors to withdraw gold.

> It is therefore *impracticable* to provide against a flight from the currency. All that it is worthwhile to aim at is a gold reserve great enough (with some margin) to meet the demands that may arise in the interval between the initiation of a credit restriction and its becoming effective.[83]

Thus, it was authoritatively admitted that shifting sand made it impossible precisely to chart the narrow and devious channel between the Scylla of the gold standard and the Charybdis of collapse.

This was precisely the reason why antibullionists opposed the gold standard. They preferred preservation of general solvency to preservation of convertibility; therefore they advocated expansion rather than contraction of bank notes in the eventuality of what would be termed today a positive shift in liquidity preference.[84] The classical school saw no cure for a serious internal drain of gold [85] other than preventing its cause: "overtrading" and the associated overexpansion of bank credit which "brings on the revulsion called a commercial crisis." [86] Ricardian bullionists interpreted any external drain as proof that bank notes should be contracted.[87] Antibullionists and most exponents of the banking school feared that such restriction might trigger a depressing internal drain that would be incurable as long as convertibility was maintained.[88] The Tooke-Fullarton-John Stuart Mill wing of the banking school argued that bank-note issue should be insulated against international bullion movements associated with unilateral payments because the latter represent temporary transfers of gold hoards unrelated to internal circulation.[89] Whether an external drain of gold signaled a temporary drawing on bank reserves and hoards that should not be allowed to affect the internal circulation, or an overexpansion of note issue that should be reversed (and, if the latter, how rapidly the prescribed cure could be administered without causing the complication of a self-inflammatory internal drain) were recurrent issues in central-bank monetary management under the nineteenth-century gold standard.[90] Distinguishing between internal and external drains of gold and isolating the cause of the latter called for a high order of discretionary judgment on the part of monetary authorities. The existence of separate national banking systems linked by a common ultimate fractional reserve compelled monetary management.[91] The "rules" of the pre-1914 gold standard required discretion in their interpretation and implementation.

One of the precautions against the vulnerability of the gold standard to internal as well as external drains was a normal maintenance of excess reserves. "Given fractional reserve banking, an international monetary standard, and such conditions of unstable equilibrium as characterize modern [in the broad sense, including the nineteenth century] economic systems, *such a degree of management of the currency as is involved in fairly large central bank reserves* would seem to be highly desirable." [92] The ratio between national gold reserves and central bank liabilities has never been uniform either among gold standard countries,[93] or in the same country through time.[94] The Bank of England reserve ratio was left largely to the discretion of the Bank directors[95]—even by the Bank Act of 1844.[96] "A standard for the exercise of this discretion was evolved empirically." [97] Successive crises raised the level of reserves which the Bank sought to keep.[98] In any case, "the amount of reserves carried by the banks, even by the central bank, was in most countries determined by the banks themselves, the state not even imposing a legal minimum." [99] Even the minimum legally required gold reserves against notes were not adhered to rigidly. "Suspension of the Bank Act in England and the provisions in German [enacted in 1875] and American law [Federal Reserve Act] involving a tax on reserve deficiencies represented situations where the reserve ratio could be lowered temporarily in order to permit an expansion of the circulating medium [independently of gold]." [100] "These are clear-cut examples of a departure from the rigid reserve relationships prescribed by automatism, in the search for a greater degree of elasticity." [101] The reserves of Federal Reserve banks were not even defined exclusively in terms of gold until 1945.[102] And long before then, the Federal Reserve Board had already consigned this policy guide to history without suggesting any precise substitute referent for the exercise of its discretion.[103] In short, the monetary management required by the augmentation of the money supply through credit media was permitted by variable central-bank reserve ratios.

Within the permissive limits of variable gold-reserve ratios, several tools of positive monetary management were developed. The central-bank discount rate was the first to be used. "The efficacy of Bank-rate for the management of a managed money was a great discovery and also a most novel one—a few years earlier the Bank of England had not had the slightest understanding of any connection between bank-rate policy and the maintenance of the standard." [104] Subsequently, passive acceptance of the monetary effects of international bullion movements was "not considered enough" to maintain "the classical gold standard." [105] "The 'rules of the game' demanded that central banks

88

should react positively to gold flows; Bank Rate is raised or lowered according to whether a country is losing or gaining gold. Such action clearly reinforces and speeds up the automatic changes in the quantity of bank deposits . . . It also provides a palliative for the situation; the change in relative interest rates causes short-term capital movements which in turn cause some reduction or even reversal of the gold flow." [106] The currency school "demurred to the [banking school] doctrine that the discounting of real bills constituted any check against overissue and immediately turned to the influence of the rate of interest as the significant controlling factor." [107] George J. Goschen's classic description of international adjustments under the gold standard assigned an important role to manipulation of its discount rate by the Bank of England.[108] The presumed automaticity of the English monetary system from 1844 to 1914 was based on the assumption that all gold movements were accounted for, fundamentally, by the balance of trade on current account.[109] Offsetting capital movements stimulated by the Bank of England's discount policies tended to be ignored.[110] Yet, it was precisely these policies that preserved the gold standard by keeping specie movements within the tolerance limits imposed by the worldwide supply and distribution of gold.[111]

Open market operations developed as another means of monetary management under the gold standard.[112] This tended further to reduce the direct connection between gold reserves and the money supply.[113] Open market transactions were used to reinforce central-bank discount policies.[114] These techniques became supplemented by others that are well known to monetary analysts.[115]

The latitude for the discretion of the monetary managers was increased under the restricted forms in which the gold standard was restored after World War I.[116] Various means of economizing the use of gold[117] freed the monetary authorities from some of the former constraints bringing about "a centralization of monetary control and management over the gold supply." [118] The gold bullion standard concentrated monetary gold stocks "in the hands of central banks and governments." [119] This, "together

89

with the reduced responsibility for redeeming other types of money in gold, *gave monetary authorities much more leeway in monetary management.* [120] Moreover, while the gold bullion standard reduced "the need for gold relative to the total money supply," [121] the gold-exchange standard made the same gold serve two masters.[122] Lending abroad would not cause the credit restriction in the reserve country that it would under an international gold standard.[123] "The abolition of the automatic effect of gold movements on the credit structure *gave the monetary authorities a new freedom of action and at the same time a new responsibility. It was up to their wisdom and insight to use the mechanism of restricting and expanding credit in accordance with the country's economic policy.*" [124] Finally, the limited gold bullion standard appeared to eliminate the dilemma of the central bank in attempting simultaneously to support the gold standard and serve as a lender of last resort. The apparent solution stemmed from the restrictions on convertibility,[125] which further reduced the gold limitation on the money supply.[126] Thus, monetary management increased as the connection between gold reserves and the money supply weakened.

Due to the entrepôt position of England in world trade and finance, the Bank of England became the primary manager of the international monetary system of the metallic-standard world in the nineteenth century.[127] "The distinguishing feature of the pre-War gold standard was the unity of policy imposed on the system through London's control over international lending, both short-term and long." [128] International capital flows were managed by the Bank of England through its discount policy in such a way as to keep specie movements within manageable proportions.[129] Angas characterized these financial arrangements as a " 'Controlled Sterling Loan' type of gold standard," "manipulated gold-loan standard," or, in other words, "very largely a sterling standard." [130] Later writers unequivocally identified the pre-World-War-I gold standard as a "sterling standard." [131] Chandler has remarked, "It is but little exaggeration to say that gold was on the sterling standard." [132] And Keynes concluded, "Gold went off sterling in 1931." [133] In short, leading authorities have conceded that there was, in the nineteenth and early twentieth centuries, no international gold standard, but a sterling standard with a managed gold mechanism for linking other currencies to the standard currency.[134] This may be one of the reasons why the classical term "gold standard" (of value) has been replaced by the rubric, "gold standard *system.*" [135]

World War I drastically modified the world financial structure. "After the First World War the conditions for a smoothly working single-centered international monetary system no longer existed. The gold standard was restored (in England in 1925), but it was a different system from that existing before 1914, and it never worked as satisfactorily. One explanation of this was that the system no longer had a single centre: New York now rivaled London as an international financial centre." [136] And the American Federal Reserve System rivaled the Bank of England in the managerial functions.[137] Some critics have viewed these changes as, in effect, transposing the so-called gold standard from a sterling to a dollar standard.[138]

Due to the isolationist sentiment prevailing in the United States after World War I, American management of the monetary system was more domestically oriented than the British had been. Not only did the Federal Reserve System neglect gold reserves in its determination of monetary policies,[139] it often pursued policies designed to offset the domestic effects of bullion movements.[140] Consequently, Federal Reserve monetary management did not limit gold movements as the Bank of England had done.[141] Countries confronted by a chronic loss of gold were forced in some measure to ape the isolationism of the United States. They weakened the connection between their moneys and gold while reorienting their monetary policies toward more domestic considerations.[142] Gold reserves became less of a guide to domestic policies and more of a pool of international liquidity designed to insulate the internal economy from foreign aberrations.[143] Hence, without fanfare, the banking school ultimately triumphed over the currency school.[144]

Gold was replaced by other criteria of monetary policy in the allegedly gold-standard world of the 'twenties.[145] The primary policy guide adopted by the Federal Reserve System in the early 'twenties was the maintenance of "sound credit conditions." [146] This was followed by the criterion of "stable business conditions." [147] The depression decade brought the guide of a stable price level to the forefront.[148] World War II added the referent of a stable interest rate.[149] In the postwar world stable high-level employment has competed with all the other criteria for the attention of policy makers.[150] And the "cold war" is shoving "growth" to the top of the list.[151] Gold is no longer the criterion of monetary policy.

Gold had ceased to be the criterion of monetary policy long before the formal abrogation of the gold standard that began in 1931. It had not been for some time the standard in any but a relatively meaningless, legalistic sense of the term. Within one century, the defenders of the gold standard had unconsciously adopted the philosophy of their antibullionist opponents, to wit: "If our national prosperity is to continue subject to the influence of circumstances over which we have no control [i.e., the luck of gold miners], or liable to the regulations of other states to whom we cannot dictate, it is plain we are then *no longer an independent nation.*" [152] Implementation of the new orthodoxy meant an actual, though unrecognized, departure from the gold standard. People, generally, were no longer willing to stabilize the monetary unit in terms of gold, come what may.[153] The connection between gold and money—already tenuous in the 'twenties [154]—was practically, though not legally, eliminated by the means already pointed out. Gold no longer served as either the standard of value for goods or the regulator of the money supply.[155] These facts removed the conceptual and empirical content from the notion of gold as standard money.

The *de facto* departure from the gold standard prior to 1931 was not generally recognized because the gold standard had become confused with the positive policies required for its implementation.[156] The continuation of these policies was necessary, but not sufficient, to preserve the gold standard. The sufficient condition was the absence of policies that offset the purpose and effect of

92

the necessary policies. But, as already indicated, precisely this offsetting effect was often the purpose of monetary policy from 1925 to 1931. Although the significance of such monetary policies generally escaped attention,[157] they implied to a few observers that the actual abandonment of the gold standard preceded its legal abrogation.[158] Its substance having been removed by monetary management according to other criteria, only the empty shell of the gold-standard mechanism remained in 1931. It crumbled like a sucked egg under the pressure of the 'thirties.

Whether the monetary system should or should not be managed is no longer an issue among knowledgeable people. The truth of Bagehot's comment that "money will not manage itself" [159] has at last penetrated the general consciousness. Like business and household management, the necessity for monetary management is now generally acknowledged.[160] The issue is *not* whether the monetary system—any more than the government in general—should run automatically by rules (laws) or be run by the discretionary management of men.[161] No such dichotomous alternatives ever existed in human society—or ever will.[162] The issue *is* whether the discretionary management of the monetary system by men should or should not be guided and judged by specific criteria.[163] This fundamental question was lost in the question-begging that has characterized monetary controversies for a century. There are, however, indications that some authorities favor guides for the inescapable management of money,[164] while others are disposed to give the managers a carte blanche to do what they think best and to constitute themselves as the sole judges of what they have done.[165] Completely unguided discretionary management by the monetary authorities is, however, a virtual impossibility. Obstacles to consistent, constructive public policy would be enormous.[166] Such difficulties may be reduced by a political consensus on objectives and determination of a generally understood criterion for the selection of monetary policies looking toward the objectives. The appropriate spheres for rules and the discretion of authorities are clarified by the concept of a monetary standard as the criterion of monetary policy.[167] The policy

93

makers' inescapable exercise of discretion should be guided by some rule or referent of monetary policy.

Implicit use of this concept of a monetary standard. After the ceremonial recitation of traditional terminology has been dispensed with, the monetary standard is often implicitly represented as the criterion of monetary policy. Though the former treatment persists in the handling of legislative history, the latter generally characterizes discussions of contemporary policy making. In Chandler's *Introduction to Monetary Theory,* most of the chapter entitled "Objectives of Monetary Policy" is devoted to what he explicitly labels "Immediate *Criteria* of Monetary Policy." [168] This section is introduced, in part, by the statement, "We must have more immediate *criteria,* or immediate *guideposts,* to show us the way to the ultimate objective." [169] Included among the sets of questions which William G. Bowen says must be considered "if wage-price relationships are to be studied rather than just debated" is "the public policy set which includes the questions of the *criteria* on the basis of which policy decisions are or should be made." [170] Referring to the 'twenties, Whittlesey said, "It was decided to base monetary policy less on gold movements which had been the *guide for central bank policy* and more on the considerably less definite goal of maintaining 'sound credit conditions.' " [171] Nevertheless, "the introduction of a paper standard is by no means the solution of all monetary problems. If the volume of money is to be managed, *criteria of control* must be ascertained." [172]

Implicit employment of this concept of a monetary standard has been typical of both the national and international approaches to the monetary system. In examining monetary policy for internal stabilization, Rollin G. Thomas explicitly identified monetary standards as "guides for monetary and credit policy." [173] Others, viewing monetary matters from the national point of view, characterized specific standards as criteria of monetary policy. Relative to Ricardo's defense of his proposed gold bullion standard, Irving Fisher said, "Ricardo advocated a constant price of gold bullion as the *criterion of monetary policy.*" [174] Lionel D. Edie advised that "the United States, in conjunction with other countries, should not trust to the automatic gold standard as the sole determinant of the volume of bank deposits and currency appropriate for a country, but should develop *criteria for deliberate policy in regulating such volume.* The criteria should include not merely reserve ratios but price indices, rates of growth of production, and speculative movements." [175] Shaw observed that "the Federal Reserve System paid little heed to its own reserve ratio as a *guide to policy*" from 1914 to 1919.[176] And, of the present, Chandler says that "gold has lost much of its popularity as a *determinant of the money supply and monetary policy.*" [177] Relative to the problem of coordinating "fiscal and monetary policy," the Committee on Public Issues of the American Economic Association commented:

> This raises broad issues . . . about the appropriate administrative and political arrangements for the control of monetary and fiscal policies and about the *standards employed to guide these policies.*
>
> . . . .
>
> In the past, also, the standards for monetary action have been very vague and broad. Some economists would favor equally broad standards for governing fiscal policy. Others would favor the acceptance of a single set of more specific *standards*—such as stability of an index of prices or employment—*to govern whatever discretionary action is authorized in both monetary and fiscal policy.*[178]

The idea of stabilizing the monetary unit in terms of goods rather than gold, which developed in the nineteenth century,[179] became in the twentieth the goods standard, wherein a stable price level is construed as the criterion of monetary policy. Irving Fisher had implied this,[180] and Keynes, interpreting him explicitly in these terms, concurred in the substance of the concept, though not in the details of its implementation.[181] Keynes called his own proposed "managed currency" a "policy," not a standard.[182] "The first question" relative to this policy, he said, "is whether the *criterion* [of monetary management] should be a precise arithmetical formula [à la Fisher's price index] or whether it should be sought in a general judgment of the situation based on all the available data." [183] Although Keynes favored

95

more latitude for discretion than was permitted by Fisher's formula, he conceded that an index of prices might be a feasible criterion for the guidance of the monetary managers.[184] "As regards the *criteria, other than the actual trend of prices,* which should determine the action of the controlling authority," Keynes added, "it is beyond the scope of this volume [on money] to deal adequately with the diagnosis and analysis of the credit cycle." [185] While Keynes spoke of the composite commodity of the official price index as the "standard of value," he explained that this is so "in the sense that . . . [the monetary authorities] would employ all their resources to prevent a movement of its price by more than a certain percentage in either direction away from normal, just as before the war they employed all their resources to prevent a movement in the price of gold by more than a certain percentage." [186] Keynes' "managed currency" was not, therefore, proposed as a monetary standard to replace gold. It was not distinguished from the gold standard by "management." He did, however, suggest a different criterion of management.

The deflation of the 'thirties increased interest in a stable price level as the guide to monetary policy. "So, today," said L. G. Melville in 1934, "the greater part of the world rejects the gold standard and pledges its adherence to some kind of goods standard. By a goods standard is meant a monetary system under which the quantity of money would be regulated rather with *reference to the prices of a selected group of goods* than with reference to the quantity of gold." [187] A few years later Donaldson remarked that "the price index as at least one of several criteria tends to be increasingly taken account of in monetary policy." [188] Interest in this criterion was reinforced by the inflation of the 'forties and 'fifties.[189] Plans for stabilizing the price level were called "stable-price-level standards." [190] "While such plans differ in details and methods," declared Woodworth, "all rely on an index of prices to *guide monetary policy.* For this reason it may also be called a 'price-index' standard." [191] Halm pointed out that "we must investigate the possible *criteria of monetary policy.* . . . A conscious control [of the money supply] needs *gauges* by which to judge

96

whether and in which direction and to which degree the monetary instruments ought to be used." [192] And he suggested a possible gauge in the form of a stable goods value for money: "Apart from this somewhat distant connection of the monetary unit with gold (which may periodically be revised through appreciation or depreciation) there are many possible *criteria for monetary management*. For instance the government may try to keep the purchasing power of money stable (*'market-basket' standard*) . . ." [193] A stable-price-level criterion for monetary policy has, therefore, been widely recognized as a possible monetary standard.

At the same time, its limitations have been noted [194] and alternative monetary standards—construed as policy guides—recognized. [195] Shaw pointed out that "market rates of interest on government securities were the *criterion of monetary policy*" in the United States from 1940 to 1948. [196] Woodworth acknowledged the concept of a labor standard under which "an official wage-rate index would become the *monetary guide,* just as an official commodity price index would show the way under the stable-price-level standard." [197] While the labor standard represented an atavism,[198] the employment standard, inspired by the great depression, has retained its modern flavor. Employment "is a very excellent *criterion* to have as a guide to monetary policy." [199] Halm confirmed that "the employment level is certainly a main *criterion.*" [200] Hart's proposed " 'gong and whistle' system" is, in effect, a dual goods and employment standard, under which the operative criterion of monetary policy would be price-level stability when the index of prices rises in excess of a specified rate, and high-level employment stability when unemployment passes stated benchmarks.[201] In their consideration of actual contemporary problems and policies—instead of terminology and legislative history—modern authorities, approaching the subject from the national point of view, have clearly construed the monetary standard as the criterion of monetary policy.

Generally, the same can be said of the modern approach from an international viewpoint. This orientation ordinarily gives primacy to ex-

97

ternal, rather than internal, stability. In the nineteenth century the degree of internal stability attainable by stabilizing money in terms of gold or silver—and, thus, the various monetary units in terms of each other—was considered by orthodox economists the most that could be achieved.[202] Many modern authorities, taking cognizance of the shrinking world and expanding market areas as well as the mounting domestic political pressures on governments, have retained or revived this attitude. In this frame of reference, stable exchange rates —instead of being considered the result of an international equation of money with metal—became internationally the criterion of national monetary policies. An early illustration of this shift in policy referents from specie reserves to exchange rates—under the supposed gold standard—was John Stuart Mill's quarrel with the currency principle.[203] The later decline in the relevance of gold reserves to monetary policy has already been described and documented.[204] The substitute— related but distinct—criterion of monetary policy under what was thought still to be the gold standard has been identified by many twentieth-century writers.[205] In describing the traditional gold-coin standard, Irving Fisher observed that "the stability of the foreign exchanges . . . became the *criterion of monetary stability*." [206] "The central bank," said Halm, "can try to accumulate 'excess' or 'buffer' reserves. Such systems may still be gold standard systems as long as the monetary authorities buy and sell gold at a fixed price and in unlimited amounts. As in the case of the automatic gold standard, maintenance of fixed gold parities (*fixed exchange rates*) *would be the ultimate guide* and objective of monetary policy." [207] The post-1925 gold standard was characterized by Dowrie in the following manner: "The volume of money and credit is as carefully 'managed' as it would be under the Keynes plan,[208] except that the stabilization of the exchange rate with the United States or England, rather than the stability of the internal price level, is the *guide*." [209] Like the nationally oriented, those who have approached monetary problems from the international viewpoint have actually understood the monetary standard—whatever it was called—to mean the criterion of monetary policy.

To the extent that member nations take their commitments to the International Monetary Fund seriously, the "new gold [exchange] standard" [210] is actually a balance-of-payments standard. This view appears to be implicitly confirmed by the recent reinterpretation of the International Monetary Fund Agreement,[211] which represented merely a formal recognition of established practice.[212] In this compromise between internal and external stability, national and international reserves have become confused, and the new tradition of including foreign exchange in monetary reserve [213]—a practice once confined largely to a few underdeveloped countries but now virtually universal— has resulted in considerable double counting of reserves.[214] The illusion has arisen that an alleged founding of domestic policies on these inflated "international reserves" represents a return to the use of gold reserves as the criterion of monetary policy: "Furthermore, the monetary authorities continually look upon *gold and foreign exchange reserves* as an essential *guidepost* because they are aware of the consequences of disorderly monetary conditions for external balance. This is self-evident, but as a matter of fact it has required, during the past decade, prolonged efforts to have the obvious relationships between money supply and *international reserves* accepted once again as a *determining consideration in domestic policy-making.*" [215] What all this appears to amount to is a search for appropriate mechanical means—or a rationalization of the present ones—of implementing the embryonic balance-of-payments guide for monetary authorities. In any case, recent discussions continue to confirm the implication that by the "monetary standard" modern writers mean the criterion of monetary policy, regardless of what they say.

CONCLUSION

Recent literature has suggested a conception of the monetary standard as the principle by which the supply of money is limited. This conceptualization has a certain plausibility. But, contrary to the impression that might be conveyed, it was not implicit in the traditional defense of metallic standards. Moreover, the modern flavor of this concept of a monetary standard is more apparent than real. Consequently, it has been quite appropriately ignored by its own authors when they addressed themselves to actual monetary problems and policy alternatives.

The idea of a monetary standard may be brought to usable fruition by construing it to be the criterion of monetary policy. This concept both distinguishes and relates the monetary phenomena that have become horribly confused, namely: objectives, policies, and standards. Furthermore, it resolves the venerable "rules-versus-authorities" issue. The monetary standard is the rule guiding the monetary authorities in their choices among alternative monetary policies for the attainment of social goals. Though never explicitly stated, this is the concept of a monetary standard that, implicitly, is most generally used today by reputable authorities when attending to present problems rather than past history.

VII

CONCLUSION

The Adam Smith cen-
tenary debate included among the "practical problems which
were to engage English political economists in the coming
decades" the "difficulties of a *conscious monetary policy* (or
'our backward condition' in respect of 'the currency')." [1]
"Conscious monetary policy" appears to mean "discretionary" monetary policy or the availability to monetary authorities of relatively unlimited choices among alternative courses
of action affecting the effective quantity of money. Classical
economists believed that as long as the policies necessary to
maintain convertibility were followed, the supply of currency
was not subject to regulation or control by either the government or the central bank.[2] Experience has since revealed their
error, but progress towards solution of the "difficulties of a
conscious monetary policy" is barely discernible. The previ-

101

ous pages have sought to show that an important reason has been a failure to appreciate the conceptual and theoretical difficulties underlying the still unresolved "practical problems" of monetary policy.[3]

SUMMARY

Concepts of a monetary standard received from the eighteenth and nineteenth centuries are irrelevant to, and unworkable in, the twentieth century. When, prior to the nineteenth century, different metals competed for use as money, the issue of the monetary standard was simply which metal should be legally designated as standard money, i.e., the money of account. The issue was one of convenience, involving the desire for greater uniformity in the pricing of products. It was resolved by a legislative fixing of the price of one of the metals, making coins of that metal standard money (e.g., the sterling pound in medieval England). Coins of another metal (e.g., the gold guinea in England) often continued to circulate as a generally acceptable means of payment, but their exchange value varied with the market price of the metal they contained. Thus, the monetary standard was construed by preclassical authorities as the material comprising standard money. With the development of token coins and bank notes, standard money became the standard for the valuation of such nonstandard forms of money. Once a uniform price system was established, the issue of the monetary standard shifted from a question of convenience to one of substance: Which metal made the more stable standard for the valuation of goods? The monetary standard then became interpreted as the material constituting such a standard of value. This concept was consistent with the classical labor theory of value and the classical doctrine that convertible paper money could only replace but not enlarge the circulation. The fact is, however, that bank notes and deposits ultimately supplemented the money supply. The actual augmentation of the circulation altered the significance of the classical concept of the monetary standard. Instead of gold

102

being the standard of value for goods, money became the standard for the valuation of gold as well as goods. Consequently, this concept of a monetary standard was reduced to the absurdity (at the present time, in contrast to the classical period) that the monetary standard is money. Escape from the absurdity is not afforded by the erstwhile distinction between standard and credit money that furnished the premise of the postclassical concept of a monetary standard as the material constituting both standard money and the standard of value. This concept fell with the postclassical version of the commodity theory of money on which it was based. Triumph of the neoclassical quantity theory over the commodity theory of money reversed the assumed causal sequence in the parity between standard and credit money. The value of gold implicitly became the result, instead of the cause, of the value of credit money. Moreover, with the growing unwillingness to accept the secularly falling price level implicit in the classical gold standard (of value)—which classicists regarded as the closest practicable approximation to a labor standard of value —the idea of the monetary standard was unwittingly inverted. Instead of money (in the classical sense, specie) being the standard for the valuation of goods, goods became the standard of value for money (in the modern sense). Therefore, neither the preclassical, the classical, nor the postclassical concepts of a monetary standard has any relevance to modern monetary issues.

Yet the outmoded terminology associated with these concepts continues to clutter the literature and obstruct monetary analysis. The anachronism is accounted for by the failure to realize that the notion of a standard measure of value, analogous to physical measures, was rendered obsolete by abandonment of the idea of intrinsic value. This oversight, in turn, resulted from misconstructions of classical monetary theory and concepts which introduced the neoclassical theoretical dichotomy that appeared to make postclassical developments in value theory irrelevant to monetary theory. Apparent confirmation of the doctrinal dualism stemmed from inattention to the subtleties of Jevons' refinement of monetary terminology and mistaking his dif-

103

ferences with classical methodology and distribution theory for disagreement with classical value theory. Jevons' use of the term "standard of value," therefore, helped to hide its inconsistency with modern value theory.

The preclassical conception of a monetary standard was revived in the financial chaos of the nineteen-thirties, reflecting the apparent desire to salvage some version of the stability implicit in the idea of a standard. The violence of price movements had made a mockery of the neoclassical notion of the standard of value. Standard money, in contrast, is fixed by definition. But its significance had declined with its diminishing relationship to either the quantity or value of money (relative to goods rather than gold). The importance of standard money was further reduced by a shift of attention and emphasis from exchange to production and employment. Stabilization of money in terms of one commodity had originated in the preindustrial society when attention was focused primarily on exchange.[4] A gradually growing awareness that money affected employment and the aggregate volume of goods to be exchanged was one of the factors which contributed to the surreptitious enfeeblement of the connection between standard money and the total money supply. Standard money became an empty legalism long before the international financial collapse of 1931–1933. In a world of more or less abstract moneys, the attempt to distinguish meaningfully between standard and nonstandard money is on all fours with the effort to nail a shadow to a wall of the Treasury Building. The received concepts of a monetary standard are utterly obsolete.[5] Their continued use in an uncongenial intellectual and institutional environment has resulted in a licentious littering of the literature with loose labels.

As a consequence of the waxing fuzziness of conception, the monetary standard has become confused with the monetary system. And this involution has included a confusion of standards and policies. Consequently, specific standards have become so ambiguous that the boundary between modification and abrogation of the gold standard has been erased, and differentiation between such supposed opposites as gold and paper standards has become impossible. The recognition that all monetary systems of modern times—even those embracing the traditional, unrestricted gold standard—have been managed and the broadened latitude for discretionary management under the restricted forms of the so-called gold standard have jointly eliminated the alleged distinction between gold and paper standards based on automaticity versus management. In the classical frame of reference "paper standard" was a contradiction of terms. If it is supposed to mean merely that the monetary unit is an abstraction without concrete definition, the label "deposit standard" would be more appropriate. "Paper standard" is a limbo term belonging neither to commodity money nor to abstract money. The expression is a negation incapable of being infused with positive content. "Paper standard" means, if anything, the absence of a standard.[6] The apparently unrecognized obsolescence of expression has seriously obstructed communication in the field of money.

The growing ambiguity of the term "monetary standard" has led, understandably, to its neglect. But the concept cannot be ignored. Some standard—or lack of standard—is as implicit in monetary behavior as in any other type of human endeavor. Ordinarily the absence of a standard is viewed as a problem, not as a principle. If monetary behavior is to be understood and rationally guided towards achievement of our social goals, the concept of a monetary standard must be restated in terms that are consistent with modern fact and theory. Otherwise, policy determination—without guide lines or direction signals —will continue to be anarchical, inconsistent, and, to some extent, self-defeating. Objectives necessitate, rather than obviate, a standard. Generally acceptable objectives are too broad to be of much help to policy makers in the day-to-day decisions required by management of the increasingly intricate and interrelated monetary-fiscal mechanism. Recent suggestions that a monetary standard is the principle limiting the money supply signify a step towards modern relevance. But this reformulation is not broad enough in conception to embrace all possible species of the genus, or any of them at all

105

times. Such breadth may be provided by the concept of a monetary standard as the criterion (referent) of monetary policy,[7] which appears to be what most modern authorities really have in mind when they address themselves to present policy issues instead of past legislation.

This is nothing more or less than an adjustment of the concept to the facts that money is no longer a concrete commodity and that value is no longer construed as an intrinsic property of things. It is merely an application of the idea of a standard in the abstract realm of values, instead of the concrete area of physical measurements. The essential relevance of this concept to theory and fact permits a resolution of terminological issues which exposes the substantive issues in monetary policy. We cannot answer the question as to what this or that monetary standard is until we know what *a* monetary standard is.[8]

The basic terminological question of whether or not a country is on the (a?) gold standard and, if not, what the appropriate name for its standard is, may now be answered by identifying the actual referent, or referents, guiding the decisions of policy makers in choosing among alternative monetary policies those which will contribute most to achievement of the social goals. If gold is the criterion, policies would be followed which would cause the money supply to vary directly with the national gold reserve, and policies which had the opposite effect would be avoided. Monetary policy may be similarly guided by silver (silver standard), either of the two metals (bimetallism), both (symmetallism), or a composite of commodities, possibly including these metals (commodity-reserve standard). When two or more countries adopt any one of these criteria, their policies fix the values of their currencies in terms of each other within the narrow limits of the cost of transporting the commodity or commodities in the foreign monetary unit to and from the foreign country. The monetary standard may then be said to be international. Another possible international standard is what might be called the balance-of-payments standard. This does not require stabilization of the monetary unit in terms of any particular thing, but merely that monetary

106

policy be guided by the balance of payments. For instance, balance-of-payments equilibrium might be the criterion of monetary policy.[9] Accordingly, a chronic deficit or surplus would require either deflationary or inflationary monetary policies, respectively, or a change in the par value of the currency. This is the standard that is implicit in the International Monetary Fund Agreement, but it is the actual standard of member nations only insofar as they adhere to the spirit as well as the letter of the agreement. Those countries not willing to accept the domestic repercussions that foreign disturbances would cause under any of the international standards may resort to purely domestic guides to monetary policy, such as a stable price level (goods standard), stable per-capita money income (labor standard), or stable growth of employment (employment standard).[10] Foreign shocks could be cushioned at national borders by flexible exchange rates or accumulation and decumulation of excess monetary reserves.

Once the century-old argument about words has been disposed of, we can devote our time, energies, and talent to the substantive matter of determining what we really want, in the light of the "opportunity costs" of our alternatives. Had the recommended generic concept of a monetary standard been accepted doctrine in the first quarter of this century, the impossibility of stabilizing money at once in terms of both one commodity (gold or silver) and many commodities [11] would not have been attempted, and the paradox in seeking to remedy an acknowledged shortage of gold relative to the claims on it, by multiplying the claims (via the gold-exchange standard),[12] would have been apparent. Hence, the international financial debacle of 1931–1933 might never have happened. If so, the great depression would have been more moderate, and the world might have been saved from some of its catastrophic consequences.

IMPLICATIONS

What does all this imply with respect to present monetary standards and current issues relative to monetary policy? The brief and general consideration of these questions presented here will be directed primarily to the situation in the United States, but implications for other countries will be more or less obvious.

If a monetary standard is conceived of as the criterion of monetary policy, the United States is not on either "the" or "a" gold standard.[13] Like other members of the International Monetary Fund, the United States is obliged to adopt a particular gold policy, but not a gold standard.[14] The United States has no ascertainable monetary standard. The Treasury policy of a fixed price for gold progressively lost its connection with the money supply —even while supplemented by policies of internal as well as external convertibility—as bank notes and deposits replaced coins as circulating media. The volume of bank credit is affected by central-bank policies, which have never been very directly related to the Treasury's gold policies. Originally, the Federal Reserve System was primarily concerned with the quality, not the quantity, of bank credit. Since the development of a regard for the quantity as well as the quality, Federal Reserve authorities have shifted about among various criteria of monetary management—such as "sound business conditions," "orderly government security market," "prevention of inflation," etc.—until the policy referent at any particular time has become utterly unidentifiable. It is the absence of such a guide that brings a policy dilemma with each recurrence of a concomitant recession and external drain of gold.[15]

The reluctance of the Federal Reserve authorities to accept a specific policy criterion is understandable because their powers were never commensurate with the responsibility for the money supply which such acceptance would imply. Government fiscal operations also have a significant impact on the money supply today. The results of this distribution of monetary control among different agencies, frequently using disparate guides to dissimilar goals, are complicated by "the inveterate tendency of the Treasury to view the management of the public debt from the angle of fiscal economy and not from the angle of its effect on prices and employment."[16] George N. Halm has succinctly summarized the situation:

108

In the United States the monetary authority rests, in the last analysis, with the Congress. The Congress, however, has delegated the authority over current monetary decisions to several agencies, particularly the Treasury and the Federal Reserve. *Unfortunately, it did this without providing clear guiding principles* and without indicating distinctly marked areas of responsibilities. Moreover, little has been done to co-ordinate and integrate the activities of different agencies in the field of monetary and fiscal policies.[17]

That Congress did not solve this problem by the Employment Act of 1946 is now widely recognized.[18] Consequently, it was said that after their so-called "accord" with the Treasury in 1951, Federal Reserve officials "now faced the task of developing new policy objectives and *guides* . . ."[19]

A workable guide to compatible objectives is not realizable until a real accord is achieved. Meanwhile, "there is a continuing tendency toward eclecticism in matters of monetary management."[20] A well-known American authority translates this British understatement into: "We have a chaos of decision-making in Monetary Management."[21] In short, we have no monetary standard. Furthermore, the United States, for example, is not presently prepared to adopt a standard. The conceptual and institutional framework is not sufficiently developed to permit a choice among the alternatives. The desideratum of "a political consensus as to when to do what"[22] is still unattainable. Even its desirability is regarded by many competent authorities as an open question.[23] Contrariwise, others have for years denied that there is any question about its propriety.[24] The question, however, that must today precede that of its desirability is the *possibility* of such a consensus in the area of money.

Agreement on a referent for the selection of those monetary policies which will be most effective in reaching our social goals requires getting on with some unfinished business in our intellectual and institutional development. There are six prerequisites for the selection of a monetary standard in the modern world:

First, we must identify our *general economic objectives.*[25] In democratic societies

109

these appear to be individual freedom, equality of opportunity, equity in the distribution of real income, conservation of natural resources, optimum economic growth, and cyclical stabilization.[26] When reasonably interpreted, these are basically compatible goals.[27] In any case, an effective guide cannot be selected until the destination is known.

Second, we must determine which of the general economic objectives can be achieved primarily (though not exclusively) by monetary measures. It should be obvious that the last objective leads the list in this respect.[28] Although the business cycle is not a purely monetary phenomenon, it originated with the modern pecuniary society. Both its anatomy and pathology are fundamentally monetary, whereas this is less true of the other general economic objectives. The contribution that monetary policy can make to the accomplishment of the other social goals is, for the most part, only indirect and is brought about primarily through the stabilization achievable by monetary policy.[29]

Third, we must understand the various interpretations of "stabilization," comprehend their interrelationship, and decide their relative priority. Stabilization may be interpreted in two ways, with each interpretation having two meanings. It may be internal or external, and in each case the object of stabilization may be the economy in general or the value of money in particular.[30] Internal stabilization means macroeconomic stabilization within a given country. It is the preservation of reasonably full utilization of a nation's resources by conscious domestic action to offset disturbances from abroad which threaten macroeconomic stability. The domestic economy may be defended against the importation of unemployment or inflation by flexible exchange rates or the depletion and sterilization, respectively, of monetary reserves. Internal stabilization of the value of money means maintaining the value of a nation's monetary unit reasonably stable in terms of commodities and services on the domestic market. Such stability of the price level is a purely monetary expression of internal stability; although it may contribute to the stabilization of the economy, it is

110

neither necessary nor sufficient to that end. Stabilizing money vis-à-vis virtually all domestically traded goods precludes stabilization of money in terms of one or two commodities à la metallic standards of yesteryear. External stabilization of the economy, on the other hand, means stabilization of the economic relations with other economies. It signifies the absence of attempts to modify the domestic impact of foreign economic disturbances. External stabilization denotes a direct linkage between the macroeconomic behavior of the domestic economy and that of foreign economies which precludes independent, autonomous policies for internal stabilization. Those disposed toward external stabilization generally assume greater compatibility of national goals, flexibility of prices, and mobility of resources than do those inclined to internal stabilization. Therefore, the former tend to rely less on government policies and more on market forces to determine the level and direction of economic activity than do the latter. Whereas reliance on internal stabilization is based on the premise that the macroeconomic effects of economic changes can be moderated most effectively by positive national public policies, the rationale of external stabilization is that the same objective can be better accomplished by dissipation of the effects through wide dissemination. External stabilization of the value of money refers to the practice of fixing the value of the domestic monetary unit in terms of foreign moneys instead of domestic goods.[31] Fixed exchange rates constitute the purely monetary aspect of external stabilization. Such fixity in the external value of money is necessary but not sufficient for external stabilization of the economy. In contrast to the external protection provided by flexible exchange rates, fixed exchange rates furnish the mechanism for transmitting changes of a macro nature from country to country, thus preserving external stability by compelling internal adjustments. But external stability cannot be preserved, despite stable exchange rates, unless domestic policy facilitates rather than obstructs internal adaptation to external change. The wider the international distribution and the quicker the transmission of the alteration, the more moderate is the adjustment within any one nation. Thus, internal stabilization necessitates external flexibility, and external stabilization requires internal flexibility in order to permit accommodation to the changes going on more or less continually in the world.[32]

Neither mechanism of adjustment is provided for in the apparent modern desire for simultaneous attainment and maintenance of both internal and external stability of the general economy as well as the value of money.[33] One of the sources of modern monetary controversy and confusion is the fact that while few seem satisfied with either internal or external stability, and many believe that we should have both, nobody—despite the exercise of enviable ingenuity—has come up with a formula assuring all this and national sovereignty, too.[34] The skepticism of an earlier age [35] has given way to expediency,[36] despair,[37] or "gadgeteering." [38] The new approaches hold little promise of delivering the long-sought dual stabilization. There are certain prerequisites. The happy combination of internal and external stability *may*, for example, be secured by nations with mobile resources and flexible cost-price structures if one of them is industrially, commercially, and financially powerful enough to prevent independent economic policies by the others and, at the same time, both willing and able to accept the responsibilities of its position. It has been thought by many that such conditions prevailed in the nineteenth century, but everyone agrees that if so, they were terminated by World War I.[39] A single nation may still enjoy the best of two worlds as long as its monetary reserves are sufficiently in excess of requirements that changes in the former can be ignored.[40] Several nations could do the same if the aggregate amount of reserves for all could be increased,[41] but a reasonable concomitance of internal and external stability is likely to be sustained only in the event of common domestic goals and appropriately similar policies.[42] Such conditions are neither existent nor expected in the forseeable future. Thus, the dollar, for example, shifting from shortage to surplus, remains a world problem as well as a world currency.

Fourth, not only must we acknowledge the distinction between general economic and monetary objectives,[43] but we must also recognize the differ-

112

ence between nonmonetary and monetary economic policies.[44] Both types of policy are required in order to reach all our economic goals. But the contribution of each type is limited primarily to its area of relevance. Attempts to attain nonmonetary ends by monetary means and vice versa lead only to frustration and confusion. Nonmonetary ends and means are beyond the scope of this study. The point to be emphasized here is that monetary measures can make a greater contribution to general economic goals than they have. This, however, requires acknowledgment that in the post-World-War-II world "monetary policy" includes not only central-bank policy (with which the term "monetary policy" has been exclusively identified) but also fiscal and debt-management policies.[45] It would be bad enough to attempt to reach noneconomic goals by all possible monetary means, but to seek such general ends by only one species of monetary policy, namely central-bank policy, is foolish. A realization of this reinforces the long-suspected (and only partially implemented) need for coordinating Federal Reserve and Treasury policies.[46] The issue of "independence versus coordination" [47] may be resolved by the concept of a monetary standard as the criterion of monetary policy. Independent criteria are neither necessary nor desirable. Here is where coordination is not only desirable but necessary if achievement of our objectives is not to be obstructed by conflicting policies. Yet independent policy implementation of the common referent may minimize the detrimental effects of occasional misjudgment by policy makers. Coordination on policy criteria does not preclude independence of policy decisions, and such independence does not require extra-legal connivance between the supposedly independent agencies.[48] Thus, the next prerequisite for the selection of a monetary standard is revealed.

This fifth prerequisite is that we must recognize the necessity for *both* "rules" and discretionary judgments by "authorities." Policy decisions are made by men, not machines; hence a certain amount of human discretion in these matters is inescapable. Since many men in different and more or less independent agencies of government are involved, a common rule (referent) guiding

113

their decisions is necessary in order to avoid a mutually nullifying inconsistency of policies. Implicit in this formulation of the matter is an affirmation of the division of labor in democratic government among voters, politicians, civil servants, and experts. Selection of general objectives is the responsibility of the voters.[49] Those politicians most successful in sensing and articulating the objectives of their constituents are elected to public offices, where they assume the responsibility for laying down the guide lines for the policy-making political appointees and policy-implementing civil servants. The experts advise all these groups in various ways ranging from the professorial podium to the President's Council of Economic Advisors. Public officials are receiving conflicting advice today partly because the legislative branch of government has defaulted on its obligation to furnish a common guide for the various monetary authorities.

The sixth and last prerequisite to the selection of a monetary standard is the acknowledgment that the monetary standard need not, and cannot, furnish a passport to the millenium. Neither official reaffirmation nor general and complete repudiation of the gold standard, for example, is the key to all current economic problems. In the modern industrial society money is of central significance, but the monetary mechanism should not be burdened with responsibilities it cannot discharge.[50] While pre-Keynesian orthodoxy neglected monetary phenomena,[51] the opposite tendency is observable in the post-Keynesian neomercantilism. Paradoxically, the value of money was stressed by the pre-Keynesians to the virtual exclusion of such real factors as output and employment, whereas real elements have been emphasized and the value of money neglected in the post-Keynesian "monetary" analysis.[52] There were, of course, historical reasons for these reversals of emphasis, but by now economists ought to have the perspective to render to money that which is money's and to other economic phenomena that which is theirs. Given such perspective, it would be more generally realized that all our economic objectives cannot be effectuated by monetary means and, by the same token, that failure to reach all economic

114

goals cannot be attributed exclusively, or even primarily, to faulty monetary policy. The necessity for supplementing monetary measures by appropriate nonmonetary policies would then be obvious.[53] Removal of some of the heat from the monetary arena would permit cooler consideration of the issues.

A rational choice of a monetary standard will be possible only after the realization of the above six prerequisites. In the absence of knowledge as to when these conditions might be fulfilled, description of the alternatives from which the choice may be made is hazardous. On the unlikely assumption that we shall be ready and willing to choose a monetary standard in the near future, certain tentative conclusions can, however, be drawn.

Metallic standards, like the labor standard, are precluded by the downward rigidity of the cost-price structure.[54] The long-run deflationary consequences of the nineteenth-century metallic standards were fortuitously circumvented by the extra-legal development of bank deposits as a generally used means of payment.[55] Feasible alternatives in the modern world are limited to those monetary standards that do not require secular deflation.[56] These fall into two categories: (1) standards based on the assumed primacy of *internal* stability and (2) standards based on the assumed primacy of *external* stability. The first group includes the commodity-reserve standard, goods standard, and employment standard. Each has its disadvantages, as well as its advantages. The commodity-reserve standard requires institutional innovations that are not apt to be adopted in the absence of a more serious economic collapse than is presently predictable. Since the price level no longer falls as much in recession as it rises in prosperity,[57] the restrictive policies required by the goods standard during expansion would not be sufficiently offset by expansionary policies during contraction to absorb the cyclically unemployed. The latter would be accomplished by the policies appropriate to the employment standard—but at the cost of aggravated secular inflation. Neither the goods nor the employment standard would produce the desired stabilization, and the effects of

115

each standard—though opinions would differ on their relative assessment—would reduce the equity of real income distribution and retard economic growth. The second category of monetary standards—those premised on the priority of *external* stability—includes the international commodity-reserve standard and the balance-of-payments standard. The institutional changes necessary for implementation of the commodity-reserve standard are no more immediately foreseeable internationally than nationally. The balance-of-payments standard necessitates no serious alteration of existing institutions, but it obliges adherents to eschew independent, autonomous monetary policies for internal stabilization. Obviously, none of these alternatives promises perfection.

Nevertheless, some day a choice may have to be made. Moreover, indications are that the day of decision is nearer than we think. In the light of existing and predictable facts, what would be a reasonable choice? Among the standards based on the assumed primacy of *internal* stability, a combination of the goods and employment standards à la Hart's "gong and whistle" [58] appears most liable to result in the maximum internal stability consistent with the other general economic objectives of democratic society. Of the two standards grounded upon the assumed primacy of *external* stability, the balance-of-payments standard can be implemented under existing institutions, national and international. Many countries are monetarily tooled up for this type of operation. The machinery is available. What is needed is the will. Now that the feasible alternatives have been narrowed to two, the question arises, which is the better? The answer depends upon whether one prefers the national or international approach to such economic stability as is attainable by monetary means. Obviously, one's preference will be colored to some extent by noneconomic considerations which transcend the boundaries of this study. But in any case the economic implications should be understood and taken into account.

The domestic economic implications have been indicated. Those relative to international institutions and policies remain to be considered.

Monetary standards oriented primarily to *internal* stability are incompatible with a combination of fixed exchange rates and fixed aggregate international reserves. This inconsistency can be removed only if the important trading nations implement the same criterion of monetary policy. In the absence of such international harmony, preservation of the desired domestic macroeconomic stability requires exchange-rate adjustment or direct controls. Without direct controls, alteration of exchange rates can be postponed only so long as the aggregate volume of international reserves is adequate and its distribution is appropriate. Under these circumstances an appropriate distribution of reserves at one time will not be suitable at another; hence enlargement of the aggregate will become necessary even though some countries may enjoy surpluses.[59] If different monetary standards manifest disparate national objectives, growth of global reserves will be necessary regardless of their distribution.[60] Either flexible exchange rates or expanding international reserves are required in order to permit trading nations to follow dissimilar guides to contrary goals without direct controls, the adoption of which raises both practical and ideological problems. Any mechanism without adequate provision for adaptation to the inevitable changes in its environment will ultimately collapse like a completely rigid metal bridge expanding under the heat of the noonday summer sun. An opting for the primacy of internal stability and monetary standards consistent with this preference would require modification but not elimination of the International Monetary Fund. On the other hand, no substantive alteration of the Fund would be necessary if at least the major member nations really accepted the primacy of *external* stability and the concomitant responsibility for undertaking the implied internal resource reallocation. The balance-of-payments standard could exist in fact as well as in the words of formal international agreements where such an attitude prevailed.[61] Stable exchange rates are not merely consistent with, but are essential to, the balance-of-payments standard.

Unlike the traditional gold standard, however, the stability of exchange rates is not the result of other policies required by the standard. Under

117

the balance-of-payments standard, maintenance of stable exchange rates is itself a policy which is ordinarily appropriate—but, at the same time, subordinate—to balance-of-payments equilibrium. If circumstances indicate that the latter may be restored most expeditiously by altering the external value of the currency, such action should be taken. The relevant exchange-rate policy is one of pegged but adjustable rates. Similarly, the price of gold is fixed but alterable in accordance with, rather than in opposition to, the standard. Gold, therefore, is merely an instrument—not a determinant —of monetary policy. It remains, under the balance-of-payments standard, an international medium of exchange (in the limited sense of a means of settlement among central banks and international monetary agencies), and it may be used as an international unit of account. In performing these functions, however, gold is the servant, not the master, of policy makers. In short, a gold policy—not a gold standard —is implied in the International Monetary Fund Agreement and the potential balance-of-payments standard.

Ultimately, internal and external stability are compatible. Preservation of reasonable internal stability by many nations would yield reasonably stable economic relations and, therefore, exchange rates among them. Likewise, general international maintenance of balance-of-payments equilibrium might reduce internal instability to tolerable and remedial proportions. However, although internal and external stability are eventually consistent, they are not *simultaneously* obtainable by *monetary* measures. In the quest for both, one must be given priority. Otherwise the monetary efforts to achieve each will be nullified by those required to reach the other. This is the story of modern monetary history, and it is this which has brought American policy makers, for example, to their present dilemma.

The time has come for some fundamental decisions. The first one to be made is whether or not we want a monetary standard—i.e., whether or not a specified criterion, or set of criteria, is preferable to the present "eclecticism in matters of monetary management"

118

currently characterized by the euphemism, "gold-exchange standard." [62] The decision to continue managing money on an *ad hoc* basis could be justified on grounds that expediency will remain the best basis for policy decisions until socio-economic objectives, national and international (regional and global), become clearer. The record of this "system" since World War II has not been bad, in view of the circumstances. Its future record might be even better if the issue is faced and rationally resolved so that the monetary managers would be freed from the limitations of the folklore surrounding the obsolete labels that have persisted. In fact, the attempt to prevent adjustment to change by either an alteration of exchange rates or domestic prices, income, and employment *requires* the absence of a particular policy referent. Both internal and external stabilization can be simultaneously pursued only by "playing it by ear." Tibor Scitovsky has followed this procedure to its logical conclusion: the necessity for continuously increasing international monetary reserves so that each country generally has all the international liquidity it wants. [63] This is not the same as the impossible attempt to supply all persons with all the domestic money they wish, because the desire of surplus countries for more liquidity will cease when they realize that the people of other countries are reaping the benefits of their industry and self-denial. [64] When this awakening occurs, however, the postponed adjustments must be made, and they will be greater for having been delayed. Meanwhile the uncertainty with respect to domestic monetary policy may retard investment and, therefore, growth. When monetary authorities are "playing it by ear," investors may be agitated by the absence of a score to follow. If they don't know the score, they fail to fully appreciate the performance. If they think they know the score (even though none exists), they may be disturbed by deviations from what they expect.

Such uncertainty may be minimized by selection of a specific monetary standard. Before this can be done, however, another basic choice has to be made. What is this choice? Before we can see what it *is,* we must recognize what it is *not.* The choice to be made

119

is neither between metallic and paper standards nor between automatic and managed standards. Before a monetary standard can be selected, the relative priority of internal and external stabilization must be determined. This determination involves the choice between internal and external criteria of monetary policy. After this decision has been made, the most workable of the alternative monetary standards will, if the above argument is correct, be obvious. But before this selection can be made, two fundamental questions must be asked—and answered. First, would we be satisfied with the *degree* of internal stability that would result from the external stability maintainable, and vice versa? In other words, would we find the domestic instability associated with external stabilization tolerable or manageable, and vice versa? The endeavor to answer this question will raise the second query. Can we develop the institutions and the nonmonetary policies necessary and sufficient to facilitate (1) internal adjustment to maintenance of external stability [65] or (2) external adjustment to maintenance of internal stability? Achievement of our social goals without drastic alteration of existing institutions depends upon our ability to find an affirmative answer.

NOTES

CHAPTER I

1 Henry V. Poor, *Money and Its Laws,* New York, 1877, pp. 317–318.
2 George Walter Woodworth, *The Monetary and Banking System,* New York, 1950, p. 47.
3 This has been called "the battle of standards." Actually, it was only *a* battle in the "war of standards," but it was the battle that enlarged the conflict to a "world war."
4 The subject was neither discussed in the Bretton Woods Conference (I am indebted to Ervin Hexner for this information) nor included in the Report of the Commission on Money and Credit (See H. Christian Sonne's dissenting note, *Money and Credit,* Englewood Cliffs, 1961, pp. 4–5). An exhausting (admittedly, not exhaustive) search through the literature has turned up only fifteen (two by one author) explicit definitions of the general concept of a "monetary standard": F. M. Taylor, *Some Chapters on Money* (printed for use of students in the University of Michigan), Ann Arbor, 1906, p. 37; Russell Donald Kilborne, *Principles of Money and Banking,* Chicago, 1927, p. 14; Sir Charles Morgan-Webb, *The Rise and Fall of the Gold Standard,* New York, 1934, p. 12; E. M. Bernstein, *Money and the Economic System,* Chapel Hill, 1935, p. 44; Anatol Murad, *The Paradox of a Metal Standard,* Washington, 1939, pp. 181–182; Eugene E. Agger, *Money and Banking Today,* New York, 1941, p. 156; Harold L. Reed, *Money, Currency and Banking,* New York, 1942, p. 52; George N. Halm, *Monetary Theory,* 2nd edn., Philadelphia, 1946, pp. 103, 105; George N. Halm, *Economics of Money and Banking,* Homewood, Ill., 1956, pp. 53–54; Major B. Foster, Raymond Rogers, Jules I. Bogan, and Marcus Nadler, *Money and Banking,* 3rd edn., New York, 1947, p. 24; Edward S. Shaw, *Money, Income, and Monetary Policy,* Chicago, 1950, p. 17; Woodworth, *op. cit.,* p. 11; Raymond P. Kent, *Money and Banking,* 3rd edn.,

New York, 1956, p. 21; and Leland J. Pritchard, *Money and Banking*, Boston, 1958, p. 81.

5 Henry Dunning MacLeod attributed the "discreditable state" of economics in his time to economists' neglect of definitions, "the only means by which a science can be founded" (*The Principles of Economical Philosophy*, 2nd edn., II, London, 1879, 381). But he made no effort to supply the most neglected definition of all.

6 *An Introduction to Money*, London, 1938, pp. 1–17.

7 *The Dollar: A Study of the "New" National and International Monetary System*, New York, 1937, p. 1.

8 *Ibid.*, p. 2.

9 No implication that this was a conscious evasion is intended. The direct transition from "the monetary standard" to "monetary standards" had become traditional long before Donaldson's time.

10 *Principles of Money and Banking*, Chicago, 1916, pp. 98–100.

11 *Money and Credit*, New York, 1935, pp. 83–88.

12 *Money and Banking*, New York, 1948, pp. 20–21.

13 *Money and Banking*, New York, 1933, pp. 73–74.

14 For a typical example of the "spontaneous generation" of the species, without any parent conception, see F. W. Mueller, Jr., *Money and Banking*, New York, 1951, pp. 48–49. The section on "Monetary Standards" in Edwin Walter Kemmerer's *Money* (New York, 1935, p. 69) begins abruptly with a chapter on "The Monometallic Standard," which, in turn, starts right off with a definition of "monometallism." Other cases in point include: Horace White, *Money and Banking*, Boston, 1895, pp. 44 ff.; *ibid.*, 6th edn. (revised and enlarged by Charles S. Tippets and Lewis A. Froman), pp. 80 ff.; Roy L. Garis, *Principles of Money, Credit, and Banking*, New York, 1934, pp. 74–76, 97 ff.; John Thom Holdsworth, *Money and Banking*, 6th edn., New York, 1937, p. 21; F. Cyril James, *The Economics of Money, Credit and Banking*, 3rd edn., New York, 1940, pp. 715 ff.; Geoffrey Crowther, *An Outline of Money*, 2nd edn., London, 1948, pp. 277 ff.; and Richard W. Lindholm, John J. Balles, and John M. Hunter, *Principles of Money and Banking*, New York, 1954, pp. 47 ff.

15 Attempts have, however, been made. For example, despite Kemmerer's utter neglect of the idea of a monetary standard, he systematically began each of his chapters on "Monetary Standards" with a definition (*op. cit.*, pp. 69, 83, and 94).

16 Milton L. Stokes and Carl T. Arlt, *Money, Banking and the Financial System*, New York, 1955, p. 99 (italics mine): "While the gold standard means different things to different economists there is a fairly general agreement as to its main characteristics. *Instead of attempting a formal definition of the gold standard most writers have contented themselves with a statement of its characteristics* and the conditions necessary for its existence." A random selection of money and banking texts would illustrate the point. Lawrence Smith (*Money, Credit, and Public Policy*, Boston, 1959, p. 121) called these characteristics "practices." Pritchard (*op. cit.*, pp. 87, 92–93) gave them the more impressive label of "principles," but he also alluded to them as "provisions" (*ibid.*, pp. 93–94). Ray B. Westerfield listed eleven "elements" (characteristics) of

122

the "gold-coin standard" and asserted: "For a country 'to go off the gold standard' means that the country completely stops some one or more of these essential features" (*Money, Credit and Banking*, 2nd edn., New York, 1947, pp. 75–76). Then he added that in 1933 "the United States was more 'off' than Great Britain" (*ibid.*, p. 77). This means that a country can "go off" the gold standard and still be "on" it—a situation supposedly designed to keep everyone moderately happy. But degrees of "offness" imply degrees of "onness" and undermine our power to distinguish the species.

17 Frederick A. Bradford, *Money*, New York, 1928, p. 33; H. F. Fraser, *Great Britain and the Gold Standard*, London, 1933, p. 3; J. Marvin Peterson, Delmas R. Cawthorne, and Philipp H. Lohman, *Money & Banking*, New York, 1941, p. 685; Lindholm, Balles, and Hunter, *op. cit.*, p. 47; Rollin G. Thomas, *Our Modern Banking and Monetary System*, 3rd edn., Englewood Cliffs, 1957, p. 33; Kent, *op. cit.*, p. 34; Lester V. Chandler, *The Economics of Money and Banking*, 3rd edn., New York, 1959, p. 354.

18 Holdsworth, *op. cit.*, p. 45.

19 Charles L. Prather, *Money and Banking*, 4th edn., Chicago, 1949, p. 95.

20 *Ibid.*, p. 117.

21 J. Whitney Hanks and Roland Stucki, *Money, Banking, and National Income*, New York, 1956, p. 40.

22 Smith, *op. cit.*, p. 263.

23 *Ibid.*, p. 279.

24 L. L. B. Angas, *The Problems of the Foreign Exchanges*, New York, 1935, p. 46.

25 *Ibid.*, p. 49.

26 Louis A. Rufener, *Money and Banking in the United States*, 2nd edn., Boston, 1936, p. 732.

27 J. Laurence Laughlin, *The Principles of Money*, New York, 1903, p. 47; Charles A. Conant, *Principles of Money and Banking*, II, New York, 1905, 431; Westerfield, *op. cit.*, p. 105; Kemmerer, *op. cit.*, p. 94; Charles R. Whittlesey, *Principles and Practices of Money and Banking*, 2nd edn., New York, 1954, p. 198.

28 Most of the distinguishing "characteristics" are government policies. See *supra*, n. 16. Stokes and Arlt (*op. cit.*, p. 97 [italics mine]) have furnished a statement which might be indicative of the mental process (or terminological trap, whichever it is) by which the "standard" has become not merely identified, but identical, with "policies": "The *development of a standard* involves more than the determination of the commodity or paper unit that is to be the money counterpart of the unit of account. *It also includes* [could refer to "development" rather than "standard"] the regulations and arrangements that relate the other nonstandard money units to the standard unit. It is the process of convertibility that permits the other money units to bear the same fixed relationship to the unit of account as that defined for the standard unit. *It is* [here "it" definitely refers to "standard" instead of "development"] a network of reserve requirements . . ." By the end of the last sentence the transition was completed. The "standard" no longer merely involved, included, or required the policies—it *was* the policies!

123

29 *The History and Theory of Money*, Philadelphia, 1893, p. 302 (italics mine). A later authority viewed this policy, when limited to gold, as the essence of the gold standard (Karl Olivecrona, *The Problem of the Monetary Unit,* New York, 1957, p. 85).

30 This, however, appears to preserve the traditionally assumed hierarchy of relationships in which subsidiary policies flow from the monetary standard. In other words, even though Sherwood called the standard a policy, he implied that it is a *major* policy. Woodworth (*op. cit.,* p. 564 [italics mine]) seemed to suggest a reversal of rank: "A fundamental *part of monetary policy* is concerned with the choice of a monetary standard . . ."

31 These matters will be given detailed consideration in Chaps. V and VI.

32 W. Stanley Jevons referred to changes in the monetary "standard" as changes in "policy" (*Money and the Mechanism of Exchange,* New York [1875], p. 133). See also the *Dictionary of Political Economy,* ed. R. H. Inglis Palgrave, London, 1894–1899, II, 801.

33 Ludwig von Mises called the *policy* of foreign exchange control "the illusive standard" (*The Theory of Money and Credit,* 2nd edn., trans. H. E. Batson, New Haven, 1953, pp. 432–433). An earlier observer had referred to monometallism as a policy (Joseph French Johnson, *Money and Currency,* Boston, 1905, p. 218). Truly, whatever its temporary disguise, the "standard" has become an illusive figure (of speech?). Changes in the United States standard have been discussed under the heading "Gold Policy" and "Results of Gold Policy" (Mueller, *op. cit.,* pp. 121–128, 129–139). At one point, Shaw (*op. cit.,* p. 17) characterized the monetary standard as a method of controlling the supply of money, and he alluded to management of the money supply as "monetary policy in the narrow sense" (*op. cit.,* p. 409). The gold standard has also been designated alternatively as a "system of rules for economic policy" and, simply, as a "policy" (Albert Gailord Hart, *Money, Debt, and Economic Activity,* 2nd edn., New York, 1953, pp. 372, 432).

34 Von Mises (*op. cit.,* p. 435 [italics mine]) has said: "There is some confused talk about stability and about *a standard* which is *neither inflationary nor deflationary*. The *vagueness of the terms* employed obscures the fact that people are still committed to the *spurious and self-contradictory doctrines* whose very application has created the present monetary chaos." Few economists would disagree with this statement. But hardly any two would agree on its interpretation. Was he (or those he criticized) talking about a "standard" that was "neither inflationary nor deflationary," or were they really referring to objectives, or to policies, or to all three? And were the contradictions within and/or among these "things"? Who can say?

35 "Stability of the weight and fineness of the metal composing the coin," a phenomenon traditionally identified as, or with, the *standard,* has been listed as an *objective* of monetary policy (Norman Lombard, *Monetary Statesmanship,* New York, 1934, p. 17). Other authorities have explicitly named the gold *standard,* for example, as a *goal* of monetary policy (Woodworth, *op. cit.,* p. 565; Halm, *Economics of Money and Banking,* p. 243). The second-edition chapter on *"Standards* of Credit and Monetary Policy" in a popular textbook became *"Goals* of

Monetary and Fiscal Policy" in the third edition (Thomas, *op. cit.,* p. 434 [italics mine]). Moreover, the first section of this renamed chapter is entitled "Quantitative *Standards* of Control" (*ibid.,* p. 439 [italics mine]), and the first two quantitative *standards* discussed are called "policy *goals*" (*ibid.,* pp. 439, 443 [italics mine]). In another book, the gold *standard* is listed and discussed as a "monetary *policy*" in a chapter of that name, which concludes with a consideration of the question of the compatibility of the various objectives (Coulborn, *op. cit.,* pp. 256–257, 261–263 [italics mine]).

36 Halm, *Monetary Theory,* p. 116.
37 Woodworth, *op. cit.,* pp. 62–64.
38 Halm, *Economics of Money and Banking,* p. 120.
39 Hart, *op. cit.,* pp. 411, 412.
40 Pritchard, *op. cit.,* p. 82: "Monetary standards have been the most controversial subject in the entire field of money—perhaps because in no other field of money is there more ignorance and misunderstanding."
41 Nevertheless, a sample (by no means intended to be complete) of the variety of names which the post-1934 monetary standard of the United States has been called might serve to remind us of the nature of the problem: *"de facto* gold standard" (T. E. Gregory, "Twelve Months of American Dollar Policy," *Economica,* N.S. I [May 1934], 141); "gold reserve standard" (Coulborn, *op. cit.,* p. 121); "international gold bullion standard" (Miroslav A. Kriz, *The Price of Gold,* Essays in International Finance, No. 15, Princeton, 1952, p. 23); " 'provisional' gold standard," "gold exchange standard," and "restricted gold bullion standard" (4th, 5th, and 6th edns. of Prather, *op. cit.,* pp. 93, 151, and 146, respectively); "type of gold standard, differing markedly from the traditional type" (Smith, *op. cit.,* p. 158); "non-fixed inconvertible paper standard" (Holdsworth, *op. cit.,* p. 45); and "gold exchange standard" (statements of Harry G. Johnson and Tibor Scitovsky, *International Payments Imbalances and Need for Strengthening International Financial Arrangements,* Hearings before the Subcommittee on International Exchanges and Payments of the Joint Economic Committee, United States Congress, June 21, 1961, Washington, 1961, pp. 173, 176). Lindholm, Balles, and Hunter (*op. cit.,* p. 63 [italics mine]) take refuge in a "practical" definition: "We shall not argue here which is the better *theoretical designation* of the monetary standard of the United States, for there is little disagreement that for *practical* economic considerations it is a *paper standard.*" Walter E. Spahr would merely remove the qualification to this definition and perhaps add a list of derogatory adjectives (see any issue of his *Monetary Notes*). However, the intriguing thing about the Lindholm, Balles, and Hunter treatment is the notion of a "practical" versus a "theoretical" definition. The significant thing about this "resolution" of the difficulty is that it illustrates the confusion of theoretical and terminological issues that obscures the whole area of monetary economics. Truly, as Sir Dennis H. Robertson has remarked, "What is a gold standard?" is "the vexed question" (*Lectures on Economic Principles,* III, London, 1959, 15).
42 The Palgrave *Dictionary* article on "classification" demonstrates both its scientific importance and its neglect by economists (when dealing

125

with money). The article quotes Mill's *Logic* to the effect that classification gives us maximum command of knowledge already acquired and leads to further acquisition. Jevons' *Principles of Science* is also quoted: "Science can extend only so far as the power of accurate classification extends" (*Dictionary of Political Economy*, ed. Palgrave, I, 303). Then, after the observation that classification is hindered by the complexity of the subject matter dealt with in the "moral and political sciences, including political economy," the following conclusion is reached: "It may almost be said that in the sphere of moral and social science the only true kinds are individuals. The most sagacious and suggestive writers upon these topics have shunned elaborate classification as they have shunned the use of highly technical language" (*ibid.*, p. 304). Granting the difficulty, let economists dedicate themselves to overcoming it! Classification and language should be no more elaborate or technical than necessary for their purposes, but in a science there are minimum requirements for both.

43 Per Jacobsson, *Towards a Modern Monetary Standard,* The Stamp Memorial Lecture, London, 1959, p. 30.

44 "It is in the simple elements that we require the most care and precision, since the least error of conception must vitiate all our deductions" (W. Stanley Jevons, *The Theory of Political Economy,* London, 1871, p. 1). Consequently, even at this late date, "something may be gained by a more thorough reflection on the fundamental notions by means of which we think and reason about economic facts . . ." (Henry Sidgwick, "Economic Method," *Fortnightly Review,* N.S. XXV [February 1879], 309). "We should make our *conceptions* as precise as possible, even when we cannot make our *statements* so. Only in this way can we keep before our minds the inadequacy of our knowledge of particulars to supply answers to the questions which our general notions lead us to ask" (*ibid.,* p. 311).

45 Some exceptions have already been noted (*supra,* n. 5).

46 Following is a random sample from the literature of the twentieth century: David Kinley, *Money,* New York, 1904, pp. 72–75; Bradford, *op. cit.,* p. 4; Steiner, *op. cit.,* pp. 53–55; White, *op. cit.,* 6th edn., pp. 26–27; Leffler, *op. cit.,* pp. 30–35; Prather, *op. cit.,* 1st edn., p. 34; Mueller, *op. cit.,* pp. 44–45.

47 Bradford, *op. cit.,* p. 373; William A. Scott, *Money and Banking,* 6th edn., New York, 1926, pp. 36–40; Rufener, *op. cit.,* pp. 35–36; Agger, *op. cit.,* p. 156; Peterson, Cawthorne, and Lohman, *op. cit.,* pp. 5–6. Occasionally the list is modified and cast in terms of the requirements for a monetary system (Prather, *op. cit.,* 1st edn., pp. 15–29; Westerfield, *op. cit.,* pp. 42–45). This procedural and terminological modification may have reflected a growing dissatisfaction with a term so ambiguous as "standard" had become in its application to money. But resort to "system" merely aggravated the ambiguity. This will be developed in Chap. V.

48 A "malleable" bank deposit is a concept to conjure! And how portable is it, i.e., what *is* the physical bulk of a bank deposit? Jevons had, in 1875, acknowledged that the growing use of representative money had reduced the question of the portability of metallic money to one of

126

"very minor importance" (*Money and the Mechanism of Exchange*, p. 199). Unfortunately, decades of subsequent writers followed neither the statement nor its wider implications. There have, of course, been isolated exceptions, e.g., "The development of credit money has changed the relative importance of these attributes, some formerly considered of great importance being given little consideration today" (Eugene S. Klise, *Money and Banking*, 2nd edn., Cincinnati, 1959, p. 9). The conventional list of characteristics appears to have originated as justification for characterizing gold and silver as "natural money," independent of law: "Gold & silver are constituted, by the nature of things, money, & universal money; independently of all convention & of all law" (Anne Robert Jacques Turgot, *Reflections on the Formation and the Distribution of Riches*, New York, 1922 [reprint of 1898 edn.], p. 39). For confirmation of this interpretation, see Sir John MacDonnell, *Survey of Political Economy*, Edinburgh, 1871, p. 151.

49 Whittlesey, *op. cit.*, pp. 34–35. Those who saw that the relevance of these characteristics had become limited to token coins usually dispensed with this ceremonial listing, along with other mechanical trivia.

50 *Supra*, nn. 17–29.

51 Almost any money and banking textbook will illustrate the point.

52 In *The War of Standards*, New York, 1896, pp. 5–17, Albion W. Tourgée defined the issue as *mono- versus bimetallism*, then announced that the remainder of the book would be devoted to the question, "What is the best monetary *policy* for the United States to adopt at this time?" (*ibid.*, p. 24 [italics mine]). Consciously or unconsciously, writers have generally followed this pattern ever since, but few have been so candid. In view of the terminological overlap already pointed out, it is, of course, impossible to determine whether this was really candor or confusion. In any event, textbook chapters on policy have generally ignored the earlier chapters on standards. Klise's only reference to any monetary standard in his two chapters on "Monetary and Fiscal Policy" in the United States since 1914 (*op. cit.*, pp. 473–527) relates to the American easy money policy during the 1920's, which was designed to hasten England's return to the gold standard (*ibid.*, p. 477). Note that the allusion is to historical facts, not contemporary issues. The latter are discussed in the final chapter which mentions no monetary standard of any kind. Those who define (whether expressly or by implication) monetary standards as systems of policies (Lindholm, Balles, and Hunter, *op. cit.*, pp. 47 ff.; *infra*, pp. 65–68) are not illogical in ignoring their own exposition of standards if they assume a "paper standard" (Lindholm, Balles, and Hunter, *op. cit.*, pp. 66, 69, *et passim*). A paper standard, according to this interpretation, implies no particular positive policies. Consequently, the policy alternatives are practically unlimited. Such a construction of the monetary standard, being virtually meaningless, is very properly ignored.

53 I have found no exception to this relative to contemporary issues. Even the exceptions in connection with past history are rare and restricted. For example, the two chapters on "Federal Reserve Policies, 1914–1954" in a recent text contain *only one* reference to the discipline of monetary policy by the gold standard, despite the fact that the authors

believed it to have existed in pure or modified form throughout the period except for brief intervals during World War I and 1933 (Stokes and Arlt, *op. cit.*, p. 535).

54 F. A. von Hayek, *Monetary Nationalism and International Stability,* 2nd edn., London, 1939, p. 82. Control of gold production implies that monetary policy is not really related to gold, but to something else. But what? Could it be the standard for controlling gold production?

55 Coulborn, *op. cit.*, p. 262.

56 Equilibration under the international gold standard requires flexible adjustment of domestic levels of prices, income, and employment. Yet, paradoxically, in the pre-New Deal era, when no one denied that the United States was on the gold standard, the Federal Reserve Board's repeated refusal to accept responsibility for stabilizing the price level never included among its reasons the limitations imposed by the gold standard on the Board's power to stabilize the price level (Federal Reserve Board, *Annual Report, 1923,* pp. 31–32; *ibid., 1926,* p. 485; *Federal Reserve Bulletin,* XXIII [September 1937], 827; *ibid.,* XXV [April 1939], 255–258).

57 James, *op. cit.*, 1st edn., pp. 325–336; *ibid.,* 3rd edn., pp. 680–714; George William Dowrie, *American Monetary and Banking Policies,* New York, 1930, pp. 244–253, 262. O. I. Stafsing proposed "an international gold standard, 'controlled' with a view to maintaining a stable world price level" (*The New Gold Standard,* a plan submitted to the League of Nations [n.p.], 1931, p. 7). Even Lester V. Chandler (who has been least guilty of these inconsistencies), despite his long historical description of United States monetary standards, devoted only two pages of a fifteen-page chapter on "Objectives of Monetary Policy" to the relevance of metallic standards; and he made no mention whatsoever of inconvertible paper standards (*op. cit.*, 2nd edn., pp. 716–731). The discrepancy between his historical material on monetary standards and his treatment of objectives has been reduced, if not eliminated, in the last edition of his book (see *infra*, n. 59).

58 Shaw, *op. cit.*, pp. 531–553 *et passim;* A. C. L. Day, *Outline of Monetary Economics,* Oxford, 1957, pp. 438–441, 482–496. Shaw's later suggestion of the possible application of the "standard" to domestic monetary matters ("Money Supply and Stable Growth," *United States Monetary Policy,* ed. Neil H. Jacoby, New York, 1958, pp. 60–65) will be noted in Chap. VI.

59 Chandler's former chapters on "Monetary Standards in the United States" have been renamed in the third edition "Monetary Policies" and removed from the front of the book to the back, where they now serve as an introduction to international finance (*op. cit.*, pp. 373–421). And the term "policy" has tended to replace "standard" in the text as well as in the titles of the chapters (*loc. cit.*). The second edition of Klise's *Money and Banking* dropped the word "Standards" from the titles of two introductory chapters and telescoped the contents into one (*op. cit.*, pp. 19–32).

60 Day, *op. cit.*, pp. 496 ff.

61 Only one participant (Edward S. Shaw) in the American Assembly symposium on *United States Monetary Policy,* New York, December

128

1958, suggested the possible relevance of the monetary standard (his suggestion will be considered in Chap. VI). Indeed, the editor dissociated the subjects at the outset by asserting that "monetary policy" (in the normal sense of the term) "sets aside other important monetary problems, including such issues as monetary standards . . ." (Neil H. Jacoby, "Contemporary Monetary Issues," *ibid.,* p. 2). James W. Angell approached "The Monetary Standard" as a cautious man might write a safe love letter—choosing his subject and carefully avoiding it (*American Economic Review,* Papers and Proceedings, XLVIII [May 1958], 76–87).

CHAPTER II

1 They were: (1) fineness of monetary metal, (2) legal fineness of standard coin, (3) legal weight of standard coin, (4) the name of the "unit of account" as distinct from its substance, (5) the substance of the unit of account ("Unit of Coinage"), (6) "Full-Legal-Tender Money," (7) "the chief coin in use," (8) standard (in contrast to token) money, and (9) "The Monetary System of a country, in general terms" (*The Silver Pound and England's Monetary History since the Restoration,* London, 1887, pp. xxi–xxii).
2 *Ibid.,* p. xxiii.
3 Inclusion of number four might seem to imply an overlap of numbers two and three. That this is not necessarily so will be elucidated later in this chapter. Horton's ninth variant will be considered in Chap. V.
4 "Standard" metal is the combination of precious metal and alloys defined by law as the legal content of specie (William Howard Steiner, *Money and Banking,* New York, 1933, pp. 59–60). The term "standard of the coinage" has been used to distinguish this from other concepts of a monetary standard (William Leighton Jordan, *The Standard of Value,* 3rd edn., London, 1883, p. 113).
5 The interpretation of "the standard of money" as the fineness of specie was categorically denied by eighteenth-century authorities, e.g., "It is carefully to be remembered, that by the *standard of money,* is always meant, the *quantity of pure or fine metal* contained in a given sum; and *not merely the degree of purity or fineness* of that metal . . ." ([Joseph Harris], *An Essay upon Money and Coins, Part I: The Theories of Commerce, Money, and Exchanges,* London, 1757, p. 55 [last two italics mine]). Indicative of the "dictionary lag," however, is the fact that the 1839 edition of Webster's *Dictionary* defined standard relating to money as "the proportion of weight of fine metal and alloy established by authority."

129

6 P.[atrick] Kelly, *The Universal Cambist and Commercial Instructor,* 2nd edn., I, London, 1835, xxviii.

7 Hiram L. Jome, *Principles of Money and Banking,* Homewood, Ill., 1957, p. 32.

8 "Standard money" is traditionally defined as "the kind of money which independently embodies the [monetary] unit and to which the values of other kinds of money are assimilated or adjusted . . ." (Horace White, *Money and Banking,* 6th edn., revised and enlarged by Charles S. Tippets and Lewis A. Froman, Boston, 1935, p. 23).

9 The Attic, Phoenician, and Gallic gold standards were described as the number of grains of gold in the respective units by which gold was measured—units which were ultimately coined (William Ridgeway, *The Origin of Metallic Currency and Weight Standards,* Cambridge, 1892, pp. 125–132).

10 Harris, *op. cit.,* p. 56: "The standard of our money, strictly speaking, remains the same, so long as there is the same quantity of pure silver in the respective coins having the old or given denominations . . . And by debasing the standard, I every where mean, the lessening of the quantity of pure silver in the pound sterling . . ."

11 Discussions relating to the early monetary legislation of the United States implied interpretation of the "monetary standard" as "standard money" (Robert E. Preston, *History of the Monetary Legislation and of the Currency System of the United States,* Philadelphia, 1896, pp. 89 ff.).

12 There were, of course, a few exceptions, e.g., Maurice L. Muhleman, *Monetary Systems of the World,* 2nd edn., New York, 1897, p. 11; and Karl Helfferich, *Money,* trans. Louis Infield, ed. T. E. Gregory, I, London, 1927, 52–66 *et passim.*

13 J. Marvin Peterson, Delmas R. Cawthorne, and Philipp H. Lohman, *Money and Banking,* New York, 1941, pp. 19, 84–85; Ludwig von Mises, *The Theory of Money and Credit,* 2nd edn., trans. H. E. Batson, New Haven, 1953, p. 429.

14 Steiner, *op. cit.,* pp. 46, 63, 81; John T. Madden and Marcus Nadler, *The International Money Markets,* New York, 1935, pp. 1–2; Ray B. Westerfield, *Money, Credit and Banking,* 2nd edn., New York, 1947, p. 80; Jome, *op. cit.,* pp. vii, 28–36, 54.

15 Ray V. Leffler, for example, used "standard of value" principally to mean the standard for valuing credit media of exchange in terms of standard money (*Money and Credit,* New York, 1935, pp. 22–23, 42–43, 88–89, 416).

16 The fixity of the standard (in this sense) existed internally and was considered obtainable externally—even in the absence of general adherence to metallic standards—by types of government action that did not violate the conservative psyche.

17 Lester V. Chandler, *The Economics of Money and Banking,* New York, 1948, p. 60:

> Monetary standards take their names from the type of standard money employed. If its standard money is gold, we say that a coun-

130

try is on a gold standard. If the standard money is silver, the country is on a silver standard. If the standard money is defined in terms of both gold and silver, the country is on a bimetallic standard. If the standard money is not kept constant in terms of any metal, the country is usually said to be on an inconvertible paper money standard.

This statement was repeated in the second edition, 1953, p. 88; and the substance of it was included in the third edition, 1959, p. 354. Rollin G. Thomas said the same thing in almost the identical words (*Our Modern Banking and Monetary System,* 2nd edn., New York, 1950, p. 28). Likewise, Charles R. Whittlesey affirmed, "To be on a particular monetary standard is to have that form or type of money as standard money" (*Principles and Practices of Money and Banking,* 2nd edn., New York, 1954, p. 19).

18 *Some Chapters on Money* (printed for use of students in the University of Michigan), Ann Arbor, 1906, p. 37. Russell Donald Kilborne used practically the same language (*Principles of Money and Banking,* Chicago, 1927, p. 14).

19 Major B. Foster, Raymond Rogers, Jules I. Bogan, and Marcus Nadler, *Money and Banking,* New York, 1936, p. 29 (italics mine). The statement was repeated verbatim in the third edition, 1947, p. 24.

20 *The Monetary and Banking System,* New York, 1950, p. 11.

21 Woodworth implicitly conceded this by interpreting the gold standard as a fixed *quantity,* not value, of gold (*ibid.,* p. 48).

22 *Money, Credit, and Public Policy,* Boston, 1959, p. 22.

23 It does not help any, either, to substitute "multiple" for "tabular" as is so often done (Charles A. Conant, *The Principles of Money and Banking,* II, New York, 1905, 431; and Westerfield, *op. cit.,* p. 105). A standard money made of "multiples" makes no more sense than one made of tables. The "tabular standard" was also known as the "commodity standard" (Westerfield, *loc. cit.*). J. Laurence Laughlin called the plan by its three "standard" names ("tabular," "multiple," and "commodity") in the same discussion—the last name in the table of contents and the other two in the text (*The Principles of Money,* New York, 1903, pp. xiii, 47). A standard money made of "commodities" has meaning, but, as already explained, not the meaning intended. Whittlesey supplied a rare example of the use of the term "multiple standard" consistent with the "standard money" conception of the monetary standard, which he implicitly adopted (*op. cit.,* p. 198). See also Edwin Walter Kemmerer, *Money,* New York, 1935, p. 94.

24 Sir George Shuckburgh Evelyn (see *Philosophical Transactions of the Royal Society of London,* 1798, Part I, pp. 175–176) has been credited with originating the "tabular standard" concept (*Dictionary of Political Economy,* ed. R. H. Inglis Palgrave, London, 1894–1899, III, 509–510). Joseph Lowe was "the first to lay any considerable stress upon its practical value" (*ibid.,* p. 510). Lowe referred, however, to the similar proposals of Arthur Young and Patrick Colquhoun (Joseph Lowe, *The Present State of England in Regard to Agriculture, Trade, and Finance,* 2nd edn., London, 1823, p. 334). G. Poulett Scrope popularized the idea

and the term (*An Examination of the Bank Charter Question,* London, 1833, pp. 25–27); and W. Stanley Jevons preserved them (*Investigations in Currency and Finance,* ed. H. S. Foxwell, London, 1884, pp. 122 ff.; and *Money and the Mechanism of Exchange,* New York, [1875], pp. 318–321, 324–326). It was pointed out in 1928 that the "tabular standard" was no recent novelty, but a proposal which had received extensive treatment in the literature on monetary standards (Joseph Stagg Lawrence, *Stabilization of Prices,* New York, 1928, p. 176).

25 *Infra,* n. 158 of this chapter.

26 Kemmerer, *op. cit.,* p. 103 (italics mine): "The *tabular standard* is a device for giving a stable standard of value for the payment of debts, particularly long-time debts. It is *concerned directly only with the standard of deferred payment function* of money, and *may be employed while any other kind of monetary* standard is serving for the medium of exchange." Paradoxically, the "tabular standard" is customarily listed among alternative monetary standards by the very authorities who associate the standard with standard money. See also Steiner, *op. cit.,* pp. 98–99; and William Howard Steiner and Eli Shapiro, *Money and Banking,* New York, 1941, pp. 66–67.

27 United States Treasury Department, *Laws of the United States Relating to the Coinage,* Washington, 1895, pp. 65–66, 69; Horace White, *op. cit.,* 1st edn., p. 59; and Charles L. Prather, *Money and Banking,* Chicago, 1937, p. 82.

28 Notwithstanding authoritative denials that the "limping standard" was a standard at all (Harold G. Moulton, *Principles of Money and Banking,* Chicago, 1916, p. 99; and D. H. Robertson, *Money,* 2nd edn., New York, 1929, pp. 73–75), its status as a standard continued to prevail. The symbol remained; only the substance changed. It became interpreted as an abstract concept distinguishable from the gold exchange standard only by the *intent* of the government (Conant, *op. cit.,* I, 279, 374–375). Another observer concluded that the "limping standard" was "a type of gold standard" (Abdus Sadeque, *The Problem of the Standard of Indian Currency,* Calcutta, 1938, pp. 22–23). Still others identified it as the gold exchange standard (Peterson, Cawthorne, and Lohman, *op. cit.,* p. 24) and as the present standard of the United States (Edward S. Shaw, *Money, Income, and Monetary Policy,* Chicago, 1950, p. 550).

29 W. A. L. Coulborn, *An Introduction to Money,* London, 1938, p. 134; and Westerfield, *op. cit.,* p. 105.

30 That premise was the classical view of the monetary standard, which will be considered in the next section of this chapter.

31 John Rooke, *An Inquiry into the Principles of National Wealth,* Edinburgh, 1824, pp. 216, 220–227, 460 ff.; Simon Newcomb, "The Standard of Value," *North American Review,* CXXIX (September 1879) 234–236; *Memorials of Alfred Marshall,* ed. A. C. Pigou, London, 1925, pp. 206–207, n. 2; Aneurin Williams, "A 'Fixed Value of Bullion' Standard—A Proposal for Preventing General Fluctuations of Trade," *Economic Journal,* II (June 1892), 280, 283, 747; J. Allen Smith, "A Multiple Money Standard," *Annals,* VII (March 1896), 207–214; Irving Fisher and Harry G. Brown, *The Purchasing Power of Money,*

New York, 1911, pp. 337–342; Irving Fisher, *Stabilizing the Dollar*, New York, 1920, pp. xxxvii–xl, 84–90, 125 ff.

32 Fisher, *Stabilizing the Dollar*, pp. 90–91. Likewise, the absence of standard money is implied by the so-called "flexible standard" (von Mises, *op. cit.*, pp. 429–430).

33 And they did, although they had their own difficulties and never found a suitable specific name for it (see *infra*, n. 173 of this chapter).

34 Leffler seemed to accept Fisher's claim that the compensated dollar plan did not represent a departure from the gold standard (*op. cit.*, pp. 100–101). To those who called the proposal an abandonment of the gold standard, Fisher answered that it would "put the standard into the gold standard" instead of take it out (*Stabilizing the Dollar*, pp. 89–90). The difference turned on the different conceptions of a monetary standard. Those, such as Leffler, who held to the concept under discussion were inconsistent in accepting Fisher's argument. A later follower in the tradition of Leffler on this matter also made the self-contradictory concession that Fisher's compensated dollar plan was a monetary standard, but he called it a "commodities . . . standard" (Lawrence Smith, *op. cit.*, p. 178).

35 On the basis of the interpretation of a monetary standard being considered, the name of this standard suggests that gold bullion would be the standard money. This is the customary answer. But may something that does not circulate as a means of payment—might even be illegal for people generally to possess—be called money? George N. Halm has said, "It is a mere terminological question whether gold bullion ought to be called standard money, considering that it would not circulate as a means of payment" (*Economics of Money and Banking*, Homewood, Ill., 1956, p. 54). A terminological question on which the determination of the monetary standard depends hardly deserves the adjective "mere." The issue is not that important for Halm because he espouses a different conception of a monetary standard. But for believers in the standard-money concept of the monetary standard it is—or should be—more than a matter of words.

36 As we "progress" down the list, the problem of identifying standard money becomes increasingly difficult.

37 "If the *standard money* is not convertible into bullion but into foreign exchange, being thus connected indirectly with the metal (gold) reserves of other countries, we have a metal (gold) exchange standard" (George N. Halm, *Monetary Theory*, 2nd edn., Philadelphia, 1946, p. 106 [italics mine]). This clearly indicates that there is a standard money in a gold exchange standard, but what is it? We have been told that the domestic currency was the "standard unit of money" (Earl Dean Howard and Joseph French Johnson, *Money and Banking*, New York, 1911, p. 191); that local money "was really token currency" (D. T. Jack, *The Economics of the Gold Standard*, London, 1925, p. 40); and that both the domestic and foreign (reserve country) currencies are standard (Eugene E. Agger, *Money and Banking Today*, New York, 1941, pp. 167–169). Maybe the "so-called *gold exchange standard*" (George William Dowrie, *Money and Banking*, New York, 1936, p. 92) is not a standard at all (J. Laurence Laughlin, *A New Exposition of Money, Credit and*

133

Prices, I, Chicago, 1931, 484; and Roy L. Garis, *Principles of Money, Credit, and Banking,* New York, 1934, p. 98), but such doubts are scarce.

38 Shaw, *op. cit.,* pp. 544–545.
39 Geoffrey Crowther, *An Outline of Money,* 2nd edn., London, 1948, p. 280.
40 Coulborn, *op. cit.,* pp. 121–124; Westerfield, *op. cit.,* p. 572.
41 Halm, *Economics of Money and Banking,* p. 178.
42 Shaw, *op. cit.,* p. 543.
43 Benjamin Graham, *Storage and Stability,* New York, 1937, pp. 49 ff.; Frank D. Graham, "Commodity-Reserve Currency: A Criticism of the Critique," *Journal of Political Economy,* LI (February 1943), 70–75; Frank D. Graham, "Full Employment without Public Debt, without Taxation, without Public Works, and without Inflation," *Planning and Paying for Full Employment,* ed. Abba P. Lerner and Frank D. Graham, Princeton, 1946, pp. 44–46 *et passim.* The usual assumption is that the standard money of this plan is the composite commodity unit with which the monetary unit is equated, but this construction contradicts the usual definition of money as a generally acceptable means of payment (e.g., Agger, *op. cit.,* pp. 31, 185–186). Whittlesey resolved this paradox by defining money as anything performing *any* of the functions of money, adding a "bank reserve" function to the conventional list (*op. cit.,* pp. 17–18). However, he conceded that the definition expands the concept of money far beyond the limits of its ordinary meaning. Only one of his three classes of United States money, for instance, *"includes what is ordinarily meant by the expression 'money supply' "* (*ibid.,* p. 34). Whittlesey achieved an exceptional consistency—by paying a price in communicability. A definition of money so far removed from normal usage has not been, and is not likely to be, widely adopted.
44 Woodworth, *op. cit.,* p. 61; Ernst Dick, *The Interest Standard of Currency,* Boston, 1926, pp. 17–18.
45 J. Allen Smith, *op. cit.,* pp. 203 ff. See also *infra,* p. 31.
46 Dick, *op. cit.,* pp. 113–116, 169. Dick's formulation of this standard, which appears to turn orthodox monetary doctrines upside down, was, according to Norman Angell (*The Story of Money,* Garden City, 1929, p. 382), founded on J. A. Hobson's contention that money is hired, not purchased like other commodities (J. A. Hobson, *Gold, Prices & Wages,* London, 1913, p. 156). The inclination of the United States Treasury, Wall Street, and the Democratic Party toward this standard is rationalized by more orthodox views.
47 Hans Glückstadt, *The Mechanism of the Credit Standard,* London, 1933, pp. 15–16, 86–87; Edward S. Shaw, "Money Supply and Stable Economic Growth," *United States Monetary Policy,* ed. Neil H. Jacoby, New York, 1958, pp. 63–64, 69–70.
48 Woodworth, *op. cit.,* p. 64.
49 Milton L. Stokes and Carl T. Arlt, *Money, Banking and the Financial System,* New York, 1955, p. 97: "Every monetary system is built upon a specific *standard* unit as the monetary equivalent or counterpart of the unit of account. The standard unit may be a certain *quantity of a commodity,* such as gold or silver, or it may be nothing more than a particu-

134

lar *type of paper* unit issued by the supreme monetary authority."
Sometimes the inconsistency is unconsciously turned into a contradiction
by defining the monetary standard as the "material" in which "money
will be redeemed" and then describing the "paper standard" as a situation wherein money "will not be redeemed" in anything (Peterson,
Cawthorne, and Lohman, *op. cit.*, p. 19). Although the implications
seem to have generally escaped attention, the fact of the discrepancy
has occasionally been recognized: "In some countries before the war
[World War I], and most countries since the war, the legal definition [of
the monetary unit as "a certain weight of gold"] has become inoperative,
the money of account being represented by *paper notes which are without definition*" (R. A. Lehfeldt, *Money*, London, 1926, p. 48 [italics
mine]).

50 Richard W. Lindholm, John J. Balles, and John M. Hunter, *Principles
of Money and Banking*, New York, 1954, pp. 47–48 (italics mine): "A
nation's money is said to be 'on the gold standard' when its monetary
unit (in paper or checkbook money) is freely convertible into a stated
quantity of gold. . . . The acceptability of paper standard money is
not based upon any intrinsic value of the backing (gold for example) of
the money unit." Another writer expressed the negation known as a
paper standard this way: "A paper standard is one in which the note
issue is *unrelated to any independent measure of value*" (F. W. Mueller,
Money and Banking, New York, 1951, p. 54 [italics mine]). For a pre-
1931 vintage of the same idea see Helfferich, *op. cit.*, p. 66.

51 This fact has become more recognizable since abstract bank deposits
have relegated paper money to the role of instruments for merely making change. Chandler implicitly recognized all this by dropping the term
"paper standard," renaming the phenomenon simply, an "inconvertible
standard" (*op. cit.*, 3rd edn., p. 354). Nevertheless, some members of
the "standard money school" of monetary standards still regard the
paper standard as a fact, that is, as indicative of something that exists—
instead of something that does not exist—and a fact which is both universal and permanent (Stokes and Arlt, *op. cit.*, p. 109).

52 Whittlesey, *op. cit.*, pp. 203–204.

53 Henry A. Miller, *Money and Bimetallism*, New York, 1898, p. 34.

54 *Money and the Mechanism of Exchange*, p. 73. Sidney Sherwood (*The
History and Theory of Money*, Philadelphia, 1893, p. 75) made the
distinction in the following manner: "This coin, which does not have in
it bullion of a market value equal to the nominal value of the coin, we
call a 'token.' On the other hand, a coin which has in it bullion of a
market value equal to its nominal value—that is, the market and the
mint value being the same—we call a standard coin." Others expressed
the same idea: Helfferich, *op. cit.*, II, 382; William A. Scott, *Money and
Banking*, 6th edn., New York, 1926, pp. 28, 93; Edwin Cannan, *Modern
Currency and the Regulation of Its Value*, London, 1931, p. 28; and
Agger, *op. cit.*, pp. 49–50.

55 Scott, *op. cit.*, p. 30. Many writers were not happy with the phraseology
that amounted to a "token standard" money, but they could not see
their way out of this glossological cul-de-sac because the difficulty was
in the premised concept of a monetary standard, which was seldom

stated and, consequently, often disregarded. For example, Charles Tippets and Lewis A. Froman observed in their revision of Horace White's classic: "It is frequently contended that a standard money can never be fiduciary, that standard money must always be full bodied [as White, himself, had contended]. There *seems, however, to be no other way* of describing certain monetary standards used in the past" (White, *op. cit.*, 6th edn., p. 23).

56 Lindholm, Balles, and Hunter, *op. cit.*, p. 63: "The minimum basic requirement of a paper standard is that all paper money be convertible into other types of money, which in turn have considerably less value as commodities than as money."

57 Conant, *op. cit.*, I, 404 (middle italics mine): *"Inconvertibility* means that the government has made *no arrangements, or inadequate ones, for converting such notes at the will of the holder into standard money.* The fact that they are *not redeemed in such money* on presentation has given such notes also the designation of *irredeemable government paper."* "Where metallic standards are dispensed with 'standard money' in the formal sense may be wanting" (Agger, *op. cit.*, p. 111).

58 Yet it is contended that "most nations today have such standards" (Lawrence Smith, *op. cit.*, p. 118).

59 "Different kinds of circulating media are kept at par with one another and no attempt is made to distinguish between 'standard' and 'token' or 'credit' moneys. Technically, *all money issued under a fiat system is 'standard money' "* (J. Whitney Hanks and Roland Stucki, *Money, Banking, and National Income,* New York, 1956, p. 51 [italics mine]). For other expressions of the same idea, see: Agger, *op. cit.*, p. 51; and Thomas, *op. cit.*, 3rd edn., pp. 24–25.

60 "The standard may be . . . some form of money itself" (Lawrence Smith, *op. cit.*, p. 22). See also *ibid.*, p. 118.

61 Coulborn, *op. cit.*, pp. 122–124, 167.

62 White, *op. cit.*, 6th edn., pp. 109–110, 112; George Francis Luthringer, Lester Vernon Chandler, and Denzel Cecil Cline, *Money, Credit and Finance,* Boston, 1938, pp. 216–217; Peterson, Cawthorne, and Lohman, *op. cit.*, pp. 35, 70.

63 Peterson, Cawthorne, and Lohman, *loc. cit.;* Dowrie, *op. cit.*, pp. 85–86.

64 Eugene S. Klise, *Money and Banking,* 2nd edn., Cincinnati, 1959, p. 31.

65 Woodworth, *op. cit.*, p. 59.

66 *Ibid.*, p. 61.

67 *Ibid.*, p. 64.

68 Lawrence Smith, *op. cit.*, p. 206.

69 Leffler, *op. cit.*, p. 97. The term could be used logically by these people only to describe such schemes as the "compensated dollar" plan, but this was not the manner of its employment. The term "flexible standard" (von Mises, *op. cit.*, p. 429) contains the same apparent contradiction.

70 Sir Dennis H. Robertson, *Lectures on Economic Principles,* III, London, 1959, 14–15.

71 *Ibid.*, p. 15.

72 Moreover, since the distinction between simultaneous comparisons, on the one hand, and time comparisons, on the other, are irrelevant to the subject under investigation, the "standard of value" will be construed as

including what is normally supposed to be meant by the "standard of deferred payments," just as it did in the classical literature before the latter phrase was "coined."

73 Henry Thornton, *An Enquiry into the Nature and Effects of the Paper Credit of Great Britain,* ed. F. A. Hayek, New York, 1939 [reprint of 1st (1802) edn.], pp. 111, 357. Notice that these pages are indexed under the topic "Gold as the standard of value" (*ibid.*, p. 365).

74 White, *op. cit.,* 1st edn., p. 31, n. 1; Whittlesey, *op. cit.,* p. 22.

75 "Chap. XVI.—An Act Establishing a Mint and regulating the Coins of the United States. (a)," 2nd Congress, 1st Session, *The Public Statutes at Large of the United States of America,* I, Boston, 1854, 248–250.

76 United States Congress, House of Representatives, Committee on Coinage, Weights, and Measures, *Hearing on the Bill (H.R. 11411) to Define and Fix the Standard of Value and for Other Purposes,* January 12, 1899, Washington, 1899, pp. 19–20, 72, 97–98; United States Congress, House of Representatives, Committee on Coinage, Weights, and Measures, *Standard of Value, etc.,* Report 1876, Part 1, 55th Congress, 3rd Session, pp. 1–4, 6, 25; *ibid., Views of the Minority,* Report 1876, Part 2, 55th Congress, 3rd Session, pp. 1 ff.; "Chap. 41.—An Act to Define and Fix the Standard of Value . . . ," approved March 14, 1900, 56th Congress, 1st Session, *The Statutes at Large of the United States of America,* XXXI, Washington, 1901, 45. In U. S. vs. Marigold, the Supreme Court interpreted the "standard of value" as the standard for the valuation of the various kinds of U. S. money, i.e., as standard money (quoted by Paul Bakewell, Jr., *Past and Present Facts about Money in the United States,* New York, 1936, p. 20).

77 Taylor, *op. cit.,* pp. 36–37; Ira B. Cross, *Domestic and Foreign Exchange,* New York, 1923, pp. 451–452; Bradford, *op. cit.,* pp. 31, 370; Dowrie, *op. cit.,* p. 51; Carl Strover, *Monetary Progress,* Chicago, 1937, p. 117; Ervin P. Hexner, "The New Gold Standard," *Weltwirtschaftliches Archiv,* LXXXV (1960), pp. 6–7 *et passim.*

78 Whittlesey, *op. cit.,* pp. 17, 19; Lawrence Smith, *op. cit.,* pp. 4–5, 19–20.

79 Thomas, *op. cit.,* 3rd edn., p. 7, n. 2 (italics mine): "When a currency is convertible into a given quantity of gold, the gold unit is sometimes looked upon as the standard of value. *This practice, however, appears to confuse the* standard monetary unit, *gold, with the standard of value which is the monetary unit in any form. Thus, the dollar is the standard of value* and has continued to be so regardless of its convertibility status since 1932."

80 See, for example, Lawrence Smith, *op. cit.,* pp. 23, 119.

81 The whole corpus of anti-gold-standard literature from the antibullionists of the early nineteenth century to modern advocates of "managed currency" could be cited here. For example, see Lawrence, *op. cit.,* p. 176 and *infra,* nn. 99, 100, 108, and 129 of this chapter.

82 *Infra,* nn. 103 and 112 of this chapter.

83 Jordan, *op. cit.,* p. 25: "The double standard of gold and silver [i.e., bimetallism] would again practically become the measure of value in all countries, though some might continue to have the gold, and others the silver standard, established by law." Marshall's preference for symmetallism was based on the belief that general commodity prices calcu-

lated in terms of both metals together would fluctuate less than they would if expressed in terms of either, alone (*op. cit.,* pp. 194–196, 206). Another bimetallist attacked the gold standard as a "desperate scheme for *appreciating the standard of value,*" maintaining that this was as unjust as depreciating the standard (H. S. Foxwell, *A Criticism of Lord Farrer on the Monetary Standard* [reprinted from the *National Review,* January 1895], London [1895], p. 24). A contemporary asserted that "standard of value" did not mean "standard money" in any sense of the latter term (Miller, *op. cit.,* pp. 34–37, 48). The House Committee on Coinage, Weights, and Measures affirmed that the commercial world determined the "real standard and measure of values" regardless of the legal enactments of Congress (*Standard of Value, etc.,* Report 1876, Part 1, 55th Congress, 3rd Session, p. 5). George Gunton distinguished between the legal fiction of "standard money" and the economic reality of the "standard of value" ("How We Came to the Gold Standard," *Lecture Bulletin of the Institute of Social Economics,* III [March 31, 1900], 610). David Kinley added that the former was invariable and the latter variable (*Money,* New York, 1904, pp. 260–261).

84 John Maynard Keynes, *A Tract on Monetary Reform,* London, 1923, p. 170; John Maynard Keynes, *A Treatise on Money,* II, London, 1930, 300–301, 338; James Dysart Magee, *An Introduction to Money and Credit,* 2nd edn., New York, 1933, pp. 471–472; Edwin Walter Kemmerer, *Kemmerer on Money,* Chicago, 1934, p. 13. For additional references see Irving Fisher, *Stable Money,* New York, 1934, pp. 94–95.

85 Irving Fisher, *The Present Chaos in Monetary Standards and How to Deal with It* (reprinted from *The Manufacturer,* March 1921), n.p., n.d., pp. 23–24. See also *supra,* n. 31 of this chapter.

86 Jordan, *op. cit.,* pp. 63–64, n.; Lesley C. Probyn, "The Maintenance by England of Her Single Gold Standard," *The Case for Monometallism* (two essays in favour of Monometallism selected by Lord Farrer), London, 1895, p. 13.

87 Taylor, *op. cit.,* p. 42. Examples of such a standard, he suggested, might include a bushel of wheat or a number of commodities comprising *"a composite or multiple standard"* (*ibid.,* pp. 42–43). "Some modern systems have forms of money which are neither standard money nor directly representative of standard bullion" (Agger, *op. cit.,* p. 159).

88 Miller, *op. cit.,* pp. 34–35.

89 Agger, *op. cit.,* p. 156. "In general, it may be said that the more extensive the area over which the money system operates, the wider must be the market for the substance that serves as a standard" (*loc. cit.*). "In different stages of economic development, various economic goods have appeared as *standards of value"* (ibid., p. 157). Two other apparent definitions of the concept evaporated in ambiguities (Sir Charles Morgan-Webb, *The Rise and Fall of the Gold Standard,* New York, 1934, pp. 12, 28–29, 45, 90, 181; Anatol Murad, *The Paradox of a Metal Standard,* Washington, 1939, pp. 4, 181–182).

90 In Volume II of Palgrave's *Dictionary of Political Economy,* p. 799, we find "Monometallism" defined as "a monetary system in which the *standard of value consists of one metal . . .* [italics mine]." Bimetallism is defined in Volume I (p. 146) as "the employment of two metals, to

138

form at the same time, in conjunction with each other, the *standard of value* [italics mine]." For other examples, see Volume III, pp. 457–458, 609, 683–684; as well as the *Encyclopaedia of the Social Sciences,* II, 1930, 546; and *Encyclopaedia Britannica,* III, 1958, 580.

91 Adam Smith, *An Inquiry into the Nature and Causes of the Wealth of Nations,* ed. Edwin Cannan, Modern Library edn. [reprinted from 5th edn.], New York, 1937, pp. 38–39.

92 For the substantive issues see Jacob Viner, *Studies in the Theory of International Trade,* New York, 1937, pp. 119–217; and Will E. Mason, "The Stereotypes of Classical Transfer Theory," *Journal of Political Economy,* LXIV (December 1956), 498–505.

93 *The Works and Correspondence of David Ricardo,* ed. Piero Sraffa with the collaboration of M. H. Dobb, Cambridge, 1951–1955, IV, 54–55 (italics mine). For his earlier expressions of this view see *ibid.,* III, 65, 68–70, 417. His "Principles of Political Economy and Taxation" implicitly reinforced this construction of the monetary standard (*ibid.,* I, 368–369). Included in a list of main conceptions said to have been treated by Ricardo in his pamphlets on the bullion question is "the nature of a *standard of value* and the use of the precious metals as such" (*Dictionary of Political Economy,* ed. Palgrave, III, 308 [italics mine]).

94 London, 1801, pp. 49–53, 66.

95 See pp. 10 and 16 of the original *Report* and pp. 12 and 16 of the reprint in *The Paper Pound of 1797–1821,* ed. Edwin Cannan, London, 1919. Frank W. Fetter has pointed out that the *Report* was not the mere carbon copy of Ricardian reasoning that many had supposed it to be ("The Bullion Report Re-examined" [reprinted from the *Quarterly Journal of Economics,* LVI (August 1942)], *Papers in English Monetary History,* ed. T. S. Ashton and R. S. Sayers, Oxford, 1953, pp. 66 ff.).

96 Lord King, in remarking on the depreciation of the paper pound, classified the indefinite postponement of sterling convertibility among the "alarming projects held out of destroying the ancient *standard of value,* and subverting the basis, and denomination, of the lawful money of the realm" (*A Selection from the Speeches and Writings of the Late Lord King,* ed. Earl Fortescue, London, 1844, p. 231). Ricardo's bullion-standard proposal received some support as a more stable standard of value than the country had yet experienced, even though it would not be perfectly stable (see, for example, Mr. Holland's statement to Sir Robert Peel's House of Commons Committee of 1819 on Resumption of Cash Payments [quoted by T.[homas] Joplin, *An Analysis and History of the Currency Question,* London, 1832, pp. 51–52]). See also the remarks of Sir Robert Peel, reported in Hansard's *Parliamentary Debates,* XL, London, 1819, column 679.

97 [Edward Copleston], *A Letter to the Right Hon. Robert Peel, M.P. for the University of Oxford, on the Pernicious Effects of a Variable Standard of Value . . . ,* 2nd edn., Oxford, 1819, pp. 11–12.

98 The exceptions among the antibullionist extremists were in the minority.

99 Thomas Smith, *Essay on the Theory of Money & Exchange,* London, 1807, p. 5; *A Reply to the Author of a Letter to the Right Hon. Robert Peel, on the Pernicious Effects of a Variable Standard of Value* [gold], London, 1819, pp. 7 ff.

139

100 S.[imon] Gray, *The Happiness of States,* 2nd edn., London, 1819, p. xi. Other expressions of essentially the same idea may be found in: Thomas Smith, *op. cit.,* pp. 5 ff.; *ibid.,* 2nd edn., 1811, pp. 35–48; John Raithby, *The Law and Principle of Money Considered,* London, 1811, pp. 24–27; T.[homas] Joplin, *Outlines of a System of Political Economy,* London, 1823, pp. 162–163. A latter-day follower in this tradition called intrinsically valuable money "barbarian money" (Edward D. Linton, *Specific Payments Better than Specie Payments,* Boston, 1876, p. 3.

101 "[Thomas] Smith on Money and Exchange," *Edinburgh Review,* XIII (October 1808), 35.

102 For a modern manifestation of this difficulty, see first quotation, *infra,* n. 216 of this chapter.

103 Thomas Smith's proposal of an abstract standard of value was written off by the elder Mill in the following manner:

> When he [Smith] discovered, accordingly, that the precious metals, on which they [orthodox writers on money] had fixed, were entirely incapable of discharging this service [of providing an invariable standard of value], it seems never to have occurred to him to suspect that possibly nothing else was more capable of discharging it. He applied himself, on the contrary, with great zeal, to discover something to which this function might be assigned; and certainly was reduced to straits in the experiment. He could find nothing, either in heaven above, or in earth beneath, to answer his purpose. But being a bold man, even this did not reduce him to despair. If he found no real standard, he found at least an imaginary one; if nothing in being could perform this service, a nonentity, he seems to have thought, might certainly accomplish it (*op. cit.,* pp. 39–40).

Other bullionists also dismissed the notion of an abstract standard of value as a contradiction of terms (R.[obert] Torrens, *An Essay on the Production of Wealth,* London, 1821, p. 65). For a brief review and commentary on this debate see R. G. Hawtrey, *Currency and Credit,* 2nd edn., London, 1923, pp. 411–415.

104 *An Inquiry into the Principles of Political Œconomy,* London, 1767, I, 527 ff.

105 *The Works and Correspondence of David Ricardo,* IV, 59. See also *ibid.,* III, 65.

106 "CAP. LXVIII. An Act to provide for a New Silver Coinage, and to regulate the Currency of the Gold and Silver Coin of the Realm [22d June 1816]," *The Statutes of the United Kingdom of Great Britain and Ireland,* LVI, London, 1816, p. 388.

107 *The Monetary Problem: Gold and Silver,* [reprint of] Final Report of the [British] Royal Commission Appointed to Inquire into the Recent Changes in the Relative Values of the Precious Metals, Presented to Both Houses of Parliament, 1888, ed. Ralph Robey, New York, 1936, p. 64 (italics mine): "That in addition to the circumstances affecting each article separately, several causes have been in operation which might have been expected to produce a fall in price without reference to the *standard of value* itself . . ." See also *ibid.,* pp. 56, 65, 67, 163, 282–283, 285–287, 291. Moreover, both Disraeli and Gladstone were reported to have interpreted the gold standard as a gold "standard of value" (Jordan, *op. cit.,* p. 39, n.; F. J. Faraday, "On Some Remarks

by the Right Hon. William Ewart Gladstone, M.P., on the relative stability of Gold and Silver as Standards of Value; being a vindication of the opinions of Ricardo and Cobden," reprint from the Seventh Volume of the Fourth Series of *Memoirs and Proceedings of the Manchester Literary and Philosophical Society*, Session 1892–1893, pp. 2–3).

108 Scrope, *op. cit.*, p. 12 (italics mine): "Thus, *where gold is, as in this country, the standard measure of value*, a change in its value occasioning a change of general prices . . . is as unjust and treacherous, as subversive of the assumed invariability of the standard, whether the change proceed from an alteration in the supply of gold or of goods." Sir David Salomons, *Reflections on the Connexion between Our Gold Standard and the Recent Monetary Vicissitudes; with Suggestions for the Addition of Silver as a Measure of Value*, London, 1843, p. vii (italics mine): "How far the plan [currency school proposal] is really practicable without producing great pressure on the industrial classes, if we persist in retaining our single [gold] *standard of value*, becomes a subject of surpassing interest." Salomons later reiterated his interpretation of the gold standard as the use of gold to "measure the value of our commodities" (*ibid.*, p. x) and "all the transactions of the country" (*ibid.*, p. xvi). See also: "Currency," *Quarterly Review*, XXXIX (April 1829), 473; James Wilson, *Capital, Currency, and Banking*, London, 1847, p. 13; [a critical notice of] "Lectures on the Nature and Use of Money by John Gray," *Westminster Review*, L (January 1849), 604; W. Cargill, *The Currency: Showing How a Fixed Gold Standard Places England in Permanent Disadvantage* . . . , London, 1847, p. 16; [John Stuart Mill], "The Currency Question," *Westminster Review*, XLI (June 1844), 581; James Maclaren, *A Letter to the Chancellor of the Exchequer, upon the Recent Decision of the German States to Adopt a Silver Standard; and on Some Circumstances which Render an Invariable Measure of Value More Important to England than to Any Other Country*, London, 1856, p. 3; N. A. Nicholson, *Observations on Coinage, and Our Present Monetary System*, 2nd edn., London, 1868, pp. 3–4; and J. Shield Nicholson, *A Treatise on Money and Essays on Monetary Problems*, 2nd edn., London, 1893, pp. 26–28, 256.

109 W. P. Tatham, *On the Restoration of the Standard of Value, and the Proper Limit to the Use of Bank Credit as Money*, Philadelphia, 1869, pp. 1–2 (italics mine): "The evils resulting from abandonment of the *gold standard of value* are so many and so great, that nearly all are agreed upon the expediency of returning to it . . . Neither can any pleasant method be devised of resuming the *specie standard of value*." This standard interpretation merely confirmed traditional American usage. Daniel Webster, a quarter of a century before, had called gold and silver at the mint ratio "the legal standard of value" (quoted by James H. Teller, *The Battle of the Standards*, Chicago, 1896, p. 4 [facing title page]). And later, the Act of 1873 was construed as affirming gold to be the legal standard of value (see, for example, the subtitle of the "Report of the Director of the Mint, Nov. 1, 1873," *Report of the Secretary of the Treasury on the State of the Finances for the Year 1873*, Washington, 1873, pp. 470, 476).

110 "There may be a great variation in respect to silver and all other commodities, but none in respect to gold, which is the *standard measure by which all fluctuations are determined, or it is not a standard"* (James G. Batterson, *Gold and Silver as Currency,* Hartford, 1896, p. 27 [italics mine except for word "standard"]). See also: Gold Standard Defense Association, Leaflet Number 1, London, 1895, p. 1; Horace White, *The Gold Standard,* an address before the Congress of Bankers and Financiers at Chicago, June 20, 1893, New York, n.d., p. 10; White, *Money and Banking,* 1st edn., p. 53; H. Parker Willis, "The History and Present Application of the Quantity Theory," *Journal of Political Economy,* IV (September 1896), 446; and the *Report of the Monetary Commission of the Indianapolis Convention,* ed. J. Laurence Laughlin, Chicago, 1898, pp. 30–32.

111 Henry D. Barrows, *International Bimetallism,* Los Angeles, 1891, p. 26: "All money-standards are variable measures of value." In the vice-presidential address delivered before the Colorado Scientific Society in Denver, December 18, 1893, O. J. Frost said: "The gold dollar at the standard weight of twenty-five and eight-tenths grains was made the unit of value for the United States by the act of [C]ongress of February, 1873, revising the coinage laws. . . . Any inquiry, therefore, into the *question of a standard of value* may properly be first directed to the suitability of gold for that purpose; and, in view of unsatisfactory financial conditions existing, the question *whether gold is a* stable *standard of value* is especially pertinent at this time" (*The Question of a Standard of Value* [n.p., n.d.], p. 1 [italics mine]). "The question at issue is the effect of the legislation in 1873 which destroyed the *bimetallic standard of value . . .*" (George H. Shibley, *The Money Question,* Chicago, 1896, p. 34). See also: Jordan, *op. cit.,* pp. xxii–xxiv; James H. Monroe, *Both Sides of the Question Relating to the Double and Single Standard of Market Values,* New York, 1893, pp. 17, 24–25; Francis A. Walker, *Bimetallism; A Tract for the Times,* Boston, 1894, p. 2; Francis A. Walker, *International Bimetallism,* New York, 1896, pp. 243, 269; John A. Grier, *Our Silver Coinage,* 6th edn., Chicago, 1896, pp. 10–11, 22; Teller, *op. cit.,* pp. 49, 116; and Francis S. Kinder, "The Effects of Recent Changes in Monetary Standards upon the Distribution of Wealth," *American Economic Association Economic Studies,* IV (December 1899), 434–435, 488, n. 1.

112 A. Barton Hepburn, *A History of Currency in the United States,* 3rd edn., New York, 1924, p. 376.

113 *Standard of Value, etc.,* Report 1876, Part 1, 55th Congress, 3rd Session, p. 4 (italics mine).

114 Salomons, *op. cit.,* pp. x–xi (italics mine): "That for us *to measure the value of our commodities by a gold currency* without any reference to the value of silver which constitutes the currency of all the neighboring states was to introduce irregularity into our transactions with foreign countries . . . And that we ought forthwith to place our currency on the same basis as that of other countries, by at once altering our system so far as to permit silver to be used as a *measure of value conjointly with gold,* I hold indisputable." Considerably later, Jevons observed: "Ever since the great discoveries of gold in California and

142

Australia began *to disturb the value of that metal relatively to silver and to other commodities,* it has been a continual subject of discussion what *standard of value* should be ultimately adopted" (*Money and the Mechanism of Exchange,* p. 133 [italics mine]). The Gold and Silver Commission proved Jevons' point (*The Monetary Problem: Gold and Silver,* ed. Ralph Robey, New York, 1936, pp. 210–211).

115 *Principles of Political Economy,* ed. Sir W. J. Ashley, London, 1936 [reprint of 1909 edn.], pp. 507–510.

116 See his "Statement of the Currency Systems of the United Kingdom, Its Colonies and Dependancies," presented to the International Monetary Conference of 1878 in Paris (*International Monetary Conference* [Proceedings], Senate Executive Document 58, 45th Congress, 3rd Session, Washington, 1879, p. 36).

117 *Investigations in Currency and Finance,* p. 319.

118 *Essays in Political Economy,* London, 1873, pp. 7–9, 11, 41, 44, *et passim.*

119 *Op. cit.,* pp. 1–3, 9; *The United Standard,* London, 1888, pp. 4, 30.

120 "A New Standard of Value," *Economic Journal,* II (September 1892), 472.

121 "Fancy Monetary Standards," *ibid.,* pp. 464–465.

122 "A Stable Monetary Standard," *Sound Currency,* II (July 1, 1895), 502–504, 509–510.

123 *Studies in Currency,* London, 1898, pp. vi–vii, xi, xv–xvi, 281–283, 312.

124 Among the less outstanding were William Leighton Jordan (*op. cit.,* pp. xx–xxi, 5–7, 12, 19–22, 33, 39, 53–54, 62); and Robert Barclay (*The Disturbance of the Standard of Value,* 2nd edn., London, 1896, pp. v, 78–79, 101, 104–105, 112–113).

125 *Op. cit.,* pp. 11–12, 15, *et passim.*

126 *Op. cit.,* pp. 190 ff., 256–257, 288–291.

127 *Money Credit & Commerce,* London, 1923, pp. 52–54.

128 Laughlin, *The Principles of Money,* pp. 41–43, 47 ff.; Laughlin, *A New Exposition of Money, Credit and Prices,* I, 224, 444–445; *ibid.,* II, 688, 692; Edward C. Towne, *The Story of Money,* New York, 1900, pp. 34–35, 74; Henry Parker Willis, *A History of the Latin Monetary Union,* Chicago, 1901, pp. 9–10; A. Barton Hepburn, *History of Coinage and Currency in the United States,* New York, 1903, p. 416; Conant, *op. cit.,* I, 275–277; *ibid.,* II, 432; Joseph French Johnson, *Money and Currency,* Boston, 1905, pp. 194, 217; Howard and Johnson, *op. cit.,* pp. 29–31, 44, 48–49, 60, 68; Sir David Barbour, *The Standard of Value,* London, 1912, pp. ix–xiii, 150, 179–180, 237–242; Moulton, *op. cit.,* pp. 98–99; Arthur Kitson, *A Fraudulent Standard,* London, 1917, p. 1; Walter T. Layton, *An Introduction to the Study of Prices,* London, 2nd edn., 1935, p. 6; George W. Edwards, *International Trade Finance,* New York, 1924, p. 58; Jack, *op. cit.,* pp. 2, 70; Lawrence, *op. cit.,* pp. 188–189; Lionel D. Edie, *Money, Bank Credit, and Prices,* New York, 1928, pp. 44–45.

129 Keynes, *A Tract on Monetary Reform,* pp. 164, 169 (italics mine): "The advocates of gold, as against a more scientific *standard,* base their cause on the double contention, that in practice gold has provided and

will provide a reasonably stable *standard of value* . . . It is natural, after what we have experienced, that prudent people should desiderate *a standard of value* which is independent of Finance Ministers and State Banks." See also Keynes' other works, e.g., *A Treatise on Money*, I, 12; *ibid.*, II, 289; and *Essays in Persuasion*, New York, 1932, p. 181. Opponents of the gold standard recommended a different standard of value—premised on the same concept of a monetary standard (Irving Fisher, *The Money Illusion*, New York, 1928, pp. 118, 156–157, 170–171; Fisher, *Stable Money*, p. 1; J. Taylor Peddie, *The Invariable Standard and Measure of Value*, 2nd edn., London, 1928, pp. 1–2, 11, *et passim*).

130 See *supra*, nn. 12–16 of this chapter.
131 This will be discussed in the next section of this chapter.
132 The impact of the varieties of this heterodoxy on the concept of a monetary standard will be considered in Chaps. V and VI.
133 The terms "standard of value" and "monetary standard" were pronounced synonyms by F. Cyril James (*The Economics of Money, Credit and Banking*, New York, 1930, p. 42). The National Industrial Conference Board announced, "The gold standard is a name applied to a system of money in which gold is the sole *standard of value*" (*The Gold Standard: Recent Developments and Present Status*, Conference Board Information Service: Domestic Affairs, Memorandum Number 5 [mimeographed], New York, 1933, p. 1 [italics mine]). Garis intoned, "The return not only of this country but of the world to *the gold standard* is deemed essential by many authorities, for the world needs a common *standard of value* to which all monetary systems [not just moneys] shall be related" (*op. cit.*, p. 129 [italics mine]). J. H. Huizinga explained, "Essentially it [the international gold standard] was a more or less tacit understanding between the nations of the world to maintain a *common measure of values* and, which is the same thing, a common standard of debts" (*Gold Points a Moral*, The Hague, 1935, p. 3 [italics mine]). Prather began his chapter on "The Gold Standard" with an elucidation of "the standard of value," explaining that *"the thing* which fixes the value of this standard [monetary] unit is called the monetary standard" (*op. cit.*, p. 33 [italics mine]). In a later edition, the statement was changed to *"The value of the thing* to which the standard unit is linked is called the 'monetary standard' " (*ibid.*, 4th edn., p. 54 [italics mine]). The chapter on "The Gold Standard" in this edition contained a section headed "Reasons for the Adoption of Gold as the Standard of Value" (*ibid.*, p. 57). This was cut from the fifth edition but restored to the sixth edition in a revised form under the heading "Why the Gold Standard?" (*ibid.*, 6th edn., pp. 115 ff.). Moreover, the first edition of Prather's text stated: "Legal bimetallism exists when provisions are made for the use of two metals, at a fixed weight proportion to each other, called the mint ratio, to form at the same time the *standard of value*" (*ibid.*, 1st edn., p. 67 [italics mine]). This definition of bimetallism, however, was not repeated in the fourth, fifth, or sixth editions. Nevertheless, it was a standard definition of bimetallism (e.g., Sadeque, *op. cit.*, p. 1), analogous to the usual definition of the gold standard (e.g., *ibid.*, p. 70). In

his National Bureau of Economic Research study, William Adams Brown, Jr., characterized the juridicial aspect of the gold standard as the "legal conception that gold was the ultimate standard of value" (*The International Gold Standard Reinterpreted 1914–1934*, I, New York, 1940, p. 29). See also Charles Rist, *History of Monetary and Credit Theory from John Law to the Present Day*, trans. Jane Degras, New York, 1940, pp. 100–101.

134 See, for example, Jay L. O'Hara, *Money and Banking*, New York, 1948, p. 27.
135 *Supra*, pp. 24–25. See also Mason, *op. cit.*, p. 495.
136 Charles A. Conant, *The Principles of Banking*, New York, 1908, p. 423 (italics mine): "The first class of proposals [for stabilizing the value of money] generally involves the creation of an *abstract standard, representing no specific tangible commodity, but a determination of value by some other process.*" Whereas Harold G. Moulton distinguished different commodity standards by the respective metals "used as the basis of the monetary system" (*op. cit.*, p. 99), he did not contend that paper was the basis of a paper standard (it would be a pretty thin basis): "With irredeemable paper money the paper is issued by the government and *declared to be the standard of value. . . . It is supposed to get its value* either from the 'fiat' of the state which issues it, or by means of a monopolistic limitation of the supply" (*ibid.*, p. 100 [italics mine]). The inconvertible paper standard had been earlier characterized as "no standard at all, because its value is subject to serious and frequently recurrent changes" (Francis Bowen, *American Political Economy*, New York, 1870, p. 294).
137 *Supra*, pp. 24–25. See also first quotation, *infra*, n. 216 of this chapter.
138 This will be developed in Chap. III.
139 Jevons, *Money and the Mechanism of Exchange*, pp. 13–15. Heretofore, the terms "standard," "measure," and their combination into "standard measure" of value had all served as tags for the process of comparing values either simultaneously or over a period of time.
140 *Ibid.*, pp. 37–38; and Francis A. Walker, *Money*, New York, 1877, pp. 8–10.
141 *Infra*, n. 144 of this chapter. F. M. Taylor furnished a good example of the unconscious neoclassical revival of the anticlassical confusion of the standard of value and unit of account:

> In the four cases which we have studied, the monetary standard has always been *a definite quantity of some material substance* or substances. We must now explain a fifth case, which is historically of great importance, wherein the standard is merely *one of the moneys* of a country,—there being nothing outside that money as money which fixes its value, neither its own substance nor any other. The best illustration of this case is furnished by *fiat money or irredeemable legal tender paper.* Take our own monetary system between 1862 and 1879. . . . But, in spite of these constant changes in the value of greenbacks, they were after all the standard of value. *For during the whole period the value of the dollar in prices*, in debts, in taxes, and so on, *kept right along with the value of the greenback. All rating of the values of things was in the greenback dollar. . . .* That fiat money can be a standard is conclusively established by an appeal to history. *It has been a standard*—it has been the thing which fixed the meaning and value of the monetary unit. It was a

145

very poor monetary standard; but the monetary standard it certainly was (*op. cit., pp.* 43–44 [fourth and fifth italics mine]).

How the abstract monetary unit could fix its own value, much less its own meaning, was not explained by Taylor, any more than it had been by the anticlassical proponents of an "ideal standard." These observations mean merely that prices are expressed in the monetary unit, or unit of account, whether or not it is linked to any concrete commodity. In other words, the monetary unit continues as long as monetary transactions, whether or not there is any ascertainable standard of value.

This same anticlassical confusion of the standard of value with the unit of account was illustrated by other neoclassicists: "The standard of value may be an intangible unit—an ideal concept in terms of which the values of all commodities are measured" (James, *op. cit.,* p. 41). Prather raised the question, "Can irredeemable money be the standard of value?" And he answered in the affirmative: "As long as there is money demand for and a limitation in the supply of irredeemable paper money, it will have value just as truly as gold coins or any other type of money. It may be a standard of value" (*op. cit.,* 1st edn., p. 124). He must have sensed that asserting that money has *some* value begs the question of the standard of value, for neither the question nor the answer was repeated in the fourth, fifth, or sixth editions. Agger concluded, "Under a fiat money system . . . the *standard money unit* may have *no clearly defined commodity equivalent.* It then *becomes simply a unit of account,* the value of which fluctuates in accordance with governmental policies of management or with shifting market conditions" (*op. cit.,* p. 49 [italics mine]).

142 Kilborne, *op. cit.,* p. 190. Taylor, too, clouded the issue with his sweeping generalization, *"Such standard money is itself the ultimate standard of the system"* (*op. cit.,* p. 170). One critic rationalized the paper standard with the impossibility of anything being its own standard by reducing the paper standard to a dependent, "secondary" status: "Secondary standards are based upon the primary [e.g., gold] in the sense that their value can-not be expressed without reference to it and that their independent existence is, therefore, impossible" (Scott, *op. cit.,* pp. 34–35).

143 Jevons conceded that the opposition of English economists to bimetallism might have been due in part to the fact that the "compensatory action," described by M. Wolowski, had been "overlooked" (*Investigations in Currency and Finance,* p. 303).

144 Walker stated that his purpose in changing Jevons' term "standard of value" to "standard of deferred payments" was to circumvent the charge that bimetallists advocated "a *double standard of value,* a phrase which savors of absurdity, and which the bi-metallists resent as applied to their scheme" (*Money,* p. 11). Another bimetallist furnished a documentation of the opponents' allegation that bimetallists proposed a double standard of value, which was alleged to be not only a practical impossibility but a contradiction of terms (Shibley, *op. cit.,* pp. 144–146, 254–255, *et passim*).

145 J. Laurence Laughlin, *The History of Bimetallism in the United States,*

New York, 1885, pp. 13 ff.; *Report of the Monetary Commission of the Indianapolis Convention*, p. 97; White, *Money and Banking*, 1st edn., p. 49; Horace White, *The History of the Gold Standard and the Present Attitude of the Currency Controversy*, address delivered at the National Currency Convention, Omaha, Nebraska, September 13, 1898 (Chicago, 1898), p. 3; Towne, *op. cit.*, pp. 105–106; and Murad, *op. cit.*, p. 18.

146 Jordan, *op. cit.*, p. xxi: "I have, however, seen no record of any such alternate premiums." Another authority asserted that as long as bimetallism exists there can be no premium on either metal, denying, therefore, the gold-standard contention that bimetallism permitted debtors to pay their debts in the cheaper metal (*Dictionary of Political Economy*, ed. Palgrave, I, 36).

147 This led some to brand bimetallism as an "alternate [or 'alternating'] standard" instead of a "double standard": Jevons, *Investigations in Currency and Finance*, p. 311; Willis, *A History of the Latin Monetary Union*, p. 8; George William Dowrie, *American Monetary and Banking Policies*, New York, 1930, p. 387; and Murad, *op. cit.*, pp. 13–14. Marshall, who was actually sympathetic to bimetallism, allowed that it was "open to the danger of becoming, and did in fact become . . . 'alternative metallism' " (*Money Credit & Commerce*, p. 62). Another bimetallist used this argument as a defense against the charge that bimetallism purported to establish a double standard of value (T. B. Buchanan, *A Plea for Silver Coinage and a Double Standard*, Denver, 1885, p. 91). Other defenders of bimetallism rejected the idea of an alternating standard as a malicious misconstruction of bimetallism by its opponents: "Lord Sherbrooke confuses alternations of gold and silver currency with alterations of the standard of value . . ." (Jordan, *op. cit.*, p. 26). Bimetallists generally insisted that it was the currency that alternated, not the standard (*Dictionary of Political Economy*, ed. Palgrave, I, 36; and Shibley, *op. cit.*, pp. 242–250).

148 Denying that bimetallism was either a "double" or "alternating" standard, some of its advocates maintained that it was a "dual" or "joint" standard: Jordan, *op. cit.*, pp. 20, 113; and Shibley, *op. cit.*, pp. 124–126, 241. This view was seldom either cogently or consistently argued —despite the fact that it had been implicit in the original report that had led to the establishment of a bimetallic standard in the United States ("On the Establishment of a Mint," *The Works of Alexander Hamilton*, ed. Henry Cabot Lodge, IV, New York [1903], 15–16.

149 Jordan, *op. cit.*, pp. 20, 27, 114; Buchanan, *op. cit.*, p. 97; Emile de Laveleye, *The Joint Standard*, an address delivered at the International Monetary Congress in Paris, October 13, 1889 (Manchester, 1889), p. 13; and W. H. Smith, *The Effects of the Gold Standard*, Chicago, 1895, p. 53. Ironically, the term "double standard" survives as a descriptive label, instead of a derogatory epithet (see, for example, Stokes and Arlt, *op. cit.*, p. 107).

150 Henry D. Barrows, *Gold and Silver: An Exposition and a Suggestion— A Composite Single Standard Deducible from a Double Standard* [n.p.], 1877, p. 1; Nicholas Veeder, *Cometallism: A Plan for Combining Gold and Silver in Coinage, For Uniting and Blending their Values*

147

in *Paper Money, and for Establishing a Composite Single Standard Dollar of Account*, Pittsburgh, 1885, pp. 32, 37–38; and *Memorials of Alfred Marshall*, pp. 204–206. "Coinage" of the term "symmetallism" has been attributed to Edgeworth, who suggested it as the appropriate label for the Marshallian variant of bimetallism (Walker, *International Bimetallism*, p. 207).

151 *Memorials of Alfred Marshall*, p. 206.
152 J. Allen Smith, *op. cit.*, pp. 191, 203 ff.
153 See Kemmerer, *Money*, p. 14, n. 2.
154 *Supra*, nn. 23–26 of this chapter.
155 See, for example, *Dictionary of Political Economy*, ed. Palgrave, I, 472; J. Shield Nicholson, *op. cit.*, p. 28; Bagehot, *op. cit.*, pp. 476–477; and J. Allen Smith, *op. cit.*, pp. 196–197.
156 In his chapter on "The Tabular Standard of Value" Miller states, "The fact that *gold would still, in any event, remain the standard of value* must not be lost sight of" (*op. cit.*, p. 285 [italics mine]). And he adds:

> *It* [tabular standard] *is not a standard of value* . . . If this so-called tabular standard of value is a standard at all, it is a standard by which to compute the amount which may be required to pay a debt, and it relates entirely to the consideration of the contract, that is, to the amount required to be paid by the debtor to discharge him from liability under his contract. The price of goods, however, for the purchase of which the debt was contracted, would be measured or expressed in terms of money, *according to the standard of value just as they are now.* . . . It is, simply, a scheme for the liquidation of debts (*ibid.*, p. 286 [italics mine]).

J. Shield Nicholson, *op. cit.*, p. 30 (italics mine): "It will be observed that, according to this scheme [tabular standard], there would be *no change in the actual currency;* the only object would be to give a more definite meaning to contracts for deferred payments by taking into account changes in the purchasing power of the sovereign." Irving Fisher interpreted the tabular standard in the same way: "The *money of the country would continue to be used as a medium of exchange and as a measure of value,* but not as a standard for all deferred payments. The standard of deferred payments, when advantage was taken of the law, would be the index number of general prices . . ." (Irving Fisher and Harry G. Brown, *The Purchasing Power of Money*, 2nd edn., New York, 1918, pp. 332–333 [italics mine]). See also *ibid.*, pp. 335, 344. E. M. Bernstein expressed the same view (*Money and the Economic System*, Chapel Hill, 1935, pp. 441–442). In their revision of White's *Money and Banking* (6th edn., p. 112) Tippets and Froman declared that the tabular standard "may not accurately be called a standard, although it is generally so designated . . ."

157 Cf. *supra*, p. 17.
158 Scrope, *op. cit.*, p. 25 (italics mine): "Now, *so long as any single commodity is employed as the standard of value, so long must that standard be liable to great variations,* with their consequent evils. . . . *Even though not employed as the legal standard, it* [the tabular standard] *might serve to determine and correct the* [evil effects of] *variations of the legal standard.*" This view of the "tabular standard" as the criterion

148

for adjusting the nominal amounts of contractual monetary payments to compensate for variations in the goods value of the standard of value has frequently reappeared in orthodox economic literature, e.g., Jevons, *Investigations in Currency and Finance,* pp. 122, 297–298; *Dictionary of Political Economy,* ed. Palgrave, III, 509; Laughlin, *The Principles of Money,* pp. 49, 51; Taylor, *op. cit.,* p. 43; Moulton, *op. cit.,* p. 100; John Thom Holdsworth, *Money and Banking,* 6th edn., New York, 1937, p. 43.

159 Orthodox economists judged that the tabular standard "comes nearer to a scientific basis than those which propose to do without a metallic standard . . ." (Conant, *The Principles of Money and Banking,* II, 428). The case for abrogating the metallic standard had been pressed by the antibullionists and their followers (*supra,* nn. 99, 100, 104 of this chapter).

160 *Investigations in Currency and Finance,* pp. 122–123; and *Money and the Mechanism of Exchange,* pp. 318, 322–323.

161 *Money and the Mechanism of Exchange,* pp. 14–15. Cf. Walker, *Money,* pp. 10–11.

162 *Money and the Mechanism of Exchange,* p. 13.

163 *Memorials of Alfred Marshall,* pp. 189–190, 196, 198–199, 207, 211.

164 *Loc. cit.* See also *supra,* nn. 144–149 of this chapter.

165 J. Allen Smith, *op. cit.,* p. 197.

166 J. Shield Nicholson, *op. cit.,* 2nd edn., p. 31; *Dictionary of Political Economy,* ed. Palgrave, III, 509; Garis, *op. cit.,* p. 264.

167 *The Money Illusion,* p. 117 (italics mine). Apparently neglecting the contractual context of such remarks by Irving Fisher, Harold G. Moulton confused Fisher's compensated dollar plan with the tabular standard (Moulton, *op. cit.,* p. 259).

168 *The Case Against Bimetallism,* 2nd edn., London, 1892, p. 214 (all except first italics, mine).

169 M. K. Graham, *An Essay on Gold: Showing Its Defects as a Standard of Value and Suggesting a Substitute Thereof,* Dallas, 1925, pp. 94–95; cf. *supra,* n. 43 of this chapter.

170 For example, Peterson, Cawthorne, and Lohman refer to both the tabular standard and Fisher's "compensated dollar" plan as "commodity standards" (*op. cit.,* pp. 38–39). Holdsworth regards the tabular standard as "the commodity standard" (*op. cit.,* p. 153) and calls Fisher's plan "the commodity dollar" (*ibid.,* p. 155).

171 *Supra,* n. 31 of this chapter.

172 See, for example, Laughlin, *A New Exposition of Money, Credit and Prices,* I, 497.

173 It should be noted that Fisher did not use the term "compensated standard." He regarded his proposal not as a standard but as a *plan* to make gold the standard of value it was supposed to be, instead of the standard of weight which (according to him) it, in fact, was (*Stabilizing the Dollar,* p. 89). Aneurin Williams, on the other hand, considered his earlier version a distinctive monetary standard. He entitled it a "fixed value of bullion standard," in contrast to his characterization of the traditional gold standard as a "fixed weight of bullion standard" (*op. cit.,* p. 283). And Laughlin said, "Thumbs wiggle wag-

149

gle"; Fisher's plan, he argued, was a new standard—but an addition, not a replacement: "In this so-called 'compensated standard' it is inherent that the existing gold standard must still be used in making up the quotations from which the index numbers will be computed, by whose changes the modifications in the gold dollar (to make it the 'virtual dollar') are to be obtained in paying debts. *Thus two gold standards are proposed for use at the same time:* one for settling debts; the other, the existing gold standard, in which price-making will go on as now" (*A New Exposition of Money, Credit and Prices,* I, 497 [italics mine]). One good absurdity ("compensated standard") deserves another (two simultaneous standards)! Kilborne distinguished the "two standards" as the "immediate standard" in the form of "the gold dollar," and the "ultimate standard" in the form of a price index, alternatively named the "multiple or tabular standard" (*op. cit.,* pp. 161–162). He did not trouble to explain precisely what "the gold dollar" would be under the compensated dollar plan. The same gap is apparent in Dowrie's explanation of the proposal: He said the plan "would retain the *gold dollar as a base* for our credit pyramid, but would have *its content adjusted* in accordance with changes in the price level" (*American Monetary and Banking Policies,* p. 248 [italics mine]). The meaning of an "adjustable base" was not revealed. Can you picture a baseball game with an adjustable home plate?

174 Fisher actually argued that control of gold was a necessary implementation of the gold standard: "Assuming that the gold standard is to be retained, credit control alone will not suffice to maintain a stable currency over long periods. *Gold control is also needed,* lest there be a conflict between the aims of credit control and the legal requirements as to gold reserve. The plans for gold control thus far proposed fall under two main heads: (1) control of gold production [proposed by R. A. Lehfeldt] and (2) control of the weight of gold in a dollar [Fisher's own proposal]" (*The Money Illusion,* pp. 185–186 [italics mine]). For Lehfeldt's plan to control the gold standard through management of gold production by "a syndicate of nations," see his *Restoration of the World's Currencies,* London, 1923, pp. 56–60.

175 Holdsworth, *op. cit.,* pp. 110–111, 162; Agger, *op. cit.,* pp. 165–167; W. J. Busschau, *The Measure of Gold* [Johannesburg] South Africa, 1949, pp. 73–74; Mueller, *op. cit.,* pp. 121, 128–129; and Leland J. Pritchard, *Money and Banking,* Boston, 1958, p. 582, n. 7.

176 J. Allen Smith, *op. cit.,* p. 187 (italics mine).

177 Mill, *Principles of Political Economy,* pp. 544–545.

178 J. Shield Nicholson, *op. cit.,* 2nd edn., p. 258; *Report of the Monetary Commission of the Indianapolis Convention,* p. 111; Laughlin, *A New Exposition of Money, Credit and Prices,* I, 487; *ibid.,* II, 755; Howard and Johnson, *op. cit.,* pp. 60–61; Kilborne, *op. cit.,* p. 60; and O'Hara, *op. cit.,* p. 42.

179 Kilborne, *op. cit.,* pp. 160–162; Bradford, *op. cit.,* pp. 35, 389.

180 The reasons why the classical school was not guilty of this *reductio ad absurdum* will be pointed out in the next chapter.

181 "The phrase *'standard of value'* . . . can only profitably be used as a *synonym of money* . . ." (Horton, *The United Standard,* p. 18 [italics

150

mine]). "Currency consists in fact of articles real or imaginary used for account, which is a highly civilized way of saying 'for measuring the relative values of different articles of use'. . ." (Sir Richard C. Temple, "Anthropology: The Evolution of Currency and Coinage," *Lectures on the Method of Science,* ed. T. B. Strong, Oxford, 1906, p. 184). Agger contended that reasoning about production and distribution "must center in that *standard of value* on which the whole economic mechanism pivots, *namely money*" (*op. cit.,* p. 9 [italics mine]).

182 *Dictionary of Political Economy,* ed. Palgrave, I, 562 (capitals in original and italics mine): "DEPRECIATION OF MONETARY STANDARD may be defined as the *lowering of the value of money in relation to goods.*"

183 An alternative, the attempt to distinguish between the "standard" and "measure" of value has not succeeded in circumventing the absurdity. It has already been pointed out that Jevons' differentiation of these terms merely provided different names for two aspects of the standard of value (*supra,* nn. 72, 139 of this chapter). Miller's effort, though potentially promising, lacked the clarity and consistency necessary to point the way (*op. cit.,* pp. 11–15, 21–22, 24–27, *et passim*). His alleged differentiation between the "standard" and "measure" of value (*loc. cit.* and *ibid.,* pp. 43–44), ultimately boiled down to classical orthodoxy (*ibid.,* p. 37). Normally "standard" was regarded merely as an adjectival modifier of "measure" (British Coinage Act of 1816, *op. cit.,* p. 388; Scrope, *op. cit.,* p. 12; J. Shield Nicholson, *op. cit.,* 5th edn., p. 312) or as a synonym (Adam Smith, *op. cit.,* pp. 36–39; Farrer, *op. cit.,* p. 5; *Dictionary of Political Economy,* ed. Palgrave, III, 609; Murad, *op. cit.,* p. 176; Prather, *op. cit.,* 6th edn., p. 1).

184 This excludes many of the authors discussed in this, as well as the first, section of this chapter, particularly those included in nn. 73–80.

185 *Supra,* pp. 21–22.

186 The argument of the more ardent monometallists of the latter nineteenth century might be added to what has already been said. They argued that the value of the standard of value, being determined by economic laws, could not be affected by standard money, which was the product of mere political laws (Farrer, *op. cit.,* pp. 7–9). Besides serving as a foundation for the defense of the gold standard, this premise was alleged to expose the fatal flaw in bimetallism: "In matters of currency, as well as in other matters, it remains true that laws cannot tie together in a fixed and permanent relation of value what natural conditions and human interests and habits have placed asunder" (*ibid.,* p. 316).

187 Harris, *op. cit.,* pp. 57–59.

188 Coming out in the early stages of the bullion controversy and demonstrating the equivocation typical of committee reports, the *Bullion Report* may afford those who are looking for it an opportunity to find affirmation, but, on balance, it appears to reflect the classical image of the monetary standard (*The Paper Pound of 1797–1821,* pp. 67–68).

189 *Dictionary of Political Economy,* ed. Palgrave, III, 395 (italics mine): "Wherever *silver coins* are full legal tender and constitute the money *in which commercial exchanges and values are measured,* and where

151

other coins are rated in their relation to silver coins, the silver standard may be said properly to exist." When J. Shield Nicholson's separate statements are put in juxtaposition, they appear to say substantially the same thing (*op. cit.,* 5th edn., pp. 20, 93, 313). Similar statements are found in Lehfeldt, *Money,* pp. 12, 15.

190 The dual meaning of "unit of value" and the slipping back and forth between implicit use of the term as, merely, the monetary unit and, alternatively, as the standard of value, makes interpretation difficult—impossible without consideration of the complete context. Even the term "standard of value" is subject to the same ambivalence. Its utilization as a standard for the valuation of moneys, on the one hand, and of goods, on the other, has already been noticed (*supra,* pp. 21–22).

191 As long as they avoid contradiction, this inference is preferable to the one that they are confused. In the following citations the page numbers before and after the slashes refer to implicit use of the "monetary standard" as, respectively, "standard money" and the "standard of value": H. F. Fraser, *Great Britain and the Gold Standard,* London, 1933, pp. 3/52; Willard E. Atkins, *Gold and Your Money,* New York, 1934, pp. 17–18/43–45; Kemmerer, *Money,* pp. 69–70, 97/84 ff.; Edwin Walter Kemmerer, *Gold and the Gold Standard,* New York, 1944, pp. 103, 138 (take your choice of interpretations)/72–73, 134; Dowrie, *Money and Banking,* pp. 27, 85, 88–89, 92, 109–110/110; Dowrie, *American Monetary and Banking Policies,* p. 230 (uses term "standard of value" to mean standard money); Holdsworth, *op. cit.,* pp. 21, 30, 40, 91/22, 43, 64, 155–156; R. G. Hawtrey, *The Gold Standard in Theory and Practice,* 5th edn., London, 1947, pp. 62, 67, 70/74; Hawtrey, *Currency and Credit,* pp. 1, 18, 172, 178, 184, 286–306, 310–312, 417–418 (standard-of-value interpretation of monetary standard); and Stokes and Arlt, *op. cit.,* pp. 97, 107/98, 104.

192 Pritchard, *op. cit.,* p. 81 (italics mine).

193 Farrer, *op. cit.,* pp. 11–12; Mueller, *op. cit.,* p. 43; Klise, *op. cit.,* p. 7.

194 This distinction is absent from the former case by definition. Its irrelevance to the latter case has already been pointed out (*supra,* p. 19).

195 Laughlin, *A New Exposition of Money, Credit and Prices,* I, 489 (italics mine): "The actual changes in general prices which have taken place *under the existing standard* (usually gold), and which have *modified the value of the standard* accordingly, may be seen during more than a century in the charts giving the course of prices . . ." One of the chief exponents of the dualistic view of a monetary standard attested to its vulnerability on this score in the following language: "The *gyrations in the value of the gold dollar* since the end of the last century have been fully as violent as during any equal period in the history of our country. . . . *It is to this unsteady monetary unit that our financial and economic systems are tied*" (Edwin Walter Kemmerer, "The Gold Standard in the Light of Post-war Developments," [reprinted from *Bankers Magazine,* CXVIII (March 1929), 355–359, 362] *The Reference Shelf, Vol. VIII, No. 7: Stabilization of Money,* New York, 1933, p. 128 [italics mine]). The fluctuating value of the fixed gold dollar was described by another observer as follows: "The

American nation and other nations came [by the time of World War I] to regard the dollar internally and externally as a sort of 'rock of ages.' This had not precluded fluctuations in the price level, booms and depressions, or even the financing of the country's part in the World War and of its stock market boom of 1928–29 by means of 'credit inflation,' assisted somewhat perhaps by the new features of the Federal Reserve System created in 1913. But all these things occurred within the framework of the 'old gold dollar,' preserved at steady gold parity" (John Donaldson, *The Dollar: A Study of the "New" National and International Monetary System*, New York, 1937, p. 20.

196 Jordan, *op. cit.*, p. 113; A. R. Burns, *Money and Monetary Policy in Early Times*, New York, 1927, p. 316; Dowrie, *Money and Banking*, pp. 72–73.

197 Harris, *op. cit.*, p. 38; Jordan, *op. cit.*, pp. 40–41, 121–122; *Dictionary of Political Economy*, ed. Palgrave, II, 222; *ibid.*, III, 395; *ibid.*, Appendix, 1908, p. 743; J. Shield Nicholson, *A Treatise on Money and Essays on Present Monetary Problems*, Edinburgh, 1888 [1st edn.], p. 340; Barbour, *op. cit.*, p. 149; Atkins, *op. cit.*, p. 45; and Rist, *op. cit.*, pp. 253–254. The above citations refer primarily to increased foreign demand for the standard metal arising from foreign adoptions of the same standard. Laughlin refers, on the other hand, to the decreased foreign demand for standard metal due to foreign abandonment of the standard (*A New Exposition of Money, Credit and Prices*, I, 319, 432–433). The following references are pertinent to both situations: *Dictionary of Political Economy*, ed. Palgrave, II, 801; Hawtrey, *Currency and Credit*, pp. 417–420; Robertson, *Money*, p. 155; Laughlin, *A New Exposition of Money, Credit and Prices*, II, 692; and Crowther, *op. cit.*, pp. 9–10.

198 This is simply the obverse of the immediately preceding postulated conditions.

199 Cannan, *Modern Currency and the Regulation of Its Value*, pp. 62–63.

200 James E. Thorold Rogers, *A Manual of Political Economy*, 3rd edn., Oxford, 1876, pp. 18–19, 27; Barbour, *op. cit.*, pp. 148–150; Hawtrey, *Currency and Credit*, pp. 177–178, 417; James, *op. cit.*, p. 106; Scott, *op. cit.*, pp. 50–55; Holdsworth, *op. cit.*, p. 151; Agger, *op. cit.*, pp. 241–242; Crowther, *op. cit.*, pp. 286–290; Chandler, *op. cit.*, 3rd edn., p. 355.

201 George Warde Norman, *Letter to Charles Wood, Esq., M.P. on Money and the Means of Economizing the Use of It*, London, 1841, pp. 30–31; Alexander Del Mar, *Money and Civilization*, London, 1886, pp. xi–xii; *The Monetary Problem: Gold and Silver*, ed. Ralph Robey, New York, 1936, pp. 55, 163–164; Albion W. Tourgée, *The War of the Standards*, New York, 1896, pp. 19–20, 36–37, 39–40, 94–96; *Dictionary of Political Economy*, ed. Palgrave, I, 192; *ibid.*, II, 222–223; *Memorials of Alfred Marshall*, p. 203; Lehfeldt, *Money*, pp. 23–24, 98; Bradford, *op. cit.*, pp. 176, 192, 215–216, 228–232, 235, 237–238; James, *op. cit.*, p. 106; Laughlin, *A New Exposition of Money, Credit and Prices*, I, 460; *ibid.*, II, 692–694, 703 ff.; Scott, *op. cit.*, p. 55; Cannan, *Modern Currency and the Regulation of Its Value*, pp. 67–68; L. L. B. Angas, *The Problems of the Foreign Exchanges*, New York,

1935, p. 16; Rist, *op. cit.*, pp. 199–200; Kemmerer, *Gold and the Gold Standard*, p. 101; Westerfield, *op. cit.*, pp. 82–83, 133; Chandler, *op. cit.*, 3rd edn., pp. 355, 357; J. W. Beyen, *Money in a Maelstrom*, New York, 1949, p. 31; Jome, *op. cit.*, pp. 33, 45; Lawrence Smith, *op. cit.*, pp. 217, 222–223.

202 Keynes, *A Tract on Monetary Reform*, pp. 173 ff.; Gustav Cassel, "The Problem of Stabilization," [reprinted from *Bankers Magazine*, CXVIII (March 1929), 415–420], *The Reference Shelf, Vol. VIII, No. 7: Stabilization of Money*, pp. 118–119; James, *op. cit.*, pp. 325–334; Cannan, *Modern Currency and the Regulation of Its Value*, p. 57; Scott, *op. cit.*, p. 55; R. G. Hawtrey, *The Art of Central Banking*, London, 1932, pp. 190–191; Donaldson, *op. cit.*, p. 63; Halm, *Monetary Theory*, p. 106; Westerfield, *op. cit.*, pp. 40–41; Chandler, *op. cit.*, 2nd edn., pp. 94–95; *ibid.*, 3rd edn., p. 359.

203 *Infra*, p. 55.

204 For years it has been recognized that nonstandard forms of circulating media did not merely replace standard money, but actually added to it to such an extent that the former has long since amounted to many times the latter. See, for example, Bradford, *op. cit.*, pp. 215–216, 229, 235; F. A. von Hayek, *Monetary Nationalism and International Stability*, 2nd edn., London, 1939, pp. 6, 8–14; Agger, *op. cit.*, p. 58; Busschau, *op. cit.*, p. 3; and Chandler, *op. cit.*, 3rd edn., p. 357.

205 This paradox was recognized by the critics of orthodoxy long before the actuality of the contradiction was so painfully demonstrated ([Thomas Barber Wright], *The Currency Question*, London, 1844, pp. 186–187).

206 Whereas originally standard money was the standard for the relative valuation of *goods*, Leffler reversed the relationship, using standard money as the standard for measuring the goods value of *money* (*op. cit.*, p. 99). Another authority explicitly denied that standard money is the standard of value: according to W. J. Busschau, war-induced credit expansion (including the expansion of credit money) has made ultimate deflation inevitable unless the gold content of currencies is reduced. Moreover, recurrent devaluation, in his opinion, would constitute preservation, not abandonment, of the gold standard—because gold standard money is the measure of gold, not the measure of values (*op. cit.*, pp. 1–14).

207 W. Stanley Jevons suggested that the gold content of the monetary unit could be reduced one per cent without affecting the standard of value (*Investigations in Currency and Finance*, pp. 246–247). See also Sir Basil P. Blackett, *Planned Money*, New York, 1933, p. 64; Leffler, *op. cit.*, p. 83.

208 Leo Pasvolsky, *Current Monetary Issues*, Washington, 1933, pp. 119 ff.; Atkins, *op. cit.*, pp. 158–161; Leffler, *op. cit.*, p. 505; Dowrie, *Money and Banking*, p. 474; Foster, Rogers, Bogan, and Nadler, *op. cit.*, p. 654; Holdsworth, *op. cit.*, pp. 111, 163; Arthur D. Gayer and W. W. Rostow, *How Money Works*, Public Affairs Pamphlet No. 45, New York, 1940, pp. 3–4; *ibid.*, 2nd edn., pp. 3–4; Peterson, Cawthorne, and Lohman, *op. cit.*, p. 39; Crowther, *op. cit.*, pp. 291–292.

209 George F. Warren and Frank A. Pearson, *Gold and Prices*, New York,

1935, pp. 200–204, 454. For this interpretation of Warren and Pearson, see, for example, Atkins, *op. cit.*, pp. 29–30, 33.

210 Conant, *The Principles of Money and Banking*, I, 276–277; Kemmerer, *Gold and the Gold Standard*, p. 104.

211 Agger, *op. cit.*, pp. 41, 58–59, 68–69.

212 *Ibid.*, pp. 240–241.

213 Chandler, *op. cit.*, 3rd edn., p. 363.

214 "But it was not the possibility of converting money into gold that gave money its value. When this right was withdrawn by the government, our money did not become less valuable. Most of us didn't notice any difference" (Gayer and Rostow, *op. cit.*, [both edns.] p. 3). In spite of his implication that the gold standard meant a gold standard of value, James observed that the gold standard no longer "implied that the value of the currency depended upon the value of gold . . ." (*op. cit.*, p. 60). By 1930 the gold standard was customarily defined as "a system by which a country maintains the value of its monetary standard and the value of a prescribed weight of gold at a parity with one another, ignoring the question of what determined that value" (*loc. cit.*). In the present setting, this view reduces the gold standard, as well as the concept of parity, to an empty legalism.

215 The paradox in the neoclassical position was succinctly stated, but apparently unrecognized, more than a half-century ago: "It is obvious that *to the extent that silver* has thus taken the place of gold, or rather, *has been made auxiliary to it, the appreciation of the latter metal has been checked.* But the *standard has all along been gold,* because the silver coin and silver notes have always been *kept at par*" (Elijah Helm, *The Joint Standard,* London, 1894, p. 203 [italics mine]). "Under a system of free and gratuitous coinage the value of the monetary unit and the value of its metallic content cannot appreciably differ. The use of token coins, of paper money of all kinds, and of checks effect an economy in the use of the standard money metal and *thereby influence the supply of standard money* and affect the value of the money unit. *The direct influence of such media of exchange upon prices is essentially the same as that of standard money*" (E. W. Kemmerer, "Prices Vary with Money Supply," *The Gold Supply and Prosperity,* ed. Byron W. Holt, New York, 1907, p. 51 [italics mine]).

216 Bertrand Nogaro, *Modern Monetary Systems* [translation of 1924 French edn.], London, 1927, p. 176:

> And even if the value of these monetary units may have been fixed by the quantity of precious metals which have been minted and so, *very indirectly,* by the cost of production, it should not be forgotten that this quantitative influence has been also exercised by the "substitutes" for metal currency, or in other words by fiduciary currency and even by such banking processes as enable unused money to be reduced to a minimum and the effective circulation to be *pro tanto* increased.

> *And so the value of monetary units appears to be independent of the circumstances which would have determined the value of the standard metal if the latter had been "a commodity like any other." On the contrary, it is the value of the standard metal which is bound up under the system of free coinage with that of the monetary unit,*

155

the variations in which are measured by the average rise and fall in prices, whatever may be the instrument in which such units are embodied.

Thus in each country the true *measure of value,* and therefore the true "standard" of values, is the national monetary unit, *the abstract unit of account* with which the precious metal is legally bought at a fixed rate, and *not the metal itself.*

"The exchange value or purchasing power of both the gold dollar [1930 vintage] and these other media, however, is determined by the *total quantity of all of them in circulation,* the velocity at which each dollar circulates, and the total volume of transactions to be performed by money and credit media" (Dowrie, *American Monetary and Banking Policies,* p. 230 [italics mine]). "We are therefore in a situation where *the value of money, in the broadest sense, determines the value of gold,* since in a gold standard country the monetary unit and a fixed weight of gold bullion are the same thing. *The causative factor is, however, money in the widest sense, and not metallic gold!"* (James, *op. cit.,* p. 106 [italics mine].)

All these comments antedated the international monetary debacle of 1931–1933. For post-1933 repetitions of the same idea, see: Robertson, *Money,* p. 86; Leffler, *op. cit.,* pp. 85, 414; Prather, *op. cit.,* 1st edn., p. 45; *ibid.,* 5th edn., p. 130; Crowther, *op. cit.,* p. 309; and Woodworth, *op. cit.,* p. 22.

217 "It may be admitted that if a calf and a sheep are exchanged either may be said to buy the other as truly as if the statement were reversed, but such a transaction bears little likeness to the relationship between money—*of any kind*—and other forms of property. *Money is the standard of value,* the common denominator by which all values are compared and exchanged . . ." ("The Gold Question" [reprinted from the *National City Bank* bulletin on Economic Conditions, March 1933, pp. 40–47], *The Reference Shelf, Vol. VIII, No. 7: Stabilization of Money,* p. 67 [italics mine]).

218 Examples were the "compensated" ("commodity dollar") standard (Kemmerer, *Money,* pp. 108–110; and Holdsworth, *op. cit.,* pp. 155–156) and the "tabular" or "commodity" standard (Dowrie, *Money and Banking,* p. 110; Holdsworth, *op. cit.,* p. 153; and Walter E. Spahr, *Alternatives in Postwar International Monetary Standards,* The Monetary Standards Inquiry, No. 7, New York, 1944, p. 19).

219 Dowrie, *Money and Banking,* pp. 109–110; Pritchard, *op. cit.,* p. 83.

220 *Ibid.,* p. 82.

221 *Ibid.,* pp. 85–86.

222 *Ibid.,* p. 100.

223 *Report of the Monetary Commission of the Indianapolis Convention,* p. 31: "The standard must have a market value as a commodity independently of any governmental fiat and of all legal-tender laws . . ." Laughlin later elaborated: "Indeed, it is unthinkable that the value of any one article could be expressed in a common denominator which itself had no value. . . . If the common denominator had no value, it could not register the value of another thing, and hence it could not be a common standard" (*The Principles of Money,* p. 14). Taylor defined the monetary standard as *"that thing the value of which fixes the*

156

value of the monetary unit" (*op. cit.,* p. 37). See also: Hawtrey, *Currency and Credit,* p. 18; and Mueller, *op. cit.,* p. 57.

224 Notice, for example: the alleged "insignificance" of the distinction between "fiat" and "commodity" money (Johnson, *op. cit.,* p. 271); the "immediate" vs. the "ultimate" standard, and "embodiment" vs. "representation" of the latter (Taylor, *op. cit.,* pp. 38, 53–54); and the semantic rationalization of the term "paper," "fiat," or "fiduciary" standard by a terminological differentiation of "standard" and "primary" money (Kemmerer, *Money,* pp. 13–15).

225 "Much of our thinking on [bank] reserves, as in other aspects of money, has been colored by the commodity origins of money . . ." (Whittlesey, *op. cit.,* p. 404). For example, as late as 1893 J. Shield Nicholson "explained" the almost "exclusive" survival of the precious metals as money: "The substance should be generally acceptable on its own account [because of its value as a commodity] if it is to serve as a medium of exchange, and no metals are more sought after on their own account than these two" (*op. cit.,* 2nd edn., p. 35). William A. Scott even criticized Nicholson for not being vigorous and consistent enough in his insistence that money must itself be a commodity possessing value independent of its use as money (*op. cit.,* 5th edn., p. 63).

226 *Dictionary of Political Economy,* ed. Palgrave, II, 787; *Memorials of Alfred Marshall,* p. 189; Holdsworth, *op. cit.,* p. 5.

227 *Supra,* p. 8.

228 Despite Whittlesey's criticism of this atavistic propensity (*op. cit.,* pp. 34–35), he defined money as a *commodity* (*ibid.,* p. 2).

229 Pritchard, *op. cit.,* pp. 82–86, 100–102; Klise, *op. cit.,* pp. 20, 24–31.

CHAPTER III

1 *The Economics of Money and Banking,* New York, 1948, pp. 2–3.
2 *Supra,* Chap. II, nn. 93–96.
3 See Will E. Mason, "The Stereotypes of Classical Transfer Theory," *Journal of Political Economy,* LXIV (December 1956), 495.
4 This was the view received by the classical school from its acknowledged predecessors:

> To avoid the great inconveniences of barter, a *material or commodity* that should be universally accepted in exchange for all other things, was soon agreed upon; and this is what we call MONEY. *As soon as this invention became established, men reckoned the value of their goods by money* . . .
>
> Thus MONEY *is a* STANDARD MEASURE, *by which the values of all things, are regulated and ascertained; and is it self* [sic], *at the same time, the* VALUE *or* EQUIVALENT, *by which, goods are exchanged, and in which, contracts are made payable. So that money, is*

157

not a pledge, to be afterwards redeemed, but is both an equivalent and a measure; being in all contracts, the very thing usually bargained for, as well as the measure of the bargain . . . ([Joseph Harris], *An Essay upon Money and Coins, Part I: The Theories of Commerce, Money, and Exchanges*, London, 1757, pp. 36–37 [first two italics mine]).

5 Early nineteenth-century authorities, therefore, did not generally use the term "standard money." Consequently, a late nineteenth-century writer found it necessary to "correct" Lord Liverpool's *Coins of the Realm* by substituting "standard coin" wherever the word "money" was used (Lord [Thomas Henry] Farrer, *Studies in Currency*, London, 1898, pp. 6–7, n. 1).

6 John Stuart Mill, *Principles of Political Economy*, ed. Sir W. J. Ashley, London, 1936 [reprint of 1909 edn.], pp. 542 *et passim*. This corollary of the classical doctrine on money was also received from earlier writers: "The *substitution* of paper in the room of gold and silver money, replaces a very expensive instrument of commerce with one much less costly, and sometimes equally convenient . . . As those notes [of a banker] serve all the purposes of money, his debtors pay him the same interest *as if he had lent them so much money*" (Adam Smith, *An Inquiry into the Nature and Causes of the Wealth of Nations*, ed. Edwin Cannan, Modern Library edn. [reprinted from 5th edn.], New York, 1937, pp. 276–277 [italics mine]). Smith later clarified precisely what he meant by his proposition that paper media of exchange were *substitutes* for money: "The whole paper money of every kind which can easily circulate in any country *never can exceed the value of the gold and silver, of which it supplies the place,* or which (the commerce being supposed the same) would circulate there, if there was no paper money" (*ibid.*, p. 284 [italics mine]). David Ricardo agreed (*The Works and Correspondence of David Ricardo*, ed. Piero Sraffa with the collaboration of M. H. Dobb, Cambridge, 1951–1955, III, 57). When Smith as well as later classical economists used the term "paper money," the adjective "paper" did not indicate, as it does today, a species of money, but rather a qualification of the term "money." Without the qualifying "paper," "money" invariably meant specie.

7 This might be the appropriate place to clarify the orthodox nineteenth-century usage of "circulation" and related terms: (1) "Money" was defined as specie (*supra*, n. 4 of this chapter). (2) "Currency" was the term applied to money *and* its substitutes, namely, bank notes (*The Works and Correspondence of David Ricardo*, III, 54–55, 57, 90; *ibid.*, IV, 276; John Stuart Mill, *op. cit.*, pp. 540, 542–543). (3) "Circulation" meant the product of the volume and velocity of currency (George Warde Norman, *Letter to Charles Wood* . . . , London, 1841, p. 9; G. Arbuthnot, *Sir Robert Peel's Act of 1884 Regulating the Issue of Bank Notes, Vindicated*, London, 1857, pp. 46 ff.; Lord Overstone, *Tracts and Other Publications on Metallic and Paper Currency*, ed. J. R. McCulloch, London, 1858, pp. 200–201).

8 "If the Bank [of England] were restricted from paying their notes in specie, and all the coin had been exported, any excess of their notes [beyond the mere replacement of specie] would depreciate the value of the circulating medium [relative to gold, the standard of value] in pro-

portion to the excess" (*The Works and Correspondence of David Ricardo*, III, 91). This doctrine was adopted by his followers, such as John Stuart Mill (*op. cit.*, pp. 543–544 *et passim*). See Mason, *op. cit.*, p. 495.

9 Mason, *loc. cit.; The Works and Correspondence of David Ricardo*, III, 37, 80, 84; John Stuart Mill, *op. cit.*, p. 554; *Dictionary of Political Economy*, ed. R. H. Inglis Palgrave, London, 1894–1899, II, 380.

10 John Stuart Mill, *op. cit.*, pp. 520–521, 523–524 ff. For restatements or indications of this classical view of deposits, see: W. P. Tatham, *On the Restoration of the Standard of Value, and the Proper Limit to the Use of Bank Credit as Money*, Philadelphia, 1869, p. 7; Henry Sidgwick, "What Is Money?" *Fortnightly Review*, N.S. XXV (April 1879), 571–572; Alexander Del Mar, *The Science of Money*, 2nd edn., London [1896], p. 36; George N. Halm, *Monetary Theory*, 2nd edn., Philadelphia, 1946, p. 186; Lloyd W. Mints, *A History of Banking Theory in Great Britain and the United States*, Chicago, 1945, pp. 77–78, 80, 83, n. 22; and Karl Olivecrona, *The Problem of the Monetary Unit*, New York, 1957, p. 57.

11 "The idea of a measure of values without any value itself is however completely at variance with the original conception of money; according to which money is itself a commodity, and price paid is a real equivalent for merchandise received" (F. A. P. Barnard, "The Possibility of an Invariable Standard of Value," *Proceedings of the American Metrological Society*, II (1878–1879), 71. Ricardo, like his classical contemporaries, never used the phrase "paper standard." He referred to the "paper circulation" in his discussion of the "standard of our currency," which, he insisted, must be a commodity in order to be the "standard by which to measure the value of other things" (*The Works and Correspondence of David Ricardo*, IV, 55). "If a *paper currency without a standard* be an improvement," Ricardo continued, "let it be proved to be so, and then let the standard be disused . . ." (*ibid.*, p. 64 [italics mine]).

12 Charles L. Prather, *Money and Banking*, 6th edn., Homewood, Ill., 1957, p. 115; Leland J. Pritchard, *Money and Banking*, Boston, 1958, pp. 94–95; Olivecrona, *op. cit.*, pp. 65–67.

13 *Supra*, p. 36. See also: Francis A. Walker, *Money*, New York, 1877, p. vi; Edwin Walter Kemmerer, *Money and Credit Instruments in Their Relation of General Prices*, 2nd edn., 1909, p. 114.

14 "If all the money of the country is convertible at par into gold, there may then be whatever, and as much, of the representative forms of currency as the convenience of the people may require" (*Report of the Monetary Commission of the Indianapolis Convention*, ed. J. Laurence Laughlin, Chicago, 1898, p. 32).

15 Following is an early example of the resulting breakdown of language, to which we have since become inured: "If there is some belief that the promise [of redeemability] will be kept, though at an uncertain time, the paper may remain in use as money, and the '*promises to pay*' *become, in fact, an imperfect standard substance*, related to the standard substance proper . . ." (Robert Giffen, *The Case Against Bimetallism*, 2nd edn., London, 1892, p. 213).

159

16 Frederick A. Bradford, *Money,* New York, 1928, p. 5.

17 Central bank notes still "promise to pay" money to the bearer, who, in actuality, can obtain in payment only a similar note (Olivecrona, *op. cit.,* pp. 49–51).

18 Eugene E. Agger, *Money and Banking Today,* New York, 1941, p. 163 (italics mine): "Domestically the full *maintenance of a money standard requires* effective interchange of standard bullion and standard money at the mint rate and provision for keeping all other kinds of circulating money at par with standard money. Internationally it requires freedom of exportation and importation of standard bullion. While through arbitrary management it may be possible to maintain a fairly stable money value [the recurrent neoclassical (not classical) ambiguity: in terms of gold or of goods in general?] without regard to these requirements, *failure to observe them under an avowed standard involves, to the extent of such failure, a sacrifice of the standard."* Note that Agger says the latter eventuality means sacrifice of a *money standard,* not merely sacrifice of the gold standard.

19 Ray V. Leffler, *Money and Credit,* New York, 1935, pp. 86–87:

> Might gold be eliminated permanently as the monetary standard without any ill effects on the monetary system of the country? Only experimentation can answer the question . . . This question does not mean that *the monetary standard* is to be abolished. It is a query about the necessity of *a particular standard.* It will always be convenient to have one money which will be the center of value for all other money by conversion. All media of exchange in a country should have the same value per unit. The standard money, however, might be paper money which has practically no commodity value. Sometime a nation may be either wise or foolish enough to abolish the use-commodity basis of its money. Then we shall learn, after a few years of observation, if statesmen, economists, and citizens have been worshiping a costly and useless god—"a golden calf."

Have we learned? If we have, the lesson is not clear. It has been obscured by retention of classical propositions (typified by the above quotation) irrelevant to abstract money. In a viable monetary system, keeping the various manifestations of abstract money at parity with each other is, in itself, no problem. In fact, the attempt to distinguish, in any substantive way, between different kinds of abstract money is absurd. Though the implications have not been followed, this has been implicitly recognized (Raymond P. Kent, *Money and Banking,* 3rd edn., New York, 1956, p. 24).

20 John Thom Holdsworth, *Money and Banking,* 6th edn., New York, 1937, p. 40: "Then in 1934 came America's voluntary abandonment of gold and the establishment of a paper standard. . . . Thus, practically throughout the world today (1937), some form of paper standard exists."

21 Milton L. Stokes and Carl T. Arlt, *Money, Banking and the Financial System,* New York, 1955, p. 109 (italics mine): "Under a paper standard such as exists almost universally today, the standard monetary unit has no fixed commodity value . . . Considered at one time as only a temporary substitute for a metallic standard, the paper standard is today considered a *permanent aspect of the monetary systems of the majority of countries."*

160

22 *Supra*, pp. 5, 28.

23 "By 'received doctrine' we mean that which has been handed down from an earlier economic period" (Karl H. Niebyl, *Studies in the Classical Theories of Money*, New York, 1946, p. 2).

24 Tenacity of the "objective value" doctrine is indicated by its paradoxical survival of the marginal-utility doctrine (e.g., James Dysart Magee, *An Introduction to Money and Credit*, 2nd edn., New York, 1933, pp. 16–17), which demonstrated the artificiality of the distinction between "value in use" and "value in exchange." Moreover, in the post-marginal-utility world the spuriousness of the conventional distinction between "subjective" and "objective" value had been recurrently pointed out (Edwin R. A. Seligman, "Social Elements in the Theory of Value," *Quarterly Journal of Economics*, XV [May 1901], 327, n.; Karl Helfferich, *Money*, trans. Louis Infield, ed. T. E. Gregory, I, London, 1927, 318–322).

25 That the labor theory of value implied the intrinsic nature of value was one thing on which the opponents as well as the proponents of the theory agreed ([Samuel Bailey], *A Critical Dissertation on the Nature, Measures, and Causes of Value* [No. 7 in the London School of Economics and Political Science Series of Reprints of Scarce Tracts in Economics and Political Science], London, 1931 [reprint of 1825 edn.], pp. 11, 23, 30–32, 120–122, 163; Lord Lauderdale, *An Inquiry into the Nature and Origin of Public Wealth*, 2nd edn., Edinburgh, 1819, pp. 21, 23–25, 33–35, *et passim;* [John Taylor], *An Essay on the Standard and Measure of Value*, 2nd edn., London, 1832, p. 20).

26 "There is no such thing as value intrinsic in any commodity . . ." (W. Stanley Jevons, *Investigations in Currency and Finance*, ed. H. S. Foxwell, London, 1884, p. 251). "Such a thing as intrinsic value is impossible. If the value [of an article] is intrinsic, it must be at all times the same. Value is a relation, and does not reside in the commodity, hence cannot be intrinsic" (James H. Teller, *The Battle of Standards*, Chicago, 1896, p. 47). "It [value] is not an attribute of matter like weight or dimension . . ." (Albion W. Tourgée, *The War of the Standards*, New York, 1896, p. 73). "Value is an intellectual conception rather than a tangible property of matter" (Charles A. Conant, *The Principles of Money and Banking*, I, New York, 1905, 148). "Value is not an organic property of anything, such as are dimensions, colour, hardness, temperature, etc. It rests far more on the relationship of the human being towards the objects of the outer world and is the expression of judgment by the human being on the importance of those outer world objects for him or for human society. . . . In so far as the process of valuation takes place in the mind of the individual it is a subjective process, and the position in the value series and the degree of value of each object is a result of this subjective process" (Helfferich, *op. cit.*, p. 318).

27 "In an economic sense, the values of two things merely express the ratio in which they do as a fact exchange for each other" (Jevons, *op. cit.*, p. 251). "But the word Value, so far as it can be correctly used, merely expresses *the circumstance of its exchanging in a certain ratio for some other substance*" (W. Stanley Jevons, *The Theory of Political*

161

Economy, 4th edn., London, 1931 [reprint of 1911 edn.], p. 77). Besides Hermann Heinrich Gossen and the familiar Austrian subjective-value theorists, see Del Mar, *op. cit.,* pp. 10–11, 15, 17–19.

28 Awareness of this fact was necessary in order to transform the dispute between Samuel Bailey and John Stuart Mill from an exercise in semantics to a division on substantive issues capable of resolution. Bailey denied that value was intrinsic and absolute, insisting that it was merely a relation between things expressing the subjective preferences of people (*op. cit.,* pp. 4–5, 8–9, *et passim*). Mill called this an argument about words ("On the Nature, Measures, and Causes of Value," *Westminster Review,* V [January 1826], 157–159), answering that Ricardo consciously used "value" in two senses: the ordinary sense of exchangeable value and the technical sense of a standard of value. Mill agreed with Bailey that it would have been better if Ricardo had limited the term "value" to its ordinary use. But he added, "It is a question of verbal convenience merely . . ." (*ibid.,* p. 159). Mill argued, in effect, that Ricardo and other authoritative economists would have willingly acquiesced to Bailey's argument—as long as it was limited to "exchangeable value." But, Mill charged, only Bailey's ignorance prevented him from appreciating his irrelevance to value in the technical sense of a standard of value. He explained that any commodity produced always by the same quantity of labor could be accepted as the means of measuring changes in the normal value (cost of production) of other commodities. "To this commodity, answering thus extensively the purpose of a test, in all changes of value, Mr. Ricardo thought that the name of *Standard of Value* might not improperly be applied; and that it might be considered as *invariable; not surely invariable in its own purchasing power;* that is a meaning which no one can for a moment suppose was applied to it by Mr. Ricardo; *but invariable in its accuracy as a test to mark the variations in the purchasing power of other commodities*" (*ibid.,* p. 160 [italics mine]). Later, Mill summarized: "When Mr. Ricardo says 'standard measure of value,' he means a commodity *invariable in the labour which goes to its production.* He does not mean invariable in its power of purchasing, quite the contrary" (*ibid.,* p. 166 [italics mine]). In short, value, in the sense relevant to the classical concept of a "standard of value," was assumed to be objective and intrinsic. The absence of the concept of marginal utility made this escape from Bailey's indictment possible and plausible. By the time the implications of marginal utility were developed by the psychological school, Bailey's book had been generally forgotten.

29 Lewis W. Judson, *Units and Systems of Weights and Measures: Their Origin Development and Present Status,* National Bureau of Standards, Circular 570, Washington, 1956, p. 2.

30 *Loc. cit.*

31 This is, in effect, what P.[atrick] Kelly said a long time ago (*The Universal Cambist and Commercial Instructor,* 2nd edn., I, London, 1835, xvi–xx). See also John Taylor (*op. cit.,* pp. 31–33, 34–41).

32 Judson, *op. cit.,* p. 8.

33 *Ibid.,* p. 11.

34 Anne Robert Jacques Turgot, *Reflections on the Formation and the*

162

Distribution of Riches, New York, 1898 [reprint of the 1770 edn.], p. 36; [Richard Page], *Letters to the Editor of "The Times".* . . , London, 1826, pp. 212–213; Francis Bowen, *American Political Economy*, New York, 1870, p. 293; *Report of the Monetary Commission of the Indianapolis Convention*, p. 31.

35 Henry A. Miller furnished a postclassical example of this usage of the terms: He described one of the functions of money as "a measure, in terms of which the prices of commodities and the extent and quantity of liabilities are expressed" (*Money and Bimetallism*, New York, 1898, p. 22). This function is merely a statement of what is implicit in the monetary unit. Then he relates the "standard" to the "measure" (unit) in the following manner: "What is here meant by the expression '*the standard of the measure of value*,' or 'the standard of value,' is that commodity which has been selected by the commercial world to serve that purpose, and by which all the different kinds of money in use are measured, and which is, consequently, that commodity to which the prices of other commodities are ultimately referred, as, for example, gold is the standard of the measure of value, a segregation or the separation of a certain fixed and definite portion of that metal into a piece called a dollar is the instrument of measure of values, and its value is determined by the quantity of gold in the piece" (*ibid.*, pp. 36–37 [italics mine]). Miller observed that in monetary lore the terms "measure" and "standard" were used indiscriminately—but implicitly "in the same sense as we here use the expression 'the standard of the measure of value,' or 'the standard of value' " (*ibid.*, pp. 43–44).

36 [James Mill], "Smith on Money and Exchange," *Edinburgh Review*, XIII (October 1808), 41–42.

37 Denials of the possibility of a standard of value antedating the marginal-utility doctrine were often, like Bailey's, simply inferences from the definition of *exchange value* (William Brown, *The Labor Question*, Philadelphia, 1872, pp. 56, 58; Henry Dunning MacLeod, *The Principles of Economical Philosophy*, I, London, 1879, 185, 298), and therefore vulnerable to characterization as arguments about words rather than substance. Although the works cited immediately above were published after the birth of marginal utility, they were apparently written before the authors were aware of the innovation (cf. *supra*, n. 28 of this chapter). Subsequent to the development of marginal analysis, protests against the idea of a "standard of value" were generally (though not universally) more substantive than terminological (S. Dana Horton, *The Position of Law in the Doctrine of Money*, London, 1882, pp. 24–25; *The Monetary Problem: Gold and Silver*, [reprint of the] Final Report of the [British] Royal Commission Appointed to Inquire into the Recent Changes in the Relative Values of the Precious Metals, Presented to Both Houses of Parliament, 1888, ed. Ralph Robey, New York, 1936, pp. 298–299; Helfferich, *op. cit.*, pp. 322–324; Ludwig von Mises, *The Theory of Money and Credit*, 2nd edn., trans. H. E. Batson, New Haven, 1953, p. 38). Karl Menger, for example, argued that "*equivalents* [of goods] *in the objective sense of the term* do not exist . . . and cannot exist . . ." (*Principles of Economics*, trans. and ed. James Dingwell and Bert F. Hoselitz [from 1st edn. published in 1871],

163

Glencoe, 1950, p. 193). Therefore he concluded that "the entire theory that presents money as the 'measure of the exchange value' of goods disintegrates into nothingness . . ." (*ibid.*, p. 273). "Though 'Standard of Value' is ever on our lips," remarked Lewis H. Blair, "a standard of value, as usually understood, is an ignis fatuus, an impossibility" (*A Standard of Value*, Richmond, 1893, p. 3). "Although standard and value, or definite invariable fact and indefinite variable state of mind, are as opposite as the poles," he explained, "yet because we can unite the words, standard and value, into a glib phrase, 'Standard of Value,' we imagine when we have done so that fact and sentiment have thereby become welded into a reality, definite and comprehensive enough to test or measure all other things, or that we really have 'a Standard of Value.' But blinded by custom, misled by authority, and confounding exchangeability with standard of value, we cannot see that though we have a name we have not a fact, and that standard of value is an impossibility, a will o' the wisp luring to ruin. Exchangeability, however great, can never be transmuted into a standard of value any more than an opinion into a fact. Exchangeability does not imply intrinsic value in the medium of exchange, for that is accepted freely which can be passed freely" (*ibid.*, pp. 6–7). "Better attempt a standard of beauty or of taste or of religion, than a permanent standard of value," he added. "If we permitted ourselves to think, we would soon perceive that we are attempting sunbeams from cucumbers . . . But because we follow in the beaten track, we still pursue with heat and passion not only one impossibility, namely a single standard, but a twofold impossibility, namely, a double standard of value—a comedy with the world for a stage, with statesmen for actors, and the fun at the expense of the people" (*ibid.*, pp. 11–12). Karl Olivecrona summed up the matter this way: "The idea of 'money' being a 'measure [i.e., standard measure] of value' seems to include that 'value' is a property of objects capable of being measured just as length is measured in feet or metres. But 'value' is no property of an object; the word is the expression of a subjective attitude with regard to the object. Moreover, it is hard to conceive how the monetary unit—if its nature is such as has been maintained here [abstract]—could be used for measuring anything at all" (*op. cit.*, p. 150). Howard S. Ellis concluded, "Enquiry into senses of the value of money fails to reveal a single instance of absolute value" (*German Monetary Theory*, Cambridge, Mass., 1934, p. 113).

38 The analogy between the standard of value and standards of physical measurement, such as the yardstick, began as an expository device for purposes of illustration, not as a mode of reasoning (Harris, *op. cit.*, pp. 39–40; Sir James Steuart, *An Inquiry into the Principles of Political Œconomy*, London, 1767, I, 534; Adam Smith, *op. cit.*, pp. 32–33). Actual analogy was not implied. In fact, Harris asserted, "Silver cannot be a fixed standard, like that of mere extension as a yard or a bushel, for measuring the values of other things" (*op. cit.*, pp. 62–63). However, some bullionists tended to reason by this analogy: "As a measure of length must itself have length—so likewise must a measure of value be something which intrinsically is valuable; for how can that be a measure of the value of other things, which is itself without value?"

164

(Page, *op. cit.*, pp. 212–213.) This far, and no further, the analogy was valid—but only so long as classical premises were accepted. Even before some of the latter lost their authenticity, however, the analogy was pushed beyond the point of legitimacy: Opponents of classical doctrines and policies called the gold standard a fraudulent standard because it was not the invariable yardstick of value people supposed it to be (G. Poulett Scrope, *An Examination of the Bank Charter Question, with an Inquiry into the Nature of a Just Standard of Value, and Suggestions for the Improvement of Our Monetary System,* London, 1833, pp. 20–21; *supra,* Chap. II, nn. 99, 100). Ironically, this heretical distortion of classical doctrine (see *supra,* pp. 24–25; and nn. 11 and 28 of this chapter), was the source of the well-worn "rubber-yardstick" cliché to be found somewhere in most textbooks of recent decades. The analogy was merely shifted from gold to money. Meanwhile, orthodox partisans of the gold standard had appropriated the weapon to their own purposes. Equating a "double standard" with double-dealing, they accused the bimetallists of advocating the absurdity of two different yardsticks of value. For a succinct statement of this argument see W. W. Baldwin, *The Gold Standard,* Burlington, 1895, pp. 21–22. Good examples of the bimetallic answer were furnished by George N. Jackson (*The Present and Future of Silver,* Chicago, 1879, p. 57) and Teller (*op. cit.,* pp. 27–28).

39 That the differences exceeded the similarities in both number and importance has long been recognized, and this awareness has not been confined to bimetallists. The observed discrepancies are: (1) Whereas the length (quality to be measured) of the yardstick is fixed, the value (quality to be measured) of the standard of value is not fixed, but variable (J. Shield Nicholson, *A Treatise on Money and Essays on Monetary Problems,* 2nd edn., London, 1893, pp. 192, 256–259; David Kinley, *Money,* New York, 1904, p. 261; Sir David Barbour, *The Standard of Value,* London, 1912, p. 110; Sir Basil P. Blackett, *Planned Money,* New York, 1933, p. 70). (2) A corollary of the first discrepancy is that in the standard of value it is the weight, not the value, which is fixed (*The Monetary Problem: Gold and Silver,* ed. Ralph Robey, p. 298; Nicholson, *op. cit.,* pp. 20, 192). (3) Whereas length is a physical attribute of a single article and can be measured by a single object, value, being a ratio, cannot be (*The Works and Correspondence of David Ricardo,* IV, 398–399, 401; R.[obert] Torrens, *An Essay on the Production of Wealth,* London, 1821, p. 65; Bailey, *op. cit.,* pp. 95–96; MacLeod, *op. cit.,* I, 295–296, 300–301; Del Mar, *op. cit.,* p. 124; Conant, *op. cit.,* pp. 148–149; Helfferich, *op. cit.,* pp. 322–323, 326–329). (4) Whereas the length of yardsticks is not affected by their number, the value of the standard of value *is* influenced by its quantity (Baldwin, *op. cit.,* p. 12; Del Mar, *op. cit.,* pp. 34–35; Teller, *op. cit.,* pp. 27–28; Bertrand Nogaro, *Modern Monetary Systems,* London, 1927 [translation of 1924 French edn.], pp. 185–186).

A recent textbook tells us, "As a standard [of value], *money is unique* in that it is an *inconstant standard* (Eugene S. Klise, *Money and Banking,* 2nd edn., Cincinnati, 1959, p. 4 [italics mine]). One should expect such a contradiction of terms to inspire a reappraisal of the concept or its label or, at least, the analogy of a constant physical standard. But instead, we are told, "In spite of its variability, money as a standard of value is indispensable" (*loc. cit.*). If we accept a contradiction as indispensable, there is something wrong with our concepts or the words we use to describe them. The persistence of the diverting analogy of the elastic yardstick defies explanation, unless it be attributable to a certain perversity or predisposition to paradox among monetary economists. For examples, see: Earl Dean Howard and Joseph French Johnson, *Money and Banking*, New York, 1911, p. 30; Irving Fisher, *Stabilizing the Dollar*, New York, 1920, p. 83; Irving Fisher, *The Money Illusion*, New York, 1928, pp. 156–157, 170–171; and Hiram L. Jome, *Principles of Money and Banking*, Homewood, Ill., 1957, p. 5. Some maintain the analogy in the face of their own recognition that money is a defective standard of value (Arthur D. Gayer and W. W. Rostow, *How Money Works*, Public Affairs Pamphlet No. 45, New York, 1940, p. 4; *ibid.*, 2nd edn., p. 4; Chandler, *The Economics of Money and Banking*, 3rd edn., p. 5; J. Whitney Hanks and Roland Stucki, *Money, Banking, and National Income*, New York, 1956, pp. 26–28; Kent, *op. cit.*, p. 10). Others persist in the analogy even though it "seems grotesque" (George William Dowrie, *Money and Banking*, New York, 1936, p. 87). Still others admit the impossibility of a standard of value like a standard of length in the very process of drawing an analogy between them (Harold G. Moulton, *Principles of Money and Banking*, Chicago, 1916, p. 7; R. A. Lehfeldt, *Restoration of the World's Currencies*, London, 1923, pp. 4, 6; Magee, *op. cit.*, pp. 37–39; Edwin Walter Kemmerer, *Money*, New York, 1935, pp. 11, 108.

40 Unfortunately, the term "standard" was preserved in "standard of deferred payments," which Walker substituted for the Jevonsonian "standard of value" (Walker, *op. cit.*, p. 11).

41 *Ibid.*, pp. 5, 7–9.

42 *Ibid.*, pp. 283–288.

43 *Ibid.*, p. 282.

44 After denying the yardstick analogy, Bailey, the contemporary critic of classicism, elaborated: "What then is it possible to do in the way of measuring value? What kind of measurement is intended, when the term is so frequently employed? All that is practicable appears to be simply this: if I know the value of A in relation to B, and the value of B in relation to C, I can tell the value of A and C in relation to each other, and consequently their comparative power in purchasing all other commodities. This is an operation obviously bearing no resemblance at all to the process of measuring length" (*op. cit.*, p. 96). Although the invariability of the standard measure of distance is essential, he explained, the value of a common denominator is irrelevant (*ibid.*, pp. 104–105). "Although the term 'measure of values' is a convenient and popular expression (so much so as to render its displacement from financial literature doubtful), yet it is not scientifically accurate, and is the cause of numerous fallacies that prevent a clear understanding of the nature of money . . . Of course, the objections here noted against the term 'measure of value,' apply with equal force against that other misnomer— 'Standard of Value' " (Jackson, *op. cit.*, pp. 55–56). His objection, like

166

that of MacLeod, Walker, et al., was that values, being ratios, cannot be measured by a single quantity. He preferred Walker's "common denominator of values" as the designation for this function of money (*ibid.*, p. 55). This point of view is reflected in Palgrave's *Dictionary of Political Economy*, II, 789: "The foregoing office of money has been termed by economists generally that of a measure of value; but that term is not descriptive and has proved highly misleading. A better statement would be that money in this connection fulfills the office of the common denominator in exchange, or denominator of values." Additional statements of this position may be found in: Walker, *op. cit.*, pp. 10–11; and Helfferich, *op. cit.*, pp. 322–325.

45 *Dictionary of Political Economy*, ed. Palgrave, II, 793 (italics mine):

> From this notion, that money measures values, has come the dictum, common to most economists, that a money of mere convention, not having INTRINSIC VALUE (*q.v.*), not being "a material recompense or equivalent" cannot perform this function, whatever it may do as a universal medium of exchange. It would appear that all this confusion has arisen from the use of a misleading term. If we read further in the works of these writers, we find that the function they are really treating of is merely that of a common denominator in exchange. *Now, it is not essentially the office of a denominator in exchange to measure values; but only to express them, as measured. . . . Probably the history of philosophy furnishes no instance of an equally mischievous result from the use of a false terminology, with that which has followed the phrase, "measure of value" in its application to money.*

Walker argued: "I apprehend that this notion of money serving as a common measure of value is wholly fanciful; indeed the very phrase seems to indicate a misconception. *Value is a relation. Relations may be expressed, but not measured* (*op. cit.*, p. 288). This was a basic contention of bimetallists:

> Money is not a measure of value in any sense so as to make such a comparison [money with a yardstick] possible. A yard-stick is a measure of fixed, unchanging length . . . *Value is not a thing; it implies a relation.* The value of anything is value in some other commodity. The value of an article cannot be mentioned without involving a reference to something else. *Value, therefore, is not, strictly speaking, measured, but expressed or stated; and money is not a measure of values, but a common denominator in terms of which values may be expressed* (Teller, *op. cit.*, pp. 27–28 [italics mine]).

The almost exclusive association of this position with the losing cause of bimetallism resulted in the loss of the argument with the cause. The monometallists used the "yardstick" to beat the bimetallists. What started as a metaphor became such an effective weapon in the battle of standards that it crystallized as the keystone of orthodox strategy. However, the idea that money is an abstract unit of account for *expressing* relative values, rather than a standard for *measuring* values, was kept alive by a few writers (e.g., Tourgée, *op. cit.*, p. 76; Helfferich, *op. cit.*, pp. 323–324; Willard E. Atkins, *Gold and Your Money*, New York, 1934, pp. 72, 82).

46 H. L. Puxley, *A Critique of the Gold Standard*, New York, 1933, pp. 13–14; Ray B. Westerfield, *Money, Credit and Banking*, 2nd edn., New York, 1947, p. 8.

167

47 J. Laurence Laughlin, *The Principles of Money*, New York, 1903, p. 14; Nogaro, *op. cit.,* pp. 175–178, 184, 186–187; Puxley, *op. cit.,* pp. 13–14; Horace White, *Money and Banking*, 6th edn., revised and enlarged by Charles S. Tippets and Lewis A. Froman, Boston, 1935, p. 21; Holdsworth, *op. cit.,* pp. 16–17, 19; Richard W. Lindholm, John J. Balles, and John M. Hunter, *Principles of Money and Banking*, New York, 1954, pp. 33–34; Klise, *op. cit.,* p. 3. The terminological involutions found in the various editions of Charles L. Prather's textbook is indicative of the problem: In the first edition he said, "By saying that money is a *standard of value* it is meant that money is the *common denominator* for expressing exchange ratios" (*op. cit.* 1st edn., p. 9 [italics mine]). This explanation of the standard of value was dropped from the fourth edition. It reappeared in the fifth edition with "common denominator" replaced by "unit" (*ibid.,* 5th edn., p. 17). The next edition tells us: "As a *standard of value,* money is more than a *common denominator* for expressing exchange ratios as prices. It . . . [is] a *standard unit* . . ." (*ibid.,* 6th edn., p. 9 [italics mine]).

48 See *infra,* nn. 57–58 of this chapter. Leffler maintained that money was a "measure of value," but he explained it as a "common denominator" (*op. cit.,* pp. 21–22). Other authorities implied their disagreement with synonymous use of all these various names for the relevant function of money. William Howard Steiner concluded, "Hence certain writers have proposed to abandon entirely the expression 'standard of value' and to term this function instead 'measure of value' or 'common denominator of value.' Thus they hope to avoid what they regard as the misleading implications of the term" (*Money and Banking*, New York, 1933, p. 28). Olivecrona observed, "The monetary unit has no function as a 'standard of value' besides that of being the unit in which prices are expressed" (*op. cit.,* p. 159). Chandler listed all the names, indicating only that they are "the most common" of the many which have "been given" to the money function in question (*The Economics of Money and Banking*, 3rd edn., p. 5).

49 *Supra,* p. 25; *infra,* nn. 55–56 of this chapter.

50 *Supra,* pp. 24–25; *supra,* n. 11 of this chapter.

51 Walker, *op. cit.,* pp. 5 ff. Cf. *supra,* n. 35 of this chapter.

52 William Huskisson implied this in his use of the terms "standard" and "denomination": The *"standard* is the precise *quantity* (ascertained by *weight* and *fineness*) fixed by law for pieces of each denomination. Thus the *standard* fineness of our gold coin is eleven parts of pure gold and one of alloy; and the *denomination* of a piece weighing 5 dwts. 9 $\frac{39}{89}$ gr. is a guinea" (*The Question Concerning the Depreciation of Our Currency Stated and Examined*, London, 1810, p. 5). "Ricardo is very sound when he insists that the measure of value should be stabilized in a standard of value" (J. Taylor Peddie, *The Invariable Standard and Measure of Value*, 2nd edn., London, 1928, p. 46, n.).

53 Sir David Barbour has furnished a good restatement of the classical position: "In the ordinary business of life everybody treats the Standard of Value which he uses, whatever it may be, as fixed and invariable in value, and looks on all changes in price as being due to economic

168

causes affecting commodities. No other course is possible, and this method of dealing with changes in prices and wages is, for practical purposes, perfectly sound and only leads to wrong results if we apply it to investigations into the general purchasing power of gold [i.e., although our standard measure of value is not fixed in value as a yard is fixed in length, our assumption that it is so fixed causes no trouble as long as we abstract from its variability] . . ." (*op. cit.,* p. 153). See also *supra,* n. 28 of this chapter.

54 Mason, *op. cit.,* pp. 495 and 498, nn. 25 and 37.

55 "Depreciation as applied to money must be understood to mean relative lowness as compared with the standard [gold], and nothing else . . ." (*The Works and Correspondence of David Ricardo,* IX, 276).

56 Classical refutation of the antibullionist confusion of the two concepts had checked the spread of the heresy during the ascendancy of the classical school (*supra,* pp. 24–25). Neoclassical and modern writers on money, without apparent realization, revived the anticlassical, antibullionist fallacy of equivocation (cf. *loc. cit.*). "The unit of account or standard of value in each country [before World War I] was a different weight of gold . . ." (D. T. Jack, *The Economics of the Gold Standard,* London, 1925, p. 25). "The standard unit of account and of value was defined by statute as a fixed weight of gold of specified fineness" (Steiner, *op. cit.,* p. 76). "The only connection between the media of payment and the unit of account is that all forms of lawful money are theoretically convertible into the unit of account" (National Industrial Conference Board, *The Gold Standard: Recent Development and Present Status,* Conference Board Information Service: Domestic Affairs, Memorandum No. 5 [mimeographed], New York, 1933, p. 3). "On the one hand, it [money] serves as a *standard of value,* an abstract unit of account in terms of which the value of any commodity or service can be measured, and by means of which the values of two or more different articles can be compared" (F. Cyril James, *The Economics of Money, Credit and Banking,* 3rd edn., New York, 1940, p. 8). "The concept of money as a standard of value is abstract" ("The Monetary System of the United States," *Federal Reserve Bulletin,* XXXIX [February 1953], 98). "Perhaps the most important function of money is that of providing a 'unit of account' or standard for measuring the relative worth of all goods and services exchanged in a nation's economy" (Hanks and Stucki, *op. cit.,* p. 26). A footnote elaborates the statement this way: "Other expressions commonly used to describe this function are *unit of value, common denominator, common measure of value,* and *standard of value*" (*ibid.,* p. 26, n. 5). "In this respect, money is frequently alluded to as a *unit of account* or as a *money of account;* but these terms are synonymous with *standard of value*" (Kent, *op. cit.,* p. 9). "It seems to be generally agreed, however, that in the modern world the basic work of money is to serve as a standard of value (or as a unit of account or common denominator, as some put it) and as a medium of exchange" (Jome, *op. cit.,* p. 27). The list of examples could be extended *ad nauseam.*

57 "However, in the case of value, there is no fixed standard despite the fact that the need for one is as great as that for a constant system

169

[i.e., standards] of weights and measures" (Prather, *op. cit.*, 4th edn., p. 55). *"A standard of value is a vague concept of an ever-changing magnitude of purchasing power, and cannot be embodied in a concrete measuring instrument"* (Anatol Murad, *The Paradox of a Metal Standard*, Washington, 1939, p. 187). "Relative stability of the value of the monetary unit [in terms of goods in general] is essential for the performance of the standard of value function" (*Federal Reserve Bulletin*, XXXIX [February 1953], 98). "The monetary unit is the country's standard of value. But until it is embodied in the form of spendable money which is measured against goods in the market place, the standard of value has little meaning" (Rollin G. Thomas, *Our Modern Banking and Monetary System*, 3rd edn., Englewood Cliffs, 1957, p. 7). "The significant factor in the concept of money value is the tendency of money value to change, and it is this tendency which keeps money from being an absolute standard of value" (Agger, *op. cit.*, p. 105). "Because of the purchasing-power concepts associated with a unit of account a *standard of value* develops . . ." (Pritchard, *op. cit.*, p. 10). "As a standard [of value], money is unique in that it is an inconstant standard. . . . The value of money, the yardstick with which we measure all economic values, may vary by any amount. For the value of money is its purchasing power" (Klise, *op. cit.*, p. 4). Attempts to explain the reasons for *variations* in the *value* of the *standard of value* (e.g., Laughlin, *The Principles of Money*, pp. 36 ff. *et passim*) should have aroused suspicion of the terms, or the reasoning, or both.

58 Lionel D. Edie, *Money, Bank Credit, and Prices*, New York, 1928, p. 27 (italics mine):

> It is said that a gold dollar is always worth a dollar. This tautology is, of course, true, because as a matter of definition a dollar is defined as a certain weight of gold. But such a statement entirely misses the significant feature of money. *The significant thing is that money should always be worth approximately the same amount of the necessities and comforts of life. The gold dollar is not the same dollar, even though it weighs the same, if at one time it buys twice as much as at another.* The notion that a dollar is always a dollar gives rise to a false sense of security under the gold standard. It is of fundamental importance to face squarely the proposition that the *gold standard does not automatically provide a true standard unit of account;* and that if it is to provide this highly essential function, *gold must be subjected to more scientific control and regulation in the future than in the past.*

These observations epitomize the neoclassical inversion of the classical standard-of-value concept. See also Peddie, *op. cit.*, p. 31; and Paul Bakewell, Jr., *Past and Present Facts about Money in the United States*, New York, 1936, pp. 101, 142–147.

59 See *supra*, pp. 24–25.

60 Thus, antibullionism finally and quietly triumphed over bullionism. This was virtually announced in the orthodox *Dictionary of Political Economy*, ed. Palgrave, II, 793 (italics mine):

> If we contemplate money of pure convention—for example, mere pieces of paper curiously engraved . . . a moment's reflection will show that, by being actually exchanged against these pieces of paper, all commodities in the market become measured as to their value, without regard to the cost of production of money itself. . . . The

170

action in the case of money of mere convention is identical [with that of commodity money]; and the results are just as exact. By the mere fact of being exchanged for any kind of money, each commodity takes its place on the price-current, high up or low down, according to the demand for it, and according to the ease or difficulty with which it can be brought to market—that is, according to demand and supply. It is this conception of the function of money as a common denominator of values which underlies the discussion of IDEAL MONEY by Sir James STEUART and Messrs. F. Percival ELIOT and Gloucester WILSON. *These writers were far nearer the truth than their critics.*

Although the victory was only partial, it was, at the same time, substantial. Money was not legally separated from gold (as antibullionists had advocated). The mechanism for maintaining a fixed price for gold was continued, but the attempt to enjoy the best of two worlds—a stable money in terms of both gold and all goods—required compromises which rendered the relationship between money and gold increasingly tenuous. Another ironic aspect of this implicit sanctification of heresy is that whereas extreme antibullionists identified the standard of value with the abstract unit of account, neglectful of the commodity origin of the predominantly commodity money of their day; neoclassical and modern writers have identified the unit of account with the commodity standard of value while commodity money and standards were being replaced by abstractions.

Acknowledgment of these facts permits resolution of the paradox in the conflicting claims that variation in the gold content of the monetary unit represented (1) abandonment of the gold standard (Bakewell, *op. cit.*, pp. 104–105; as well as most orthodox opponents of Fisher's "compensated dollar" plan, and of the New-Deal devaluation of the dollar), and (2) establishment of a "real" gold standard (e.g., Fisher; see *supra*, Chap. II, nn. 85, 173, 174). The former was an inference from the premised classical view of the standard of value (as a basis for comparing the relative monetary values of goods), whereas the latter was an inference from the "modern" application of the term "standard of value" to the concept of a "unit of account" (for historical comparisons of the goods value of money). In his support of the former, Roy L. Garis illustrated the difference between the two views of the standard: (1) fixed as a physical thing, or (2) fixed in terms of the value of everything (*Principles of Money, Credit, and Banking,* New York, 1934, pp. 273–274).

61 Robert Barclay, *The Disturbance of the Standard of Value,* London, 1893, p. 28: "The standard must be a true equivalent of the value which it measures . . . Representative money in bank notes could not fulfill these conditions because it has no intrinsic value . . ."

62 Palgrave's *Dictionary of Political Economy,* III, includes an article on the "Standard of Value" which accepts the concept as well as the term (*ibid.,* pp. 457–458), despite admitted weaknesses, and elaborates: "Such invariability [as that sought in the standard of value] is impossible of achievement, impossible even of conception, if we require the same standard to be invariable for all persons and all times. The impossibility arises out of the human element in value, from the fact that value has reference not to a property inherent in a commodity, but to

the estimate by a person of the desirability of the possession of the commodity. . . . The position of the standard of value depends on circumstances extraneous to itself" (*ibid.*, p. 458). See also: George H. Benton, *The Evaluation of the Gold Standard,* Minneapolis, 1896, p. 11; Laughlin, *The Principles of Money,* pp. 14–16, 60; Conant, *op. cit.,* p. 23; Bakewell, *op. cit.,* pp. viii, 9; Dowrie, *Money and Banking,* pp. 5, 27; Agger, *op. cit.,* p. 98; Murad, *op. cit.,* pp. 176–177; and Klise, *op. cit.,* pp. 3, 5 (n. 3), 7.

63 That this was not merely a matter of words is indicated by the persistence of "objective, intrinsic value," along with the notion of a "standard of value." This was the way value was treated by lawmakers and the courts until the gold-clause cases of the 'thirties (Del Mar, *op. cit.,* pp. 7–8; Bakewell, *op. cit.,* pp. 66–67). A few based their retention of "intrinsic value" on an outright denial that value is relative (B. M. Anderson, Jr., *Social Value,* Boston, 1911, pp. 184, 197–199; B. M. Anderson, Jr., *The Value of Money,* New York, 1936, pp. 6–7 *et passim;* Bradford, *op. cit.,* pp. 373–379). But the term "intrinsic value" (alternatively, "objective value") and the notion it was supposed to represent continued to be used by some authorities who believed in the relative nature of value (Conant, *op. cit.,* pp. 5–6; Russell Donald Kilborne, *Principles of Money and Banking,* Chicago, 1927, p. 10; Walter E. Spahr, *Alternatives in Postwar International Monetary Standards,* The Monetary Standards Inquiry, No. 7, New York, 1944, p. 19; *Dictionary of Political Economy,* ed. Palgrave, II, 455–456 [cf. *ibid.,* III, 610]). MacLeod was truly prophetic when he said, "The expression Intrinsic Value is so common that persons are apt to overlook its incongruity of idea" (*op. cit.,* I, 290).

CHAPTER IV

1 The labor theory of value is a species of the genus cost-of-production theory, all of whose species imply the notion of intrinsic value. It is the latter implication that is relevant to this study. Therefore, no attempt will be made to distinguish or evaluate the various interpretations of the labor theory of value. Where the term "labor theory of value" is used here, it will mean merely a form of the cost-of-production theory of value on which all classicists agreed. "For the purpose of an elementary survey of the history of the theory of value we may roughly divide the various theorists into two 'schools'—the 'cost of production' school and the 'utility' school" (*Dictionary of Political Economy,* ed. R. H. Inglis Palgrave, London, 1894–1899, I, 762).

2 Henry Dunning MacLeod maintained that the postmercantilist practice of determining what was wealth by the useful qualities of things "led

writers to speak of *Intrinsic Value"* (*The Principles of Economical Philosophy*, 2nd edn., London, 1879, I, 288). He forthwith elaborated:

Then they [economists] began to consider that things would exchange in proportion to the labour employed in producing them. Thus the value of a thing was considered to depend on the quantity of labour employed to produce it. Thus the quantity of labour embodied as it were in the thing came to be counted as its value, and value thus came to be called *Intrinsic,* and many of the most eminent Economists consider value to be some inherent quality of a thing conferred by labour. This unhappy phrase, *Intrinsic Value,* meets us at every turn in Economics, and yet the slightest reflection will shew that to define Value to be something *external,* and then to be constantly speaking of *Intrinsic Value,* are utterly self-contradictory and inconsistent ideas (*ibid.,* p. 289).

"The unfortunate confusion of ideas between the Value of a quantity being any other quantity a thing will exchange for, and the quantity of labor embodied in obtaining the quantity itself, has led not only to the mischievous expression, Intrinsic Value, the source of endless confusion, but also to the search for something which reflection would have shown to be impossible, viz., an *Invariable Standard of Value"* (*ibid.,* p. 293).

3 John Maynard Keynes, *The General Theory of Employment Interest and Money,* New York, 1936, pp. 292–293; Henry H. Villard, "Monetary Theory," *A Survey of Contemporary Economics,* [I], ed. Howard S. Ellis, Philadelphia, 1948, 322, n. 15; Joseph A. Schumpeter, *History of Economic Analysis,* ed. Elizabeth Boody Schumpeter, New York, 1954, p. 1088; Overton H. Taylor, *A History of Economic Thought,* New York, 1960, pp. 474, 476.

4 The brief treatment here will be elaborated in another study which is presently in preparation.

5 *The Works and Correspondence of David Ricardo,* ed. Piero Sraffa with the collaboration of M. H. Dobb, Cambridge, 1951–1955, I, 11–12; [John Stuart Mill], "On the Nature, Measures, and Causes of Value," *Westminster Review,* V (January 1826), 167–168.

6 John Stuart Mill, *op. cit.,* p. 168.

7 *Ibid.,* p. 167; Ricardo, *op. cit.,* p. 12.

8 James Mill, *Elements of Political Economy,* London, 1821, pp. 68–69. Classical writers regarded "labor" and "cost" (real) as close enough approximations of each other to be used as synonyms.

9 John Stuart Mill, *op. cit.,* p. 168.

10 The classical school's views on this range of topics were received, at least in an embryonic state, from Adam Smith (*An Inquiry into the Nature and Causes of the Wealth of Nations,* ed. Edwin Cannan, Modern Library edn. [reprinted from 5th edn.], New York, 1937, pp. 31–33, 36–37, 186).

11 Donald F. Gordon, "What Was the Labor Theory of Value?" *American Economic Review,* Papers and Proceedings, XLIX (May 1959), 472.

12 Smith, *op. cit.,* pp. 34–35, 187.

13 *Ibid.,* pp. 36–37.

14 *Ibid.,* pp. 32–33, 37; *The Works and Correspondence of David Ricardo,* IV, 54–55, 364, 366–368, 372–373, 390–391, 397, 401, 405–406; [John Stuart Mill], "The Currency Question," *Westminster Review,* XLI (June 1844), 581. See also *supra,* Chap. III, n. 28.

173

15 Lord [Thomas Henry] Farrer, *Studies in Currency*, London, 1898, pp. 306–308; F. W. Taussig, *The Silver Situation in the United States*, New York, 1893, pp. 107–108; John Cummings, "Monetary Standards," *Journal of Political Economy*, II (June 1894), 354–357.

16 George H. Shibley, *The Money Question*, Chicago, 1896, p. 722. See also *supra*, Chap. III, nn. 58, 60. For a theoretical denial of the possibility see Feliks Mlynarski, *The Functioning of the Gold Standard*, Geneva, 1931, p. 107.

17 *Supra*, Chap. III, n. 60.

18 Again, the classical monetary theory and its neoclassical misconstruction will only be summarized here since elaboration of the details and documentation will be furnished in the study already mentioned (*supra*, n. 4 of this chapter).

19 John Stuart Mill, *Principles of Political Economy*, ed. Sir W. J. Ashley, London, 1936 (reprint of 1909 edn.), pp. 488, 499, 504, 523, 626.

20 *Ibid.*, pp. 504–523.

21 Money not offered in exchange for goods was not considered part of the money supply (*ibid.*, pp. 490, 496), and plate was the principle means of storing value.

22 *Ibid.*, pp. 624–626.

23 From the point of view of monetary theory, the term "neoclassical" is applied here to those postclassical writers who associate themselves with classical monetary theory, claiming only to interpret it.

24 *Money*, New York, 1877, pp. 56–57.

25 *A Treatise on Money and Essays on Monetary Problems*, 2nd edn., London, 1893, pp. 69–71.

26 *Ibid.*, p. 70.

27 *Ibid.*, p. 71.

28 The static analytical and quasi-dynamic historical senses of the terms "short run" and "long run" have been pretty generally confused ever since. The terms will be subsequently enclosed in quotation marks (except where the meaning appears to be clear) as a warning of their ambiguity.

29 John Stuart Mill, *Principles of Political Economy*, p. 523.

30 The discussion of this, too, will be brief as the complete argument and supporting evidence will be available in the forthcoming study previously mentioned (*supra*, n. 4 of this chapter).

31 Taussig, *op. cit.*, p. 90; Edwin Walter Kemmerer, *Money and Credit Instruments in Their Relation to General Prices*, 2nd edn., New York, 1909, pp. 140–141, 144, 147; Edwin Walter Kemmerer, *Money*, New York, 1935, pp. 57, 65.

32 Irving Fisher and Harry G. Brown, *The Purchasing Power of Money*, New York, 1911, pp. 55 ff., 159–161.

33 *Supra*, n. 3 of this chapter.

34 Henry V. Poor, *Money and Its Laws*, New York, 1877, p. 6. See also the article on "Intrinsic Value," *Dictionary of Political Economy*, ed. Palgrave, II, 455–456. Evidence of the persistence of this doctrine in monetary analysis is ample, e.g., Roy L. Garis, *Principles of Money, Credit, and Banking*, New York, 1934, p. 11 (italics mine): "Obviously every article possessing value can be compared with other articles hav-

ing value only by reference to some *standard which itself possesses value.*"

35 *Supra*, pp. 47–49.

36 *Money and the Mechanism of Exchange,* New York [1875], p. 74; *supra*, Chap. III, n. 26.

37 Jevons, *op. cit.*, pp. 14–15. Cf. *supra*, Chap. II, nn. 93–96.

38 Jevons, *op. cit.*, pp. 14–15 (italics mine): *"We must not suppose that the substance serving as a standard of value is really invariable* in value, but merely that it is chosen as that *measure by which the value of future payments is to be regulated.* Bearing in mind that value is only the ratio of quantities exchanged, it is certain that no substance permanently bears exactly the same value relatively to another commodity; but it will, of course, be desirable to select as the standard of value that which appears likely to continue to exchange for many other commodities in nearly unchanged ratios." The classical school judged the stability of the standard of value in terms of labor, not goods (*supra*, nn. 13–14 of this chapter).

39 *Op. cit.*, pp. 13–15. See also *supra*, Chap. II, nn. 139, 160–162.

40 *Op. cit.*, pp. 13–15; Walker, *op. cit.*, p. 11.

41 J. Allen Smith placed Jevons with those who interpreted the ideal standard of value as a constant quantity of commodities, in contrast to the classical interpretation as the product of a constant quantity of labor ("The Multiple Money Standard," *Annals*, VII [March 1896], 181, n.).

42 See *supra*, p. 22.

43 Consequently, he preferred the tabular standard for deferred payments as a means of compensating for the inequities of the gold standard of value, over modification or control of the gold standard (*supra*, p. 30).

44 For example, in denying the claim of creditors to compensation for loss of real income resulting from a fall in the value of gold, Jevons said: "All such claim seems to be done away with by the fact that, generally speaking, *the Legislature never obliged contracts to be made in gold money.* Though very rightly selecting gold as the best obtainable standard and providing a gold currency as a public convenience, *it never professed to make gold an invariable measure of value,* and accordingly never prevented any person from selecting other standards if they desired . . .

. . . .

Thus it seems obvious, that the law of England has always carefully avoided guaranteeing gold or any other commodity as a real standard of value. It has *never guaranteed amounts of value at all, but only amounts of* [a] *commodity"* (*Investigations in Currency and Finance,* ed. H. S. Foxwell, London, 1884, pp. 97, 99 [all except first italics mine]). Jevons then reaffirmed his faith in gold as "the preeminent and natural standard of value" (*ibid.*, p. 101).

45 *Money and the Mechanism of Exchange,* pp. 66–67.

46 Therefore, if schools of economics are distinguished by their respective treatments of value theory, as they generally are, the customary practice of terminating the classical school with John Stuart Mill or John Elliot Cairnes and classifying Jevons with the "Austrian," "utility," "psycho-

logical," or "subjective value" school is wrong. For examples of this error see: Othmar Spann, *The History of Economics*, trans. Eden and Cedar Paul [from 19th German edn.], New York, 1930, pp. 255–256; Alexander Gray, *The Development of Economic Doctrine*, London, 1931, pp. 285–286; Erich Roll, *A History of Economic Thought*, New York, 1940, pp. 369–371, 376. Schumpeter associated Jevons with the Austrians on a different criterion (*op. cit.*, pp. 918–919). Although Schumpeter's linkage is quite legitimate, it is irrelevant to the point under discussion here. Incidentally, the name "Austrian" is an ironical (one might even suspect, a satirical) label for a school founded by two Frenchmen (Auguste Walras and his son Leon), a German (Herman Heinrich Gossen), and an Englishman (Jevons)—as well as an Austrian (Karl Menger). (See Gray, *op. cit.*, pp. 333, 336, 341, 345.)

47 In a letter to J. L. Shadwell, Jevons clearly indicated that his *Theory of Political Economy* represented a refinement, not a repudiation of the labor theory of value (*Letters & Journal of W. Stanley Jevons*, ed. Harriet A. Jevons, London, 1886, pp. 268–269). Moreover, in a letter to Leon Walras, the reluctance of Englishmen to accept his theory of value was attributed to the opposition of John Stuart Mill's disciples "to any innovation *upon* his [Mill's] doctrine" (*ibid.*, p. 332 [italics mine]). Notice that Jevons characterized his theory as an "innovation *upon*," not a refutation—or even a correction—*of*, Mill's value theory. Jevons' disagreement with received doctrine was confined to methodology and distribution theory (*infra*, nn. 68, 70 of this chapter). George J. Stigler has recognized the essentially classical character of Jevons' analysis (*Production and Distribution Theories*, New York, 1941, p. 13).

48 After an apparent effort to prove otherwise, Erich Roll finally admitted that Jevons "abandoned half-way his attempt to give an explanation of the origin of value in terms of utility, in favor of a purely 'functional' theory" (*op. cit.*, p. 378).

49 Cf. *supra*, p. 53.

50 *Supra*, p. 53. Appreciation of the classical position and Jevons' essential agreement with it was eclipsed by the excesses of the pseudoclassical and Marxist partisans, on the one hand, and the anticlassicists, on the other hand, who claimed that labor or utility, respectively, was *the cause* (i.e., source) of value.

51 *Letters & Journal of W. Stanley Jevons*, pp. 151–152 (italics mine).

52 *The Theory of Political Economy*, London, 1871, pp. 155–156 (first italics mine):

> The preceding pages contain, if I am not mistaken, an explanation of the nature of value which will, for the most part, *harmonize with previous views on the subject*. Ricardo has stated, like most other economists, that utility is absolutely essential to value; but that "possessing utility, commodities derive their exchangeable value from two sources: from their scarcity, and from the quantity of labour required to obtain them." Senior, again, has admirably defined wealth, or objects possessing value, as "those things, and those things only, which are transferable, are limited in supply, and are directly or indirectly productive of pleasure or preventive of pain." Speaking only of things which are transferable, or capable of being passed from hand to hand, we find that the two clearest statements of the nature of value available, recognize *utility* and *scarcity* as the requisites.

176

But the moment that we distinguish between the total utility of a mass of commodity and the degree of utility of different portions, we may say that scarcity is that which prevents the fall in the final degree of utility.

53 *Ibid.*, pp. 58, 168–169.

54 *Ibid.*, pp. 157–161.

55 This distinction was missed by no less an authority than Allyn A. Young: "Finally, it is obvious that his [Jevons'] criticism of the 'cost of production theory of value' had no bearing upon the prevalent form of that theory, which was simply a statement of admitted facts relative to long-period price tendencies under conditions of free competition" ("Jevons' 'Theory of Political Economy,' " *American Economic Review*, II [September 1912], 586).

56 H. Winefred Jevons and H. Stanley Jevons, "William Stanley Jevons," *Econometrica*, II (July 1934), 234; E. W. Eckard, *Economics of W. S. Jevons*, Washington, 1940, p. 91; Young, *op. cit.*, p. 582.

57 His son attributed the misconstruction of Jevons' *Theory of Political Economy* to the latter's abstraction from ideas presumed to be familiar to the professional readers for whom the book was written (H. Stanley Jevons, "Appendix I, Note by the Editor on the Author's Theory of Interest," *The Theory of Political Economy* by W. Stanley Jevons, 4th edn., London, 1931 [reprint of 1911 edn.], pp. 279–280).

58 *The Theory of Political Economy*, 1st edn., p. 181 (italics mine). In a later edition the statement was made even more explicit: "It may tend to give the reader confidence in the preceding theories when he finds that they lead directly to the well-known law, as stated in the ordinary language of economists, that *value is proportional to the cost of production*. As I prefer to state the same law, it is to the effect that *the ratio of exchange of commodities will conform in the long run to the ratio of productiveness*, which is the reciprocal of the ratio of the costs of production" (*The Theory of Political Economy*, 4th edn., p. 186 [italics mine]). This confirmation of classical long-run value theory was reiterated in his elementary primer (*Political Economy* [one of the] Science Primers, ed. Professors Huxley, Roscoe, and Balfour Stewart, New York, 1878, pp. 101–103). Cf. *supra*, p. 53.

59 *Money and the Mechanism of Exchange*, pp. 242–245; *Political Economy* (primer), pp. 98, 104–106; *Investigations in Currency and Finance*, p. 99.

60 *Investigations in Currency and Finance*, pp. 33, 108, 315; *Letters & Journal of W. Stanley Jevons*, p. 166; *Money and the Mechanism of Exchange*, p. 186. Jevons cleaved to the classical proposition that only when paper was inconvertible could it augment, rather than merely replace, money (i.e., standard coin). True to classical orthodoxy, he called this a "forced currency of paper" (*Investigations in Currency and Finance*, p. 355). Also he appeared to imply that checking deposits were substitutes that did not supplement the money supply (*Money and the Mechanism of Exchange*, pp. 188–189, 282).

61 *Political Economy* (primer), pp. 105–106.

62 *Investigations in Currency and Finance*, p. 318 (all except first italics mine). Jevons' other discussions, particularly of the point made in the

last sentence of the quotation, clearly reinforce the implication that he did not mean to limit the long run in the field of money to a duration of centuries (*ibid.*, pp. 109–110, 131–132, 311). For other statements by Jevons supporting the cost-of-production explanation of the long-run value of money, see *ibid.*, pp. 15, 18, and 69.

63 Gray, *op. cit.*, pp. 291–292; Roll, *op. cit.*, p. 376. After making this erroneous classification, Allyn Young reported, "His doctrines have been absorbed into the general structure of economic theory and *reconciled with the political economy of the Ricardian line in a manner which we may suppose Jevons would have neither imagined nor wished*" (*op. cit.*, p. 589 [italics mine]). On the contrary, this was precisely what Jevons desired. His disappointment was that it did not happen in his lifetime. His letters make this quite clear. In any case, the fact of such a reconciliation should have made Young suspicious of his interpretation of Jevons as an opponent of the classical theory of normal value (*supra*, n. 55 of this chapter). Although Schumpeter's association of Jevons with the Austrians was based primarily on other criteria (*supra*, n. 46 of this chapter), he seems to have gone further in the direction of identifying Jevons with Austrian value doctrine than appears to be justified by what Jevons said (Schumpeter, *op. cit.*, p. 922).

64 In his review, John Elliot Cairnes remarked, "He [Jevons] will have in the opinion of many, a better claim to be heard because his divergence from the old [classical] results is scarcely so great as he seems to imply . . . In fact, we have been struck by his general agreement with the writers to whose authority he declines, and rightly declines, to yield unreasoning obedience" ("Jevons on the Theory of Political Economy," *Saturday Review*, XXXII [November 11, 1871], 624). Both Jevons and a more favorable reviewer thought Cairnes' review an unfair one, based on a failure fully to comprehend Jevons' analysis (*Letters & Journal of W. Stanley Jevons*, p. 327; George H. Darwin, "The Theory of Exchange Value," *Fortnightly Review*, N.S. XVII [February 1, 1875], 247 ff.). Despite Cairnes' above statement, he interpreted Jevons as reviving the notion that value is explained exclusively by utility (*Some Leading Principles of Political Economy Newly Expounded*, New York [1874], p. 17). This was, perhaps, the seed that was responsible for the harvest of misinterpretation and the ultimate misplacement of Jevons. Darwin denounced this aspect (among others) of Cairnes' review, offering in substitution the view that Jevons reconciled the cost and utility doctrines on value (*op. cit.*, pp. 243–244, 250, 252). Jevons agreed with Darwin's interpretation of his work (*Letters & Journal of W. Stanley Jevons*, pp. 311, 327).

65 Alfred Marshall did not repeat Cairnes' mistake. In his review of Jevons' *Theory of Political Economy*, Marshall saw less than Cairnes to be critical of, but little more to be enthusiastic about. He characterized the difference between Jevons and Ricardo as "a difference in form." "We may, for instance, read far into the present book," Marshall continued, "without finding any important proposition which is new in substance" (*Memorials of Alfred Marshall*, ed. A. C. Pigou, London, 1925, p. 93). "We continually meet with old friends in new dresses . . ." (*ibid.*, p. 95). Jevons was not pleased with the negative tone of this

178

review, but he did not disagree with its characterization of his work as a supplement to, not a refutation of, classical theory (*Letters & Journal of W. Stanley Jevons*, p. 309).

66 *Memorials of Alfred Marshall*, p. 128, n. 3: "I hold that much of what Professor Jevons says about 'final utility' is contained, implicitly, at least, in Mill's account: but he has brought out with excellent distinctness many vital points connected with this notion, and has thereby made one of the most important of recent contributions to economics." No doubt Jevons was among those Marshall had in mind when he wrote the Preface to the first edition of his magnum opus (*Principles of Economics*, 8th edn., London, 1936 [reprint of 1920 edn.], p. v). Moreover, the rationalization of Jevonsonian and classical value theories in Marshall's *Principles* carried the marginal notation, "Jevons' position less different [from the classical] than it appears" (*ibid.*, p. 820).

67 *Memorials of Alfred Marshall*, pp. 99–100, 163.

68 One of the reasons for the general characterization of Jevons as an opponent of the classical school was the failure to recognize Jevons' distinction between short-run (market) and long-run (normal) values (Marshall, *Principles of Economics*, pp. 90 [n. 1], 817–821; Edwin R. A. Seligman, "Social Elements in the Theory of Value," *Quarterly Journal of Economics*, XV [May 1901], 337; Young, "Jevons' 'Theory of Political Economy,'" *op. cit.*, p. 586; Allyn A. Young, "Economics," *Encyclopaedia Britannica*, 14th edn., VII, London, 1929, 930; Gray, *op. cit.*, p. 344; Eckard, *op. cit.*, pp. 34–35, 84–85, 88–89). In contrast to the relative classical neglect of market value (*Memorials of Alfred Marshall*, p. 130), Jevons addressed himself to the task of providing the missing details in the classical treatment of short-run value. His *Theory of Political Economy* was primarily an explanation of *market*, not "natural," value. A difference in emphasis has been misinterpreted as a difference in kind.

69 *Supra*, pp. 28, 30, 58.

70 Jevons' work had neither the purpose nor the effect of replacing classical doctrine by a subjective theory of value, as the Austrians sought to do. He merely elaborated classical theory by means of a mathematical methodology. His utility theory resulted not from any peculiar psychological premises, but simply from a mathematical treatment of orthodox classical premises (Jevons, *Theory of Political Economy*, 1st edn., pp. vi–ix, 3–4, 11, 13–14, 24, 33–37, 56; cf. James Bonar, "The Austrian Economists and Their View of Value," *Quarterly Journal of Economics*, III [October 1888], 2–3). In the formative stage of the development of his utility theory, he described it as "entirely mathematical in principle," adding: "Nevertheless, *I obtain from the mathematical principles all the chief laws at which political economists have previously arrived,* only arranged in a series of definitions, axioms, and theories almost as rigorous and connected as if they were so many geometrical problems" (*Letters & Journal of W. Stanley Jevons*, p. 151 [italics mine]). See also: *Dictionary of Political Economy*, ed. Palgrave, I, 73; *ibid.*, II, 60–61, 477; Young, "Jevons' 'Theory of Political Economy,'" *op. cit.*, pp. 583–585; and Eckard, *op. cit.*, pp. 24–25, 88. Jevons' formulation of what was subsequently converted into the concept of marginal utility

179

was not inconsistent with classical value theory. He could, and probably would, have sided with John Stuart Mill against Samuel Bailey (cf. *supra*, Chap. III, n. 28).

The traditional identification of Jevons with the Austrian psychological school may have been due to a misinterpretation of his antipathy to John Stuart Mill's *Logic* as a general disagreement with the latter's *Principles of Political Economy* (see *Letters & Journal of W. Stanley Jevons*, pp. 331, 334, 409) and a mistaking of Jevons' criticism of classical *distribution* theory for dissent from classical *value* theory (see, for example, Jevons' "Preface to the Second Edition 1879," *The Theory of Political Economy*, 4th edn., pp. xliv–lii; and W. J. Ashley, "The Present Position of Political Economy in England," presidential address, August 1, 1907, before Section F, Economic Science and Statistics, *Report of the Seventy-Seventh Meeting of the British Association for the Advancement of Science*, London, 1908, pp. 583–584).

71 *Supra*, pp. 28, 30, 58.

72 The postclassical bifurcation of economic thought and the application of the resulting dualistic approach to Jevons was well illustrated by Henry Higgs' characterization of Jevons as "a pioneer in pure theory, [and] an authoritive writer upon such *practical matters* as Money and Banking, Currency and Finance . . . [etc.]" ("Editor's Preface" [to] *The Principles of Economics: A Fragment of a Treatise on the Industrial Mechanism of Society and Other Papers* by the late W. Stanley Jevons, London, 1905, p. v [italics mine]). In the same vein, Schumpeter said of Jevons, "During his life he was better known for his writings on *money and finance and other practical questions* of current interest . . . than for the performance that was to make him immortal" (*op. cit.*, pp. 825–826). Some reasons for the traditional "practical" orientation of monetary "theorists," which helps to explain the lag of monetary theory behind value and distribution theory, are given in Robert Giffen, "Fancy Monetary Standards," *Economic Journal*, II (September 1892), 465. In recent years there has been a tendency for monetary theory to be eclipsed by macroeconomic theory.

CHAPTER V

1 *Money, Banking, and National Income*, New York, 1956, p. 36.

2 *Loc. cit.* (last italics mine).

3 *Money and Banking*, 3rd edn., New York, 1956, p. 21. Georg Friedrich Knapp had earlier observed the tendency for the term "standard" to encompass the "system," but he acknowledged a dual meaning of "standard"—the "narrow sense" and the "larger sense" (*The State*

Theory of Money, trans. H. M. Lucas and J. Bonar, New York, 1924, p. 111).

4 *The Principles of Money and Banking,* I, New York, 1905, 275, 284.
5 *Money,* trans. Louis Infield, ed. T. E. Gregory, I, London, 1927, 34 ff.
6 *Ibid.,* II, 352.
7 *Ibid.,* pp. 363–364.
8 See, for example, D. S. Edwards, *A Critical Study of Gold Reserves and the Monetary Standard,* London, 1933, p. 72; and Royal Institute of International Affairs, *The Future of Monetary Policy,* London, 1935, pp. 18–19, 122–123.
9 *Supra,* pp. 3–4, 13.
10 League of Nations, *Report of the Gold Delegation of the Financial Committee,* Geneva, 1932, pp. 50, 70; L. L. B. Angas, *The Problems of the Foreign Exchanges,* New York, 1935, p. 133; George N. Halm, *Monetary Theory,* 2nd edn., Philadelphia, 1946, pp. 208, 209; R. G. Hawtrey, *The Gold Standard in Theory and Practice,* 5th edn., London, 1947, pp. 240, 246; Charles R. Whittlesey, *Principles and Practices of Money and Banking,* 2nd edn., New York, 1954, p. 305; International Monetary Fund, *International Reserves and Liquidity,* Washington, 1958, p. 3; A. C. L. Day, *Outline of Monetary Economics,* Oxford, 1957, pp. 438, 482, 493. The League of Nations Gold Delegation explicitly called the gold standard "a system of monetary and credit policy" (*op. cit.,* p. 9).
11 F. W. Taussig, "International Trade under Depreciated Paper. A Contribution to Theory," *Quarterly Journal of Economics,* XXXI (May 1917), 394, 396; R. G. Hawtrey, *The Art of Central Banking,* London, 1932, p. 264; Edwin Walter Kemmerer, *Money,* New York, 1935, p. 228.
12 Kemmerer, *op. cit.,* p. 94; J. Marvin Peterson, Delmas R. Cawthorne, and Philipp H. Lohman, *Money & Banking,* New York, 1941, pp. 703–704; Karl H. Niebyl, *Studies in the Classical Theories of Money,* New York, 1946, p. 9; Ray B. Westerfield, *Money, Credit and Banking,* 2nd edn., New York, 1947, pp. 42, 75, 138 ff.; J. W. Beyen, *Money in a Maelstrom,* New York, 1949, pp. 25, 30, 38, 181; Richard W. Lindholm, John J. Balles, and John M. Hunter, *Principles of Money and Banking,* New York, 1954, pp. 47–49; Day, *op. cit.,* p. 494; Rollin G. Thomas, *Our Modern Banking and Monetary System,* 3rd edn., Englewood Cliffs, 1957, p. 33; Lester V. Chandler, *The Economics of Money and Banking,* 3rd edn., New York, 1959, pp. 355–356, 359, 370–371; Lawrence Smith, *Money, Credit, and Public Policy,* Boston, 1959, pp. 187–188, 265.
13 Kemmerer, *op. cit.,* pp. 105, 108.
14 Erik T. H. Kjellstrom, *Managed Money,* New York, 1934, p. 96; Halm, *op. cit.,* p. 207; Beyen, *op. cit.,* p. 38; Chandler, *op. cit.,* p. 354.
15 Oliver M. W. Sprague, "The Working of the Gold Standard under Present Conditions," *Proceedings of the Academy of Political Science,* XIII (January 1930), 524; Angas, *op. cit.,* p. 258; Frank A. Southard, Jr., Philip F. Swart, Jr., and A. N. Gentes, *Foreign Exchange Practice and Policy,* New York, 1940, p. 150; Hawtrey, *The Gold Standard in Theory and Practice,* p. 240; Day, *op. cit.,* p. 439.
16 Lionel D. Edie, *Dollars,* New Haven, 1934, p. 65; Horace White, *Money*

181

and Banking, 6th edn., revised and enlarged by Charles S. Tippets and Lewis A. Froman, Boston, 1935, pp. 91–93; Chandler, *op. cit.,* 2nd edn., p. 89; Hiram L. Jome, *Principles of Money and Banking,* Homewood, Ill., 1957, p. 367.

17 F. W. Mueller attributed the drawbacks of the gold standard to "the mismanagement of the *system* rather than the deficiencies of the *standard*" (*Money and Banking,* New York, 1951, p. 778 [italics mine]). Although Mueller appears here to distinguish between the "standard" and the "system," he seems at other times to regard them as identical. He later stated, "All monetary *systems* are and must be managed to some extent" (*ibid., p.* 779 [italics mine]). But earlier in the same book he had said, "All *standards* are to some degree managed standards" (*ibid., p.* 56 [italics mine]). See also: Edwards, *op. cit.,* pp. v–vi, 93–96, 125, 146; Westerfield, *op. cit.,* p. 576; Chandler, *op. cit.,* 2nd edn., pp. 88–89; *ibid.,* 3rd edn., p. 371; and Ralph A. Young, "Tools and Processes of Monetary Policy," *United States Monetary Policy,* ed. Neil H. Jacoby, New York, 1958, pp. 14, 16, 33.

18 John Donaldson, *The Dollar: A Study of the "New" National and International Monetary System,* New York, 1937, p. 2 (italics mine): "It is unnecessary to deal here with all the different *monetary standards or systems* which in monetary history have been used or advocated, such as gold, gold exchange, silver, bimetallic, symmetallic, limping, fiat, tabular." See also Mueller, *op. cit.,* p. 48; Harold G. Moulton, *Principles of Money and Banking,* Chicago, 1916, p. 98; Leo Pasvolsky, *The Necessity for a Stable International Monetary Standard,* Paris [1933], p. 29; F. Cyril James, *The Economics of Money, Credit and Banking,* New York, 1930, p. 63; Royal Institute of International Affairs, *op. cit.,* pp. 205–206; Angas, *op. cit.,* p. 5; Thomas, *op. cit.,* pp. 33, 48–49; Day, *op. cit.,* pp. 438–439; Smith, *op. cit.,* pp. 136, 175–176, 279–280; and U. S. Treasury Department, *Facts about United States Money* [mimeographed release], Washington, 1960, p. 16.

19 Hanks and Stucki explained including the "entire monetary system" in their monetary standard concept (*supra,* n. 2 of this chapter): "If the standard is based on gold, then the monetary unit is defined in terms of gold, but *the monetary standard includes all credit moneys together with the rules, regulations, and practices* associated with the operation and administration of that standard" (*op. cit.,* p. 37 [italics mine]). Kent elaborates his definition of a monetary standard as a monetary system (*supra,* n. 3 of this chapter) in a similar fashion: "A monetary standard includes within its scope not only the designation of a standard of value, but also *all other regulations and arrangements of a monetary character* . . ." (*op. cit.,* p. 21). See also League of Nations, *Second Interim Report of the Gold Delegation of the Financial Committee,* Geneva, 1931, p. 9; William Howard Steiner, *Money and Banking,* New York, 1933, p. 97; and Day, *op. cit.,* pp. 438–439, 482 ff.

20 *Money,* 2nd edn., New York, 1929, p. 69.

21 Edie, *op. cit.,* p. 90; Sir Charles Morgan-Webb, *The Rise and Fall of the Gold Standard,* New York, 1934, p. 181.

22 Pasvolsky, *op. cit.,* p. 12; Steiner, *op. cit.,* pp. 75–76; George Francis Luthringer, Lester Vernon Chandler, and Denzel Cecil Cline, *Money,*

Credit and Finance, Boston, 1938, p. 179; Peterson, Cawthorne, and Lohman, *op. cit.,* p. 685; George Walter Woodworth, *The Monetary and Banking System,* New York, 1950, pp. 48, 56; Lindholm, Balles, and Hunter, *op. cit.,* pp. 48–49; Milton L. Stokes and Carl T. Arlt, *Money, Banking and the Financial System,* New York, 1955, pp. 99–100; Hanks and Stucki, *op. cit.,* pp. 38, 45.

23 See, for example, the last note immediately above, as well as almost any textbook that might be at hand.

24 See, for example, citations of Peterson, Cawthorne, and Lohman; Steiner; and Woodworth; *supra,* Chap. II, nn. 13, 14, and 20, respectively.

25 Stokes and Arlt, *op. cit.,* p. 98; Leland J. Pritchard, *Money and Banking,* Boston, 1958, p. 81.

26 Charles L. Prather once appeared to have made this distinction: "The gold standard exists wherever the value of money is kept equal to a fixed amount of gold. The *mechanism whereby this end is achieved* varies from country to country" (*Money and Banking,* Chicago, 1937, p. 35 [italics mine]). He then described the different characteristics (i.e., policies) of the various varieties of the gold standard (*ibid.,* p. 35). But the distinction was dropped from later editions, and Prather has apparently adopted the synonymous use of "standard" and "system" (*ibid.,* 7th edn., p. 23).

27 Eugene E. Agger, *Money and Banking Today,* New York, 1941, p. 47 (italics mine): "Gold has been pushed off the monetary throne and, *instead of dictating policy,* has itself become a mere *instrument of policy."* Frederick Soddy, who was advertised as the founder of the "New Economics" before Keynes' *General Theory* was published, added the following observation: "For over a century there simply has not been nearly enough gold and silver in the world for the requirements of a pure barter-currency [i.e., pure full-bodied money]. As regards actual present conditions in this country [England] and elsewhere, since the final breakdown of the 'gold standard,' we are now committed to an almost pure credit-debt money, but *instead of any definite standard we have entered upon a stage of 'monetary policy'* in which the price-level is modified deliberately from time to time by irresponsible judges according to what they conceive to be 'policy' . . ." (*The Role of Money,* London, 1934, p. 32 [italics mine]).

28 Edwards, *op. cit.,* pp. v–vi, 93–96 ff.

29 Conant, *op. cit.,* p. 275.

30 Chandler, *op. cit.,* 2nd edn., p. 88.

31 *Ibid.,* p. 106. The negative connotation of this species of the standard has been further highlighted by Chandler's simplification of the term to "inconvertible standard" (*ibid.,* 3rd edn., pp. 370–371).

32 After dividing monetary standards into two classes, *"commodity standards"* and *"fiat standards,"* Kent concedes "a fiat standard can be described [only] in a *negative sense* as a monetary system in which the value or purchasing power of the monetary unit is not kept equal to the value of a specific quantity of a particular commodity or of a group of commodities" (*op. cit.,* pp. 21–22). It is, therefore, understandable that, in contrast to his handling of "commodity standards," he attempts no

183

positive identification of "fiat standards," despite the plural form of the term.

33 Hanks and Stucki, *op. cit.,* p. 50. Commodity standards, which no longer exist, consume twelve and one-half pages of this book (*ibid.,* pp. 36–50), whereas domestically inconvertible standards, which now pervade the world, take up only two and one-third pages (*ibid.,* pp. 50–52). See also *supra,* n. 32 of this chapter.

34 Hanks and Stucki, *op. cit.,* p. 40.

35 The ambiguity of the term has not gone entirely unrecognized. See Chandler, *op. cit.,* 1st edn., pp. 76–77; and Smith, *op. cit.,* p. 188. Nor has it been rectified (*ibid.,* pp. 188–202).

36 John Maynard Keynes, *A Tract on Monetary Reform,* London, 1923, pp. 170 ff.

37 Ira B. Cross, *Domestic and Foreign Exchange,* New York, 1923, p. 468; Agger, *op. cit.,* pp. 200–201. According to this school of thought, convertible money is made legal tender by "law," whereas inconvertible media are made legal tender by government "decree or fiat" (Prather, *op. cit.,* 4th edn., p. 116).

38 Horace White, *Money and Banking,* 1st edn., p. 231; William A. Scott, *Money and Banking,* 6th edn., New York, 1926, pp. 81–82.

39 Edwards, *op. cit.,* pp. 66–67.

40 Kent, *op. cit.,* p. 22.

41 Chandler, *op. cit.,* 1st edn., pp. 76–77.

42 Almost any modern textbook will illustrate the point. See, for example, Lindholm, Balles, and Hunter, *op. cit.,* pp. 63–64.

43 Russell Donald Kilborne, *Principles of Money and Banking,* Chicago, 1927, p. 58; John T. Madden and Marcus Nadler, *The International Money Markets,* New York, 1935, p. 1.

44 Sir David Barbour, *The Standard of Value,* London, 1912, p. 150: "It has been the habit of Mono-metallists to ascribe all the economic gains since 1870 to maintenance of the single gold standard of England and other countries." Edward C. Towne concludes his *Story of Money,* New York, 1900, pp. 234–236, with a section entitled "Human Progress Means Gold [standard]."

45 Towne, *op. cit.,* p. 34: "A supreme service rendered by gold is that of a standard of honest reality in values. The intense scorn and hatred of gold which politicians have been known to feel or to affect, has been in great part the revolt of a sort of rascal libertinism against a veritable rule of honest reality. To speculative libertinism in politics, the dream of making that real which is not real, and finding thereby a short and easy way to success in life, finds gold as a standard of reality in value very much in its way." Subsequently, Towne quotes Senator Jones as saying, in 1874, "Gold is so exact a measure of human effort that when it is exclusively used as money it teaches us the very habit of honesty" (*ibid.,* p. 35). Relative to the use of gold as a "measure of value" as well as a medium of exchange, Hawtrey remarked, "Economists have at times been inclined to teach that this usage is so firmly established that it approximates to a moral principle, as if the use of a metallic currency were somehow essential to honest dealing" (*The Gold Standard in Theory and Practice,* p. 1). It was probably just such a reverential atti-

184

tude toward gold that accounted for Conant's reference to "the *perfected gold coin and check and deposit system of to-day* [1905]" (*op. cit.,* p. vi [italics mine]). Robertson noted a similar overzealousness among the financial leaders of London (*op. cit.,* p. 157).

46 Such was the common theme of the antibullionist and bimetallist heterodoxies (*supra,* Chap. II, nn. 99, 100, 108, 111). Keynes climaxed the conversion of old heterodoxy into a new orthodoxy even before the collapse of the interwar gold standard, which he had foreseen (*supra,* Chap. III, n. 60). "In truth," he remarked, "the gold standard is already a barbarous relic" (*op. cit.,* p. 172).

47 Jome, *op. cit.,* p. 359. See also Beyen, *op. cit.,* pp. 66–67.

48 Morgan-Webb, *op. cit.,* p. 20.

49 For one of the best reinterpretations, see Ervin P. Hexner, "The New Gold Standard," *Weltwirtschaftliches Archiv,* LXXXV (1960), 1–33.

50 Miroslav A. Kriz, *Gold in World Monetary Affairs Today,* Essays in International Finance No. 34, Princeton, 1959, pp. 29–30.

51 *Op. cit.,* 2nd edn., p. 88. Chandler explained that the various gold standards "bear only faint family resemblances" to each other (*loc. cit.*). Angas identified "seven different forms of the gold standard," including a "variable gold standard [variable price for gold]" (*op. cit.,* pp. 45–47).

52 Edie, *op. cit.,* p. 65 (italics mine): "The monetary standard of the future will doubtless include *some provision for gold, and therefore may be called a gold standard."* However, Edie conceded in the next sentence that "any such arrangement would have the *form but not the substance* of the traditional gold standard [italics mine]." See also: H. L. Puxley, *A Critique of the Gold Standard,* New York, 1933, pp. 168 ff.; W. A. L. Coulborn, *An Introduction to Money,* London, 1938, pp. 168, 171; Geoffrey Crowther, *An Outline of Money,* 2nd edn., London, 1948, pp. 289–290; W. J. Busschau, *The Measure of Gold,* [Johannesburg] South Africa, 1949, pp. 5–6 *et passim;* Edward S. Shaw, *Money, Income, and Monetary Policy,* Chicago, 1950, pp. 532–533; and Chandler, *op. cit.,* 3rd edn., pp. 356, 359–360. Apparently, "great changes can be made in our actual use of gold as money without causing even a ripple of excitement on the placid surface of our contented use for it. So long as there is *enough gold about it to justify retaining the name of gold standard,* we are satisfied" (M. K. Graham, *An Essay on Gold: Showing Its Defects as a Standard of Value and Suggesting a Substitute Therefor,* Dallas, 1925, p. 109 [italics mine]).

53 Donaldson, *op. cit.,* p. 141, n. 15: "It is unnecessary to point out here, despite the increasing questioning of the gold standard on theoretical grounds, and the so-called abandonment of that standard by practically all nations at the present time, that gold is still closely related to existing currency and credit systems, and remains a large factor in the national and international situation." "The phrase 'going off gold' does not mean the elimination of gold for monetary purposes. If so, one would have to speak of a demonetization of gold" (Peterson, Cawthorne, and Lohman, *op. cit.,* p. 701, n. 3). "But to suggest that the gold standard mechanism will not come back does not mean to say that gold could not perform an eminently useful role in a modern international payments system. The question is partly a terminological one. If we broaden the meaning of

185

the term 'gold standard mechanism' sufficiently, we may even apply it to a payments system in which gold parities are not unalterably fixed and in which the monetary gold serves predominantly or even exclusively as an asset of highest international liquidity (without being locked away by obsolete backing requirements)" (Halm, *op. cit.*, p. 207).

54 Calling such a scheme a "gold standard" amounts to confusing the gold standard with a gold *policy* designed for some particular purpose. For examples, see: Irving Fisher, *Stabilizing the Dollar*, New York, 1920, pp. xxxvii–xxxviii; Angas, *op. cit.*, p. 256; Crowther, *op. cit.*, pp. 289–290; Shaw, *op. cit.*, pp. 544–545; and Woodworth, *op. cit.*, p. 565. E. M. Bernstein recognized that such "management" of the gold standard constituted "in fact an abandonment of the gold standard" (*Money and the Economic System*, Chapel Hill, 1935, p. 455). Edward Jerome implied that the idea of a "fluctuating gold standard" was compatible with classical premises (*Governments and Money*, Boston, 1935, p. 118). During the suspension of specie payments in England, the classical school still regarded gold as the standard, but not as a fluctuating standard. They viewed gold as the standard for measuring the fluctuating value of the currency (Will E. Mason, "The Stereotypes of Classical Transfer Theory," *Journal of Political Economy*, LXIV (December 1956), 495–496, 503, n. 52).

55 Jome, *op. cit.*, p. 377 (italics mine):

It will be a long time before we restore the gold-coin standard, perhaps never . . . Internationally, however, the gold standard *in some form* will long be with us, though it is *doubtful whether sovereign countries will let the principles on which it is based work out freely or completely.* The emphasis on monetary and fiscal controls and influences indicates that *people may not be willing to rely too much on the operation of the gold standard.* They may often resort to even more arbitrary and direct measures.

56 See, for example, Beyen, *op. cit.*, pp. 38–39; and Smith, *op. cit.*, p. 258.

57 Kriz, *op. cit.*, p. 4. A few supply the reasoning for their choice, e.g.,

The term "The Gold Standard" embodies a fallacy, one of the most expensive fallacies which have deluded the world. It is the fallacy that there is one particular gold standard, and one only. There are *innumerable* possible gold standards. The assumption that the *widely divergent* standards of currency masquerading under the name of the gold standard are identical has recently brought the world to the verge of ruin . . . One of the main difficulties which the ordinary business man finds in understanding what is meant by 'the gold standard' is that the term comprises so many *contradictory meanings* (Morgan-Webb, *op. cit.*, pp. 11, 19 [italics mine]).

58 John A. Todd, *The Fall of Prices*, London, 1931, pp. 58–59; Prather, *op. cit.*, 1st edn., pp. 34, 82; Luthringer, Chandler, and Cline, *op. cit.*, pp. 179–180, n. 1; Stokes and Arlt, *op. cit.*, p. 101. Another writer has argued, on the other hand, that "the Standard of International Trade . . . is not adequately described as being either 'The Gold Standard' or *a* gold standard" (Jerome, *op. cit.*, p. 142).

59 Edwin Walter Kemmerer distinguished between "the genus *gold standard* and . . . its three principal species" (*Gold and the Gold Standard,* New York, 1944, p. 134): "the gold-coin standard" (*ibid.*, pp. 151–152), "the gold-exchange standard" (*ibid.*, pp. 152 ff.), and "the gold-bullion standard" (*ibid.*, pp. 174–176). Hanks and Stucki identified two additional

species, concluding that "there is no such thing as a single gold standard" (*op. cit.*, p. 37).

60 *Supra,* Chap. II, nn. 93–96; Chap. IV, n. 14.

61 *Supra,* Chap. II, n. 215.

62 This possibility appears to be implicit in Chandler, *op. cit.,* 3rd edn., pp. 355–356 (italics mine): "The term 'gold standard' is a generic term applied to a broad category of *monetary systems* that have one common characteristic: their monetary units are in *some sense* kept at a constant value in terms of gold. But this common characteristic should not be allowed to obscure the numerous and highly important differences among the *many systems that have been called gold standards."*

63 Our friends in the "hard sciences" tell us, moreover, that there is only one natural and stable isotope of the element, gold.

64 John Thom Holdsworth, *Money and Banking,* 6th edn., New York, 1937, p. 21 (italics mine): "The concensus of opinion among monetary economists is that the abandonment [of the gold standard] is only temporary and that 'there will be a general return to it, either in a *pure* or *modified* form.' " The quotation within the above quotation is from Walter E. Spahr, *Economic Principles and Problems,* 2nd edn., I, New York, 1934, 409. See also Holdsworth, *op. cit.,* pp. 110–111.

65 The "free gold standard" (i.e., the traditional, nineteenth-century gold-coin standard) has been called the only true "full-fledged gold standard" (Pritchard, *op. cit.,* p. 93).

66 Whittlesey, *op. cit.,* pp. 20, 24; Stokes and Arlt, *op. cit.,* pp. 139, 141, 144; Pritchard, *op. cit.,* p. 582.

67 Lauchlin Currie, *The Supply and Control of Money in the United States,* 2nd edn., Cambridge, Mass., 1935, p. 104.

68 Holdsworth, *op. cit.,* p. 162. On the contrary, Currie insisted, "To achieve a pure gold standard may require a high degree of conscious management of money" (*op. cit.,* pp. 104–105).

69 R. A. Lehfeldt, *Restoration of the World's Currencies,* London, 1923, pp. 56 ff.; R. A. Lehfeldt, *Controlling the Output of Gold,* London, 1926, pp. 3–5, 10, 20 ff.

70 Mueller, *op. cit.,* pp. 121, 128–129.

71 Pritchard, *op. cit.,* p. 97. See also Busschau, *op. cit.,* pp. 73–74.

72 Currie, *op. cit.,* p. 105; Busschau, *op. cit.,* p. 73; Whittlesey, *op. cit.,* p. 24.

73 Currie, *op. cit.,* p. 105. He adds that "there has been a general tendency in postwar [post World War I] years for gold standards to become more impure . . ." (*loc. cit.*).

74 *Monetary Nationalism and International Stability,* 2nd edn., London, 1939, p. 17.

75 Edwards refers to his suggested managed gold standard as "the reformed gold *system"* and as "a reformed 'gold' monetary *structure"* (*op. cit.,* pp. 125, 146 [italics mine]). See also von Hayek, *op. cit.,* p. 17.

76 Hanks and Stucki, *op. cit.,* p. 37.

77 For a brief account of this conceptual transformation, see Frank W. Fetter, "European Convertibility," *American Economic Review,* Papers and Proceedings, XLVII (May 1957), 588–589.

78 "In the sense in which the word convertible is generally used today—

absence of exchange control on current transactions—all European currencies were convertible within a few months, at most, after the Armistice of 1918, even though in the economic terminology of that day they may have been called inconvertible" (*ibid.*, p. 588). External inconvertibility lasted longer after World War II.
79 Chandler, *op. cit.*, 2nd edn., p. 89.
80 *Ibid.*, 3rd edn., p. 371.
81 Edwin Walter Kemmerer, *Kemmerer on Money*, Chicago, 1934, p. 5.
82 *Op. cit.*, p. 540.
83 *Money*, London, 1926, pp. 106–108. Resolution 11 of the Genoa Conference of 1922 had recommended restoration of the gold standard with regulation of credit such as to prevent "undue fluctuations in the purchasing power of gold" (*Papers Relating to International Economic Conference, Genoa, April–May, 1922*, London, 1922, p. 62).
84 Attention to historical examples alleged to demonstrate preservation of the fiction but not the substance of the gold standard never, unfortunately, resulted in a precise delineation of the distinction (Coulborn, *op. cit.*, p. 139; Chandler, *op. cit.*, 2nd edn., p. 141).
85 Federal Reserve Bank of New York, *Monthly Review*, XXXV (February 1953), 20; *Annual Report of the Secretary of the Treasury*, Washington, 1954, p. 290.
86 Almost any page of any issue of Walter E. Spahr's *Monetary Notes* will be found to support this interpretation. See also Agger, *op. cit.*, pp. 232–233.
87 Kent, *op. cit.*, p. 98. See also Whittlesey, *op. cit.*, pp. 197–198.
88 Holdsworth, *op. cit.*, p. 23; Pritchard, *op. cit.*, p. 582, n. 7; Eugene S. Klise, *Money and Banking*, 2nd edn., Cincinnati, 1959, p. 31.
89 Angas, *op. cit.*, pp. 256, 258.
90 Louis A. Rufener, *Money and Banking in the United States*, 2nd edn., Boston, 1936, p. 732.
91 Smith, *op. cit.*, p. 279.
92 *Ibid.*, p. 280.
93 For erstwhile acknowledgment of the irony, see Rufener, *op. cit.*, p. 732.
94 See, for example, *supra*, nn. 90 and 91 of this chapter.
95 Smith, *op. cit.*, pp. 175–176 (italics mine).

CHAPTER VI

1 One other possibility might be mentioned—interpreting the "monetary standard" as the immediate objective of monetary policy. Lester V. Chandler appears to intimate the conceivability of this alternative (*The Economics of Money and Banking*, 3rd edn., New York, 1959, p. 354) although he, himself, does not use it (*ibid.*, pp. 354, 366–367, 370–371). This construction would merely substitute the confounding of standards

188

and objectives for the more usual confusion of standards and policies. Moreover, this view is inconsistent with the current characterization of all monetary standards as more or less managed. One does not manage an objective. One manages the means of attaining the objective. Finally, how can one among many objectives be singled out as *the* immediate objective? If the criterion for this distinction in the levels of significance among objectives can be identified, perhaps it, rather than the objective, is the standard.

2 Raymond Mikesell suggested this interpretation to me about twenty years ago.

3 *Money and the Economic System,* Chapel Hill, 1935, pp. 43–44.

4 The significance of this qualification is not clear, but in the light of his subsequent discussion, it might be interpreted as a concession that the statement represents an oversimplification.

5 Bernstein, *op. cit.,* p. 44 (italics mine).

6 *Monetary Theory,* 2nd edn., Philadelphia, 1946, p. 103 (italics mine).

7 Cf. Bernstein, *op. cit.,* p. 44; and *supra,* Chap. II, nn. 215, 216. Strangely, Halm later revived the association of the value as well as the quantity with the monetary standard (*op. cit.,* p. 105).

8 Cf. *supra,* Chap. V, nn. 19–27. Moreover, this tendency toward confusion was reinforced by Halm's later substitution of "regulating" for "limiting" the money supply (*op. cit.,* p. 105; *Economics of Money and Banking,* Homewood, Ill., 1956, pp. 53–54). Also, Halm appears to contradict this interpretation of a monetary standard by subsequently implying that a monetary standard is the material constituting standard money: "The choice of the standard money and of the methods by which other kinds of money are related to standard money establishes what is broadly and vaguely referred to when we speak of a monetary standard, such as the gold standard, silver standard, bimetallic standard, or *inconvertible paper standard*" (*ibid.,* p. 54 [italics mine]). Inclusion of an "inconvertible paper standard" in this list of possible standards seems to preclude a rationalization of the two views of a monetary standard. This ambiguity persists in the revised edition (*ibid.,* 2nd edn., p. 59).

9 *Money, Income, and Monetary Policy,* Chicago, 1950, p. 17.

10 For an objective statement of the argument, see Leland J. Pritchard, *Money and Banking,* Boston, 1958, pp. 91–92. For repeated restatement and defense of this position, see any issue of Walter E. Spahr's *Monetary Notes,* e.g., XXI (September 1, 1961), 1–2.

11 *Money,* 2nd edn., New York, 1929, pp. 69–70 (italics mine). See also *ibid.,* p. 91. Robertson later abandoned this concept of the monetary standard when he recognized that the mechanism did not control the quantity of money as directly as had been thought (*Lectures on Economic Principles,* III, London, 1959, 14–15).

12 Lauchlin Currie, *The Supply and Control of Money in the United States,* 2nd edn., Cambridge, Mass., 1935, p. 104: "If the country is on a gold standard . . . the *ultimate determinant of the supply of money* is the extent of the gold holdings of the reserve banks [i.e., the central bank] in conjunction with the central bank reserve ratio." In the same vein, Raymond P. Kent observed, "Whatever may be said in criticism of the

189

gold standard, it nevertheless remains true that it places *maximum limits* upon the creation of hand-to-hand money and bank demand deposits, for if the promise of redemption is to be fulfilled, the volume of credit money cannot be permitted to exceed predetermined multiples of the gold reserves; otherwise, the reserves might be quickly exhausted through demands for redemption" (*Money and Banking,* 3rd edn., New York, 1956, p. 64 [italics mine]). See also: Joseph French Johnson, *Money and Currency,* Boston, 1905, pp. 177–178; Hans Glückstadt, *The Mechanism of the Credit Standard,* London, 1933, pp. ix, 84–85; Leo Pasvolsky, *The Necessity for a Stable International Monetary Standard,* Paris [1933], p. 39; R. G. Hawtrey, *The Gold Standard in Theory and Practice,* 5th edn., London, 1947, pp. 14–16; and Geoffrey Crowther, *An Outline of Money,* 2nd edn., London, 1948, pp. 16–17, 281, 286.

13 Willard E. Atkins, *Gold and Your Money,* New York, 1934, pp. 95–96.

14 J. Marvin Peterson, Delmas R. Cawthorne, and Philipp H. Lohman, *Money & Banking,* New York, 1941, p. 32 (italics mine): "Such [government credit] money is issued, not as a substitute for coin as is the case with representative money, but as a *means of expanding the money supply beyond the limits imposed by the available metallic base."* See also Alvin H. Hansen, *Monetary Theory and Fiscal Policy,* New York, 1949, p. 13.

15 Lesley C. Probyn, "The Maintenance by England of Her Single Gold Standard," *The Case for Monometallism* (two essays in favour of monometallism selected by Lord Farrer), London, 1895, p. 15:

> The confusion between the standard commodity and money is answerable for what is known as the quantitative theory. The basis of the argument brought in support of this theory by one of its most distinguished advocates is an imaginary system of money, whose value depends entirely on scarcity, without any commodity operating as a standard of value at all! And the same economist, so far from admitting that the commercial value of the commodity chosen as the standard must regulate its exchange value, uses "the merchandise [i.e., commodity] theory" as an expression of contempt! And so it is frequently insisted that the quantity of gold in existence is insufficient to enable that commodity to operate properly as a standard of value. With almost equal justice it might be said that the quantity of diamonds is too small for their value to be accurately denoted. The standard depends not on the quantity but on the value of the commodity selected.

The traditional monometallist emphasis on the distinction, rather than connection, between the standard and the quantity of money is also clearly illustrated by the following defense of the gold standard against the bimetallist attack: "Accordingly, the contention of some advocates of silver in 1896, that the proposed change from a one hundred-cent to a fifty-cent dollar [a footnote explains, "Measured in gold at the value it had in 1896"] was justified, as being a fair offset to the change which in fact had taken place from a one hundred to a two hundred-cent dollar [a footnote elucidates, "As measured in gold at the value it had in 1873"] was wholly fallacious. . . . The offset would not in any case have been a fair one, since the injury to creditors from an *instantaneous lowering of the standard* would be far greater than the injury to debtors from an equal change in the opposite direction *spread over many years"*

190

(F. M. Taylor, *Some Chapters on Money* [printed for the use of students in the University of Michigan], Ann Arbor, 1906, pp. 246–247 [first italics mine]). Bimetallism was generally viewed by its advocates—who reasoned from the quantity theory premise—as making gold *and* silver a "joint standard" (Sir David Salomons, *Reflections on the Connexion between Our Gold Standard and the Recent Monetary Vicissitudes; with Suggestions for the Addition of Silver as a Measure of Value*, London, 1843, pp. 76 ff.; Henri Cernuschi, *Bi-metallic Money*, London, 1876, p. 3 ("Author's Note"); Elijah Helm, *The Joint Standard*, London, 1894, p. 15; James H. Teller, *The Battle of Standards*, Chicago, 1896, p. 42). See also *supra*, Chap. II, n. 148. On the other hand, monometallists—oriented to the commodity-theory of money—interpreted bimetallism as purporting to maintain the conceptual or practical absurdity of a "double" or "alternating standard" of gold *or* silver (*supra*, Chap. II, nn. 145, 147). Nineteenth-century proponents of the gold standard minimized the significance of the quantity of money (stressed by bimetallists) and emphasized the direct depreciation of the standard which bimetallism represented in their view (Henry Farquhar, "A Stable Monetary Standard," *Sound Currency*, II [July 1, 1895], 500; J. Laurence Laughlin, *A New Exposition of Money, Credit and Prices*, I, Chicago, 1931, 454–455).

16 It was also a premise of the original Federal Reserve Act. Notice, for example, the stated purposes of the act and the rules for the eligibility of paper for discounting. "It was unfortunate that the main instrument of credit policy which was originally at the disposal of the Reserve banks, the discount policy, was misconstructed owing to the commercial loan theory" (Halm, *Economics of Money and Banking*, 1st edn., p. 245). Moreover, this "theory" continued to guide the Federal Reserve Board in its early years (Federal Reserve Board, *Annual Report, 1923*, p. 33; Lloyd W. Mints, *A History of Banking Theory in Great Britain and the United States*, Chicago, 1945, p. 265; Karl R. Bopp, "Three Decades of Federal Reserve Policy," *Federal Reserve Policy*, Board of Governors of the Federal Reserve System Postwar Economic Studies No. 8, Washington, 1947, pp. 2–3, 11–12; Shaw, *op. cit.*, pp. 426, 447). In 1945 devotees of this doctrine were believed to be still in the majority (Mints, *op. cit.*, p. 258).

17 J. Laurence Laughlin, *The Principles of Money*, New York, 1903, pp. 411–412; Charles Rist, *History of Monetary and Credit Theory*, trans. Jane Degras, New York, 1940, pp. 41, 197–198, 227–228, 238. "In short, convertibilty is not a mere device for limiting [the] quantity [of bank notes]; convertibility gives notes legal and economic qualities which [government] paper money [which Rist, in agreement with the banking school, categorically distinguished from bank notes] does not possess, and which are *independent of quantity*" (*ibid.*, p. 200). Those who recognized the essential similarity of the forms of bank credit extended the "real bills" doctrine to include bank deposits as well as notes: "Credit is thus converted into credit-money: the amount of credit money is easily adapted to circumstances, and *its limits are difficult to define*" (R. A. Lehfeldt, *Money*, London, 1926, p. 36).

18 *Supra*, n. 13 of this chapter.

191

19 Horace White, *Money and Banking*, 6th edn., revised and enlarged by Charles S. Tippets and Lewis A. Froman, Boston, 1935, p. 83 (italics mine): "The chief reason for selecting the gold-bullion standard is to *economize on gold.*" See also: Richard W. Lindholm, John J. Balles, and John M. Hunter, *Principles of Money and Banking*, New York, 1954, p. 54; and Chandler, *op. cit.*, pp. 358, 389.

20 [Ragnar Nurkse], *International Currency Experience* [Geneva], 1944, p. 7: "The gold exchange standard was successfully extended in the 'twenties, thus meeting a substantial part of the total demand for international currency in the form of foreign exchange reserves instead of gold." Milton L. Stokes and Carl T. Arlt, *Money, Banking and the Financial System*, New York, 1955, p. 127 (italics mine): "The widespread use of the gold exchange standard [in the 1920's] reflected the official recommendation of the Genoa Conference in 1922, the general desire *to economize on the use of gold and to free the domestic money supply from a direct relationship with the supply of gold,* and at the same time to acquire the advantages of stable exchange rates." See also: Norman Lombard, *Monetary Statesmanship*, New York, 1934, p. 21; George Walter Woodworth, *The Monetary and Banking System*, New York, 1950, p. 51; Lindholm, Balles, and Hunter, *op. cit.*, p. 55; A. C. L. Day, *Outline of Monetary Economics*, Oxford, 1957, p. 494; Rollin G. Thomas, *Our Modern Banking and Monetary System*, 3rd edn., Englewood Cliffs, 1957, p. 45; and Chandler, *op. cit.*, p. 361.

21 W. H. Steiner and Eli Shapiro, *Money and Banking*, 3rd edn., New York, 1953, p. 45; Stokes and Arlt, *op. cit.*, p. 7, n. 7; Chandler, *op. cit.*, pp. 358–359.

22 Stokes and Arlt, *op. cit.*, p. 8.

23 *The Works and Correspondence of David Ricardo*, ed. Piero Sraffa with the collaboration of M. H. Dobb, Cambridge, 1951–1955, I, 353–354; *ibid.*, IV, 59.

24 *Ibid.*, IV, 62–63; *ibid.*, I, 352, 356–357, 361; *supra*, pp. 53–56.

25 *Supra*, pp. 23–25, 53–55. Ricardo denied that the value of money could be meaningfully measured in terms of "commodities generally" (*The Works and Correspondence of David Ricardo*, IV, 59–62).

26 *Ibid.*, p. 64; *supra*, pp. 55–56. The persistence of the classical emphasis on the cost rather than the quantity of money was illustrated by W. Stanley Jevons, *Investigations in Currency and Finance*, ed. H. S. Foxwell, London, 1884, p. 318. See also Marion Bowley, *Nassau Senior and Classical Economics*, New York, 1949 (reprint of 1937 edn.), pp. 217, 220.

27 *The Works and Correspondence of David Ricardo*, IV, 55–58.

28 *Supra*, Chap. III, nn. 6, 7.

29 Bernstein, *op. cit.*, pp. 44–45; Crowther, *op. cit.*, p. 288, n. 1. The limitation to the volume of exchange media is referred to as an "ultimate" limitation (Currie, *op. cit.*, p. 104). Like other concepts of a monetary standard, this one is developed in early textbook chapters on "Metallic Standards" and utterly ignored in the later chapters on "Monetary Policy and Economic Stabilization" dealing with transitional problems such as cyclical fluctuations (Halm, *Monetary Theory*, pp. 103–107, 434 ff.).

30 [Joseph Harris], *An Essay upon Money and Coins, Part I: The Theories*

of Commerce, Money, and Exchanges, London, 1757, pp. 80–83; *The Works and Correspondence of David Ricardo,* I, 365; John Stuart Mill, *Principles of Political Economy,* ed. Sir W. J. Ashley, London, 1936 (reprint of 1909 edn.), p. 550; Jevons, *op. cit.,* pp. 318–319; Howard S. Ellis, *German Monetary Theory,* Cambridge, Mass., 1934, p. 113.

31 Mill, *op. cit.,* p. 551; Jevons, *op. cit.,* p. 319.

32 See Charles F. Dunbar, "Deposits as Currency," *Quarterly Journal of Economics,* I (July 1887), 402–403, 406, 409, 411; John Cummings, "Monetary Standards," *Journal of Political Economy,* II (June 1894), 350, 365–366; Willard Fisher, "Money and Credit Paper in the Modern Market," *Journal of Political Economy,* III (September 1895), 392–393; and Laughlin, *Principles of Money,* pp. 319–320. The "real bills" doctrine helped to preserve the disconnection between gold reserves and aggregate bank credit (Shaw, *op. cit.,* p. 426). The doctrine was so firmly entrenched in France that no reserve against deposits was required during her adherence to the traditional gold standard (Shaw, *op. cit.,* p. 472).

33 *Supra,* nn. 19, 20 of this chapter. See also League of Nations, *Interim Report of the Gold Delegation of the Financial Committee,* Geneva, 1930, pp. 18–20; *Second Interim Report of the Gold Delegation of the Financial Committee,* Geneva, 1931, p. 17; Feliks Mlynarski, *The Functioning of the Gold Standard,* Geneva, 1931, p. 74.

34 Lawrence Smith, *Money, Credit, and Public Policy,* Boston, 1959, p. 340: "Congress would be likely to lower gold reserve requirements in the face of a real credit shortage. They were lowered in 1945. Contemporary society shows no tendency to let technical monetary requirements, whether prudent or not, stand in the way of high employment, high incomes, and economic growth."

35 George William Dowrie, *Money and Banking,* New York, 1936, p. 85; Peterson, Cawthorne, and Lohman, *op. cit.,* p. 21.

36 The point has been made by Chandler (*op. cit.,* p. 367), among others.

37 The dual use of the term "standard" is clearly illustrated by Bernstein, *op. cit.,* p. 441 (italics mine): "In favor of the *tabular standard* it can be said that it would provide a means of securing stability in purchasing power in long term contracts; and that it would cause no forced disturbance in existing contracts, as would result from a *change in the monetary standard.*" See also *ibid.,* p. 502.

38 *Ibid.,* p. 57; Halm, *Monetary Theory,* p. 112.

39 Bernstein, *op. cit.,* pp. 52, 62.

40 Yet, writers who expressly interpret a monetary standard as the principle for limiting the money supply concede that the gold standard may be managed for other purposes. See, for example, Bernstein, *op. cit.,* p. 58; Halm, *Monetary Theory,* pp. 203–204, 207–208; and Shaw, *op. cit.,* pp. 17–19, 531–533, 544–545. Halm appears to recognize the incongruity: "Even a gold-standard system today would be a highly managed affair. *The growing tendency to manage the money supply independently of the supply of gold violates the original philosophy of the gold standard* and explains why the relics of the gold standard which are still found in modern monetary systems are so incongruous" (*Economics of Money and Banking,* 1st edn., p. 55 [italics mine]). Moreover, in his suggested

reinterpretation he changed "gold *standard* mechanism" to "gold-*flow* mechanism" (*ibid.*, p. 471 [italics mine]). The difficulty appears to be a confusion of gold policies with the gold standard (see, for example, Shaw, *op. cit.*, pp. 544–545) or a more general confusion of monetary policies with monetary standards (*supra*, pp. 66–67). The latter confusion is illustrated by the statement, "Different monetary standards are fundamentally nothing but different *methods* of regulating the supply of money . . ." (Halm, *Economics of Money and Banking*, 1st edn., pp. 53–54). "Method" means policy, not principle or standard. In his earlier book, Halm had distinguished just two "methods" of "limiting" the money supply: the automatic method of metallic standards and the discretionary method of managed standards (*Monetary Theory*, pp. 115–116). It has already been pointed out that the so-called "automatic operation" of the gold standard refers not to the standard, but to the policies necessary (though not sufficient) to implement the gold standard in fact as well as in law (*supra*, p. 66). The discretionary method of determining monetary policies means, simply, that there is no standard for determination of monetary policies. Halm is therefore comparing policies, not standards, and the concept of the standard becomes obscured in the process (*Monetary Theory*, pp. 203–204, 207). Shaw appears actually to identify the monetary standard as an optional *policy* (alternative to central-bank and fiscal policy) for regulation of the money supply (see references to Shaw in this note and in n. 9 of this chapter).

41 It does not appear to have been taken seriously by even those who professed it as they implicitly returned to a more traditional view of the monetary standard. Their discussions of specific standards often imply the classical concept of the standard as the material constituting the standard of value (Bernstein, *op. cit.*, pp. 46, 58–59, 439; Shaw, *op. cit.*, pp. 531, 637; Halm, *Economics of Money and Banking*, 1st edn., p. 54).

42 Glückstadt, *op. cit.*, p. ix.

43 I am indebted to the late Frank D. Graham for this suggestion. In a publication subsequent to our discussion of the subject, he implicitly confirmed my interpretation of his earlier observations: "A so-called managed gold standard is, however, not a gold standard at all, since, by the very fact of management, *the criterion or referent, the standard, by which the supply of money has been determined,* is subtly changed" (*Fundamentals of International Monetary Policy*, Monetary Standards Inquiry, No. 3, New York, 1943, p. 17).

44 Cf. *supra*, pp. 17–20, 27–30, 34–38, 66–67.

45 "The reasons which once led to the adoption as currency of a commodity of intrinsic value . . . have been eliminated by the development of adequate banking machinery" (Anatol Murad, *The Paradox of a Metal Standard*, Washington, 1939, p. 173). Much of the difficulty with the concept of a monetary standard has stemmed from its failure to reflect the increasingly abstract nature of money (e.g., Pritchard, *op. cit.*, pp. 99–100; Ralph A. Young, "Tools and Processes of Monetary Policy," *United States Monetary Policy*, ed. Neil H. Jacoby, New York, 1958, pp. 14, 16, 33). Clinging to the concrete commodity concept of a monetary standard, John Thom Holdsworth concluded that "nationaliza-

194

tion of gold and silver" practically precluded "any standard at all" (*Money and Banking*, 6th edn., New York, 1937, p. 31). See also *infra*, n. 174 of this chapter.

46 The interest-rate standard or "government-bond standard," which appeared to be the standard, if anything did, from the beginning of World War II to 1951 (Kenneth E. Boulding, *Principles of Economic Policy*, Englewood Cliffs, 1958, p. 226), may qualify as such an addition. Although there is little authoritative sympathy with such a criterion of monetary policy (Shaw, *op. cit.*, pp. 403–404), interest in it was not entirely destroyed by the accord of 1951 (Charles R. Whittlesey, *Principles and Practices of Money and Banking*, 2nd edn., New York, 1954, p. 398).

47 This is simply the monetary application of the term "policy," which means "a course or line of action" (William J. Baumol and Lester V. Chandler, *Economic Processes and Policies*, New York, 1954, p. 9).

48 Moreover, it no longer makes any sense to distinguish fiscal policy and debt management policy *from* "monetary policy." Due to the relative size of the public sector of even private enterprise economies in the modern world, both fiscal and debt management policies have at least as much impact on the quantity and velocity of money today as what is called "monetary policy" had in the 1920's. Consequently, the former are as much monetary policies as the latter. The time has come to extend the coverage of the term "monetary policy" to include fiscal and debt management policies, as well as central-bank policy to which the term has been traditionally limited (Stokes and Arlt, *op. cit.*, p. 498; Pritchard, *op. cit.*, p. 489; Smith, *op. cit.*, pp. 573–574, 578–579). Therefore— instead of distinguishing fiscal policy and debt-management policies *from* monetary policy—fiscal, debt-management, and central bank policies should all be identified as species *of* monetary policy.

49 E. F. M. Durbin, *The Problem of Credit Policy*, London, 1935, pp. 25– 26; Boulding, *op. cit.*, p. 17.

50 J. W. Beyen, *Money in a Maelstrom*, New York, 1949, pp. 37–38, 154.

51 Henry C. Wallich, "Postwar United States Monetary Policy Appraised," *United States Monetary Policy*, p. 102. Other cases in point abound, e.g., "Price Stabilization" and "A *Policy* of Neutral Money" are listed as "Objectives of Monetary Policy" (Halm, *Economics of Money and Banking*, 1st edn., pp. 120–121). In other words, a "monetary policy" is an "objective of monetary policy"!

52 Under the heading, "Some Basic Objectives of Monetary Policy," we find the following statement: "This list is not inclusive of all the *objectives* which have been suggested as *guides* for monetary policy" (J. Whitney Hanks and Roland Stucki, *Money, Banking, and National Income*, New York, 1956, p. 467 [italics mine]). For another synonymous use of "guide" and "goal" see: Whittlesey, *op. cit.*, p. 364.

53 In his "Appraisal of the Stable-Price-Level Standard," Woodworth said, "The conclusion seems clear that pursuit of the *price-stability objective* alone is unwise . . . Nevertheless . . . it should be regarded as a legitimate *goal*. It should be one of the *guiding factors*, but by no means the only *criterion, of monetary policy*" (*op. cit.*, pp. 62, 64 [italics

195

mine]). "There is a strong tradition in economics in favor of letting monetary and fiscal policy be *guided* strictly *by a goal* of price level stabilization. Following this *rule* [a "rule" is clearly a "guide" rather than a "goal"] would mean taking measures to expand the stock of cash (and perhaps, also, to reduce the demand for cash assets) in case prices begin to fall, and taking contractional measures in case prices began to rise" (Albert Gailord Hart, *Money, Debt, and Economic Activity,* 2nd edn., New York, 1953, p. 411 [italics mine]). Hart seems to be groping towards my concept of a monetary standard, but confusion results from his failure to complete the transition. We are not *guided by* an objective; we are *guided to* an objective by a referent. A pilot is guided by the stars to his earthly goal beyond the horizon. Imagine the consequences of his mistaking the guide for the goal!

54 Whittlesey, *op. cit.,* pp. 561–562; Stokes and Arlt, *op. cit.,* pp. 499–505.

55 Stokes and Arlt, *loc. cit.* The "gold movements" in the heyday of the gold standard, for instance, are referred to as "guides to monetary policy" (*ibid.,* p. 500).

56 Changes in the United States monetary standard since March 1933 have been examined under the headings "Gold Policy" and "Results of Gold Policy" (F. W. Mueller, *Money and Banking,* New York, 1951, pp. 121, 139).

57 Frank D. Graham and Charles H. Seaver, for example, pointed out that the gold standard *was* the identification of money with gold and that the standard was *maintained by a policy* of free coinage or unrestricted Treasury purchases and sales of gold at a fixed price (*Money, What It Is and What It Does,* New York, 1936, pp. 43–45). A more recent instance of such exceptional discrimination is found in the following statement: "A silver standard is in its structure essentially like the gold standard. The monetary unit is defined as a fixed amount of silver, and all forms of money are maintained at a parity with the defined quantity of silver. The *methods of maintaining parity* are the same, involving the unobstructed flow of silver bullion into the monetary system, the redemption of all forms of money in silver at the established rate, and the free movement of silver in and out of a country" (Smith, *op. cit.,* p. 159 [italics mine]). Generally speaking, modern writers appear to be unaware of the formerly recognized distinction between the monetary standard and the "necessary regulations" associated with it. Evidence of the earlier perspicacity is found in the *Dictionary of Political Economy,* ed. R. H. Inglis Palgrave, London, 1894–1899, II, 220. For the conventional failure to differentiate between the monetary standard and the policies required for its maintenance, see: Woodworth, *op. cit.,* p. 48; Stokes and Arlt, *op. cit.,* p. 107; and Kent, *op. cit.,* pp. 21, 66–67. Woodworth regards "the choice of a monetary standard" as merely a "part of monetary policy" (*op. cit.,* p. 564).

58 The same thing—e.g., a stable price level, interest rate, money supply, etc.—is often alternatively labeled by the same author as an objective of monetary policy, a criterion or guide for monetary policy, or, simply, a monetary policy (Lombard, *op. cit.,* pp. 16–17, 23–24, 27, 32, 143–144; Chandler, *op. cit.,* 2nd edn., pp. 716, 718, 720; Thomas, *op. cit.,*

2nd edn., pp. 741, 745, 753–754; *ibid.*, 3rd edn., pp. 434–435, 437, 439, 443, 449). See also Halm, *Economics of Money and Banking,* 1st edn., pp. 55, 120–121, 247; and Per Jacobsson, *Towards a Modern Monetary Standard,* The Stamp Memorial Lecture, London, 1959, pp. 8, 12–30.

59 Henry C. Simons, "Rules Versus Authorities in Monetary Policy," *Readings in Monetary Theory,* ed. Friedrich A. Lutz and Lloyd W. Mints, New York, 1951, pp. 337 ff.

60 Joseph Stagg Lawrence, *Stabilization of Prices,* New York, 1928, p. 3.

61 *Lombard Street,* New York, 1887, p. 20. "Even the best monetary system is not a machine which functions quite automatically. In fact, every monetary system, if it is to fulfill the purposes for which it is intended, requires an active controlling force to regulate it continually and intelligently" (Karl Helfferich, *Money,* trans. Louis Infield, ed. T. E. Gregory, II, London, 1927, 407).

62 Henry Thornton, *An Enquiry into the Nature and Effects of the Paper Credit of Great Britain* (1802), ed. F. A. von Hayek, New York, 1939, pp. 123, 127, 208–211, 230 ff., *et passim.* Bagehot, *op. cit.,* p. 35: "In consequence all our credit system depends on the Bank of England for its security. On the wisdom of the directors of that one Joint Stock Company, it depends whether *England shall be solvent or insolvent.* This may seem too strong, but it is not." Francis Horner had expressed some misgivings about this transfer of public responsibility to a private corporation ("Thornton on the Paper Credit of Great Britain," *Edinburgh Review,* I [October 1802], 196).

63 Bagehot, *op. cit.,* p. 20.

64 G. L. Bach, "Monetary-Fiscal Policy Reconsidered," *Readings in Fiscal Policy,* ed. Arthur Smithies and J. Keith Butters, Homewood, Ill., 1955, p. 253 (italics mine). For further confirmation of this proposition see: Paul A. Samuelson, "Principles and Rules in Modern Fiscal Policy: A Neo-Classical Reformulation," *Money, Trade, and Economic Growth,* [essays] in Honor of John Henry Williams, New York, 1951, pp. 162–166; and Walter W. Heller, "CED's Stabilizing Budget Policy after Ten Years," *American Economic Review,* XLVII (September 1957), 639–640.

65 The term "managed currency" has been called a misnomer: "All currency is managed currency, though mostly mismanaged" (Carl Strover, *Monetary Progress,* Chicago, 1937, p. 225).

66 This was implicitly conceded by the defense of the gold standard contained in the *Report of the Monetary Commission of the Indianapolis Convention,* ed. J. Laurence Laughlin, Chicago, 1898, pp. 21 ff. A later defender of the gold standard observed, "There was thus, in the operation of the pre-war [World War I] gold standard, no real automatism, but a good deal of what in more recent times has become known as 'monetary management' " (Pasvolsky, *op. cit.,* p. 18). See also: Atkins, *op. cit.,* pp. 149–150; Erik T. H. Kjellstrom, *Managed Money,* New York, 1934, p. 34; Lombard, *op. cit.,* pp. 155–156; L. L. B. Angas, *The Problems of the Foreign Exchanges,* New York, 1935, p. 177; Bernstein, *op. cit.,* pp. 45–46, 61; and Nurkse, *op. cit.,* p. 88.

197

67 Ray B. Westerfield, *Money, Credit and Banking,* 2nd edn., New York, 1947, p. 89; Kent, *op. cit.,* p. 31; Ludwig von Mises, *The Theory of Money and Credit,* 2nd edn., trans. H. E. Batson, New Haven, 1953, p. 416.

68 *Supra,* p. 66. "The principles of the gold standard, as it began to operate in the latter half of the 19th century, were arrived at after much painful experience, and much hard work by many able men. However, once the basic principles had been grasped, they appeared almost self-evident and people even began talking about 'the automatic gold standard' " (Jacobsson, *op. cit.,* p. 5). For examples of such talk see: F. Cyril James, *The Economics of Money, Credit and Banking,* New York, 1930, p. 90; Edwin Walter Kemmerer, *Gold and the Gold Standard,* New York, 1944, p. 49; and Hiram L. Jome, *Principles of Money and Banking,* Homewood, Ill., 1957, p. 367. Writers less enamored of the gold standard have implicitly recognized that its alleged automaticity related to the monetary *system* rather than the standard: "Since no *system* has yet been found which could be fully automatic in its *operation,* the difference between metallic standards and inconvertible paper standards is not quite so important as it may seem. Even a *gold-standard system* today would be a highly managed affair" (Halm, *Economics of Money and Banking,* 2nd edn., p. 60 [italics mine]). Whittlesey recognized the central bank operations originally designed to facilitate rather than resist the "automatic forces" as "a deviation from strict principles of an automatic monetary *system*" (*op. cit.,* p. 307 [italics mine]). Even Kemmerer said it was the "system" which was "automatic" (*op. cit.,* p. 49).

69 *Supra,* pp. 66–67.

70 *Loc. cit.*

71 "It was not, in any accurate sense of the term, an *automatic* foreign exchange *policy,* but the management responsibilities which it placed upon the banking authorities were relatively simple, provided the authorities would follow wherever the policy led" (Frank A. Southard, Jr., Philip F. Swart, Jr., and A. N. Gentes, *Foreign Exchange Practice and Policy,* New York, 1940, p. 165 [second italics mine]). "Monetary policies have always, even under the gold standard, been managed in some degree" (J. B. Condliffe, *The Reconstruction of World Trade,* New York, 1940, p. 236).

72 Recognition of the past and present lack of automaticity spread in the twentieth century: "The idea that the gold standard today is, or can be, 'automatic' is wrong. As we have seen, gold is now far more influenced by banking policy than by its use in the arts for dentistry, gilding picture frames or making gold watches, rings and jewelry" (Irving Fisher, *The Money Illusion,* New York, 1928, p. 157). "In using the expression, a managed currency, it must not be forgotten that the gold standard, even in its purest form, the pre-war gold circulation standard, was always a *managed system;* the post-war gold bullion standard was more clearly, quite obviously, a managed system. The difference between a gold standard currency and a free currency is not the absence or presence of *management in the system;* management, in the sense of regulation,

there is always; the difference lies in the object or purpose of the management . . ." (W. A. L. Coulborn, *An Introduction to Money*, London, 1938, p. 144 [italics mine]). See also: Holdsworth, *op. cit.*, pp. 42–43; Eugene E. Agger, *Money and Banking Today*, New York, 1941, p. 621; Chandler, *op. cit.*, 2nd edn., pp. 97–98, 165; *ibid.*, 3rd edn., pp. 365–367; and *supra*, Chap. V, n. 17.

73 R. G. Hawtrey has observed, "With a fully developed credit system the currency must be 'managed'; it *cannot* be automatic" ("Keynes: A Tract on Monetary Reform," *Economic Journal*, XXXIV [June 1924], 234).

74 *A Treatise on Money*, I, London, 1930, 16. "This growth of conscious control has doubtless been an incidental outgrowth of the general evolution of credit and currency as the dominant portions of the nation's total means of payment" (Lionel D. Edie, *Money, Bank Credit, and Prices*, New York, 1928, p. 61). "Since the issue of bank-notes by authorized banks, and since the development of deposit banking with chequing accounts, the operation of the gold standard has never been entirely automatic . . ." (H. F. Fraser, *Great Britain and the Gold Standard*, London, 1933, p. 21). "No currency system which involves the use of credit has been, or will be, 'automatic' in any but the most superficial sense . . ." (Royal Institute of International Affairs, *The Future of Monetary Policy*, London, 1935, p. 205). "Of course, even under the gold standard the internal paper notes and bank-credit money of a country were 'managed,' but the management was dictated from without by external forces rather than from within by a definite political or economic policy" (Angas, *op. cit.*, pp. 54–55). "The value of the standard metal in a modern monometallic system depends at least as much on monetary management as on the monetary supply of the standard metal. This is so because the value of money is determined partly by its quantity and because the quantity of money in circulation depends on the whole monetary system, that is, on the superstructure of money which can be based on the metal reserve" (Halm, *Monetary Theory*, p. 106). Even Spahr acknowledges that the existence of credit money reqires monetary management under any monetary standard, including the traditional, unrestricted gold-coin standard that he would like to see restored (*Monetary Notes*, XIX [September 1, 1959], 2). See also: John Maynard Keynes, "The Return to the Gold Standard," *Essays in Persuasion*, New York, 1932, pp. 184–185; H. L. Puxley, *A Critique of the Gold Standard*, New York, 1933, pp. 52–53; Ellis, *op. cit.*, p. 121; Dowrie, *op. cit.*, p. 108; and W. J. Busschau, *The Measure of Gold*, [Johannesburg] South Africa, 1949, p. 10.

75 Royal Institute of International Affairs, *op. cit.*, p. 124: "In fact, to be on the gold standard meant that, although the various national currencies were not exclusively composed of the precious metals, yet they were to be managed as if they were. . . . The preservation of the system clearly depended upon the policies of Central Banks reflecting such variations as would have occurred under an automatic system of purely metallic currencies with no other types of money."

76 Continental countries, too, generally had no specified gold cover or reserves against bank deposits. "The increased use of cheques and bank transfers deprived the minimum gold cover [for bank notes] of its

restrictive influence on the monetary circulation" (Beyen, *op. cit.*, p. 31).

77 Keynes, *Treatise on Money*, I, 17.
78 Dowrie, *op. cit.*, p. 492; F. A. von Hayek, *Monetary Nationalism and International Stability*, 2nd edn., London, 1939, p. 76.
79 William Howard Steiner, *Money and Banking*, New York, 1933, p. 94 (italics mine): "Central banking was relied upon to achieve greater *stability and elasticity* than gold unaided could achieve."
80 Busschau, a proponent of the gold standard, affirmed that "while in a world without credit prices would vary in relation to the stock of commodity money, *in a world with credit disciplinary measures are necessary to make the gold standard work*" (*op. cit.*, p. 78 [italics mine]). "However, the limited degree of management in the pre-war gold standard does not make it inappropriate to designate such a monetary *system* an 'automatic' gold *standard*. It was automatic in that *control was exercised with the strictly limited objective of making the gold standard work* more smoothly and effectively. Fundamentally, the quantity of money was determined by the size of the monetary gold stock, and *management was directed towards facilitating appropriate adjustments in the volume of money as variations in the size of monetary gold stocks occurred*" (George Francis Luthringer, Lester Vernon Chandler, and Denzel Cecil Cline, *Money, Credit and Finance*, Boston, 1938, p. 211 [italics mine]). Relative to the British gold standard of 1925–1931, Beyen remarked: "Though gold movements no longer had an automatic effect on the credit structure they continued to define the policy of the monetary authorities. Under such a system it was only natural that the guardian of monetary policy should be the Central Bank and not the Government: if the policy of the government threatened to endanger the external value of the currency the Central Bank had to have the power to oppose that policy" (*op. cit.*, p. 33). See also, *The Works and Correspondence of David Ricardo*, III, 75–76; John Leslie Foster, *An Essay on the Principles of Commercial Exchanges*, London, 1804, pp. 166–167; R. G. Hawtrey, *The Art of Central Banking*, London, 1932, pp. 177–179; Fraser, *op. cit.*, p. 21; and Bernstein, *op. cit.*, p. 61.
81 Whittlesey, *op. cit.*, p. 304. According to his son, John Charles Herries believed the crisis of 1847 was "intensified, if not caused, by the restrictions imposed upon the Bank [of England] by the Act of 1844 . . . He could not be persuaded that a law was a good one which involved the necessity of its own periodic violation by the assumption of a 'dispensing power' on the part of the Crown" (Edward Herries, *Memoir of the Public Life of the Right Hon. John Charles Herries in the Reigns of George III., George IV., William IV. and Victoria*, II, London, 1880, 231). See also Thornton, *op. cit.*, pp. 104, 112, 124, 126; and Bagehot, *op. cit.*, p. 28.
82 *The Art of Central Banking*, p. 189 (italics mine).
83 *Ibid.*, p. 259. Mints implies that Wheatley and Ricardo would have agreed with the substance of Hawtrey's statement (*op. cit.*, p. 55, n. 50).
84 Thornton, *op. cit.*, pp. 114, 128, 259.
85 Mints, *op. cit.*, p. 191.
86 Mill, *op. cit.*, pp. 531–536, 654–655.

87 Will E. Mason, "The Stereotypes of Classical Transfer Theory," *Journal of Political Economy*, LXIV (December 1956), 492–493, 499.
88 *Ibid.*, p. 501, n. 44; Thornton, *op. cit.*, pp. 122, 152–153, 226–227.
89 Mill, *op. cit.*, pp. 665 ff.; Mason, *op. cit.*, p. 500, n. 44.
90 Mints, *op. cit.*, pp. 120–121.
91 Von Hayek, *op. cit.*, pp. 76–78.
92 Mints, *op. cit.*, p. 193 (italics mine).
93 Nineteenth-century reserve requirements generally applied only to notes, not to deposits; and they varied from a one hundred per cent gold reserve in Peru, through fixed fractional percentages or gold cover for notes in excess of a fixed fiduciary issue, to no gold reserve for gold-exchange-standard countries (John T. Madden and Marcus Nadler, *The International Money Markets*, New York, 1935, p. 1, n. 1). See also Mlynarski, *op. cit.*, p. 5.
94 Hawtrey, *The Art of Central Banking*, pp. 195–199.
95 Edward Jerome, *Governments and Money*, Boston, 1935, p. 127 (italics mine): "As to the principles upon which the monetary institutions of Great Britain operated from 1819 until 1844, it is to be observed that one was that of the gold reserve,—although there was *no statutory requirement in that respect. . . .*" A contemporary observer remarked, "It does not appear that the circulation has ever been regulated on that principle" (Salomons, *op. cit.*, p. xii). Likewise, "no condition as to metallic reserve" was imposed on the Bank of France (Hawtrey, *The Art of Central Banking*, p. 197). See also Thornton, *op. cit.*, pp. 110–111.
96 Hawtrey, *The Art of Central Banking*, p. 196.
97 *Loc. cit.*
98 *Loc. cit.*
99 Westerfield, *op. cit.*, p. 84.
100 Whittlesey, *op. cit.*, p. 305.
101 *Ibid.*, pp. 304–305.
102 The original Federal Reserve Act specified a gold reserve for only Federal Reserve notes in circulation. Reserves against Federal Reserve deposits could be either gold *or lawful money* (*The Statutes at Large of the United States of America*, XXXVIII, Part 1, Washington, 1915, 266). The amendment of 1945 designated a twenty-five per cent minimum reserve of gold certificates against both notes and deposits (*ibid.*, LIX, Part 1, 237).
103 Federal Reserve Board, *Annual Report, 1923*, pp. 30 ff.; *Federal Reserve Bulletin*, XXIII (September 1937), 827–828. See also Mints, *op. cit.*, p. 267.
104 Keynes, *Treatise on Money*, I, 17.
105 Day, *op. cit.*, pp. 440–441.
106 *Ibid.*, p. 441. See also: *ibid.*, p. 483; Southard, Swart, and Gentes, *op. cit.*, pp. 165–166; Mints, *op. cit.*, pp. 187–189; and Stokes and Arlt, *op. cit.*, p. 500.
107 Mints, *op. cit.*, p. 85.
108 *The Theory of the Foreign Exchanges*, 14th edn., London, 1890, pp. 133–134.
109 Coulborn, *op. cit.*, pp. 136–139; Mlynarski, *op. cit.*, pp. 15–16.

110 Mlynarski, *loc. cit.*
111 *Infra*, n. 129 of this chapter.
112 Mints, *op. cit.*, p. 276; Edie, *op. cit.*, p. 61.
113 Beyen, *op. cit.*, p. 31.
114 William Ward, *On Monetary Derangements*, London, 1840, pp. 29, 37; Edie, *op. cit.*, p. 52; Hawtrey, *The Art of Central Banking*, p. 188; Atkins, *op. cit.*, pp. 150–151; Edwin Walter Kemmerer, *Kemmerer on Money*, Chicago, 1934, pp. 4–5; Whittlesey, *op. cit.*, p. 307.
115 Mints, *op. cit.*, pp. 191–196; Whittlesey, *op. cit.*, pp. 307–308.
116 Keynes argued that the British Act of 1925 "established . . . a pure Managed Money," which was not "rigidly linked in quantity to the supply of 'commodity' money" (*Treatise on Money*, I, 20).
117 John A. Todd, *The Fall of Prices*, London, 1931, p. 58; Charles O. Hardy, *Is There Enough Gold?* Washington, 1936, pp. 5–6. See also *supra*, nn. 19, 20, and 33 of this chapter.
118 Stokes and Arlt, *op. cit.*, p. 104.
119 Chandler, *op. cit.*, 3rd edn., p. 358.
120 *Loc. cit.* (italics mine).
121 *Loc. cit.*
122 Hans Glückstadt, *Theory of the Credit Standard*, London, 1932, pp. 33–35; Edwin Walter Kemmerer, *Money*, New York, 1935, pp. 154 ff.; Madden and Nadler, *op. cit.*, p. 7; Beyen, *op. cit.*, pp. 31–32.
123 Beyen, *op. cit.*, p. 32.
124 *Loc. cit.* (italics mine). "But their freedom of policy remained subordinated to the ulterior aim of keeping the currency in line with other currencies. . . . In using this power they could not go *too* far" (*ibid.*, pp. 32–33 [italics mine]).
125 Chandler, *op. cit.*, 3rd edn., pp. 358–359.
126 Todd, *op. cit.*, p. 19.
127 Fraser, *op. cit.*, p. 26: "It is only in these post-War days that the world has come to realize the debt it owes to Great Britain for the successful working of the gold standard throughout the nineteenth century and up to 1914. She became the custodian of the international gold standard, and with large experience and great financial power, she learned and practiced all the arts of management. In all of this London and especially the Bank of England played the most important part." See also Bagehot, *op. cit.*, pp. 32–33; W. Stanley Jevons, *Money and the Mechanism of Exchange*, New York [1875], pp. 297–298; Lombard, *op. cit.*, pp. 155–156; Jerome, *op. cit.*, pp. 132–134; Brown, *op. cit.*, II, 774–778; W. M. Scammell, *International Monetary Policy*, London, 1957, p. 10.
128 Royal Institute of International Affairs, *op. cit.*, p. 17. See also *ibid.*, pp. 148–149.
129 Angas, *op. cit.*, p. 49:

> Gold movements and movements in internal prices were largely ironed out by varying sterling loans; the system was, in fact, a kind of British-controlled 'World Exchange Equalization Fund,' operated by turning on and off the tap of sterling loans.
>
> The system worked satisfactorily (a) because England had a large annual surplus income from foreign investments and (b) because the Bank of England manoeuvred the bank rate wisely. Gold as

metal was not hoarded by England, and the international distribution thereof was reasonably maintained.

Shaw reaffirmed this interpretation: "Great Britain was the pre-1914 International Monetary Fund. Her loans to countries having temporary difficulty with their balances of payments saved the borrowers from gold exports, exchange depreciation, or internal deflation. Also, as an international central bank, she held out valuable clearing services to her satellites, so that each member of the gold-standard community could settle in sterling for its net debts to all other members" (*op. cit.*, p. 567). See also: Beyen, *op. cit.*, pp. 13–14; Brown, *op. cit.*, II, 774–778; and Norman S. Buchanan and Friedrich A. Lutz, *Rebuilding the World Economy*, New York, 1947, pp. 17–18.

130 *Op. cit.*, pp. 47–49.

131 National Industrial Conference Board, *The Gold Standard: Recent Developments and Present Status,* Conference Board Information Service: Domestic Affairs, Memorandum No. 5 [mimeographed], New York, 1933, p. 5: "Owing to the tremendous financial power of Great Britain, the pre-war international gold standard was actually a British standard." Sir Charles Morgan-Webb called it "the international, exchange-stabilizing, sterling standard" (*The Rise and Fall of the Gold Standard,* New York, 1934, p. 5). Shaw observed that "any satellite could meet the terms of the gold standard by being on the sterling-exchange standard" (*op. cit.*, p. 567). Day labeled the system of gold-exchange standards linked to the United Kingdom in the 'twenties as "the sterling exchange standard" (*op. cit.*, p. 442). Furthermore, he added, "In a significant sense, the pre-1914 system was a sterling exchange standard, not a gold standard" (*ibid.*, p. 494). Allan Sproul had earlier remarked that the nineteenth-century gold standard "rapidly became more of a sterling standard than a gold standard" (Federal Reserve Bank of New York, *Monthly Review,* Supplement, XXIX [January 1947], 4). See also Miroslav A. Kriz, *The Price of Gold,* Essays in International Finance, No. 15, Princeton, 1952, p. 9.

132 *Op. cit.*, 3rd edn., p. 381.

133 Quoted by Beyen, *op. cit.*, p. 65.

134 Georg Friedrich Knapp, *The State Theory of Money,* trans. H. M. Lucas and J. Bonar, New York, 1924, p. 279; David Davidson, *The Rationalization of the Gold Standard,* Uppsala och Stockholm, 1933, pp. 70–73. "The [Interim] Report [of the Cunliffe Committee (England, August 1918)] recognized the truth, which had been suppressed hitherto, namely, that the gold standard was virtually non-existent" (Coulborn, *op. cit.*, p. 141).

135 See Davidson, *op. cit.*, pp. 1–2, 44, 60–63, *et passim.* "By the *substance* of the international gold standard we mean the whole institutional pattern of trade and of finance that breathes life into these forms of law and practice, and that works out its contribution to economic progress through them. In the pre-war world this was the London-centered *system* of international finance based upon British predominance in international trade" (Brown, *op. cit.*, I, 28–29 [second italics mine]). See also *supra*, Chap. V, nn. 2–6.

136 Day, *op. cit.*, p. 494.

137 John Maynard Keynes, *A Tract on Monetary Reform*, London, 1923, p. 175; Gustav Cassel, *Post War Monetary Stabilization*, New York, 1928, p. 75.

138 Fisher, *The Money Illusion*, p. 158; George William Dowrie, *American Monetary and Banking Policies*, New York, 1930, p. 385; Morgan-Webb, *op. cit.*, p. 5.

139 Justification was found in the attribution of postwar gold movements to the war and its aftermath, factors unrelated to business conditions (Federal Reserve Board, *Annual Report, 1923*, pp. 30, 37–38). Whatever the cause, the resulting excess reserves enabled the Federal Reserve banks to determine their policies more or less independently of international gold movements (James Harvey Rogers, *America Weighs Her Gold*, New Haven, 1931, pp. 96–97). See also: Chandler, *op. cit.*, 2nd edn., p. 98; and Whittlesey, *op. cit.*, p. 305.

140 Keynes, *A Tract on Monetary Reform*, p. 167; "The beginnings of this change in the operation of the gold standard date back to the pre-war period, for even in those days its automatic operation was more of a legend than an historical truth. Since the war, this change has become so apparent that, to-day, the non-existence of such an automatism [as was formerly assumed to characterize the gold standard] is unquestioned, and it is generally held that the gold standard now is, and must be in an increasing degree, a manipulated standard" (Mlynarski, *op. cit.*, p. 16); Friedrich A. Lutz, *International Monetary Mechanisms: The Keynes and White Proposals*, Essays in International Finance, No. 1, Princeton, 1943, p. 4; Nurkse, *op. cit.*, pp. 73–75; Whittlesey, *op. cit.*, p. 305.

141 Jome, *op. cit.*, p. 373. France aggravated the situation by preventing the inflation that would have stopped her disproportionate accumulation of gold (Westerfield, *op. cit.*, p. 565).

142 Madden and Nadler, *op. cit.*, p. 15; Westerfield, *op. cit.*, pp. 565, 576; Crowther, *op. cit.*, pp. 315–321; Woodworth, *op. cit.*, pp. 53–54; Chandler, *op. cit.*, 2nd edn., p. 98; *ibid.*, 3rd edn., pp. 366, 390–391.

143 Dowrie, *American Monetary and Banking Policies*, p. 390; Beyen, *op. cit.*, pp. 29–30; J. Herbert Furth, "The World Dollar Problem," *World Politics*, XI (January 1959), 276–277. Chandler concludes his survey of the changing monetary roles of gold by saying: "Its role as a determinant of domestic monetary policy is . . . far smaller than it once was. Its most important remaining role is as a form of international reserve—as something that is generally acceptable in international payments and as a medium for stabilizing exchange rates" (*op. cit.*, 3rd edn., pp. 367–368). The compatibility of the dual monetary functions of gold had been an issue in the English currency controversy of the middle-nineteenth century (*supra*, nn. 91–101 of this chapter). By the third decade of the twentieth century, the issue was only partially resolved:

> These two functions are to some extent antithetical. The more closely a central bank's policy is dominated by the necessity of maintaining a given reserve ratio, the less can it allow gold flows to operate as a cushion. On the other hand, to the extent to which variations in a central bank's gold holdings in themselves adjust changes in the balance of payments, more discretion is permitted

central bank administrators in their domestic monetary policies. The trend of central banking theory and practice has been in the direction of allowing more discretionary power to central banks. Hence the amount of *excess* reserves rather than the amount of required reserves has been assuming more importance. This trend, needless to say, tends to make for greater variations in the gold-money ratio (Currie, *op. cit.,* p. 109).

See also the League of Nations, *Second Interim Report of the Gold Delegation of the Financial Committee,* pp. 16–18.

Domestic convertibility was finally abandoned in the 'thirties because gold drains and economic contraction were recognized as mutually aggravating. A fractional gold reserve was, in the nature of the case, not large enough to stop a serious internal drain before its complete exhaustion. Now we are discovering that national gold pools of international liquidity dissociated from national monetary policies—whatever their size—are not large enough to stop external drains. Recognition of this fact has inspired proposals for continuous expansion of international reserves by empowering the International Monetary Fund to create them (Robert Triffin, *Gold and the Dollar Crisis,* New Haven, 1960, pp. 102 ff.) or by periodically raising the world price of gold (Sir Roy Harrod, "A Plan for Increasing Liquidity: A Critique," *Economica,* N.S. XXVIII [May 1961], 201; Sir Frederick Leith-Ross, "The Dollar's Relations with Gold: Call for Orderly Realignment of Currencies," *Times* [London], November 10, 1960, p. 19). See also International Monetary Fund, *International Reserves and Liquidity,* Washington, 1958, pp. 41–44, 66, 72, *et passim.*

144 Cf. *supra,* pp. 86–87.

145 Kjellstrom, *op. cit.,* pp. 34–35. "In contrasting prewar and postwar international standards, the significant point is not the similarity in management but the dissimilarity in the objectives of management" (Peterson, Cawthorne, and Lohman, *op. cit.,* p. 690). It has already been pointed out that a confusion of objectives (goals) and criteria (guides) has been typical of monetary literature (*supra,* nn. 52–54 of this chapter).

146 Federal Reserve Board, *Annual Report, 1923,* pp. 32–39. See also *infra,* n. 171 of this chapter.

147 The idea dawned at the 1922 Genoa conference of experts and was carried forward by the "American experiment" of "enfeebling the link which binds the supply of money to the supply of gold, by varying the proportion which the Central Bank keeps between its reserves and its deposits" (Robertson, *Money,* p. 160).

148 The American priority of the internal over the external stabilization of the value of the dollar stymied the London Economic Conference of 1933 and set the style for the period (Morgan-Webb, *op. cit.,* pp. 130–131; Beyen, *op. cit.,* pp. 93, 96, 98). "The gold standard does not fit in with the American conception of stabilization—stabilization of prices" (Morgan-Webb, *op. cit.,* p. 181). See also: Puxley, *op. cit.,* pp. 25, 28; John Donaldson, *The Dollar: A Study of the "New" National and International Monetary System,* New York, 1937, p. 4; and Myra Curtis and Hugh Townshend, *Modern Money,* New York, 1938, p. 244.

149 Shaw, *op. cit.,* p. 440: "War finance took charge [of the money supply]

in 1940–45. Since 1945 the money supply has been suited to the relative demand of commercial banks and the public for government securities vis-à-vis cash at a stable pattern of interest rates." See also *infra*, n. 196 of this chapter.

150 The Employment Act of 1946 made it official. Edwin G. Nourse, "Ideal and Working Concepts of Full Employment," *American Economic Review*, Papers and Proceedings, XLVII (May 1957), 100 (italics mine): "The declaration of *policy* in the Employment Act does not specify full or even 'maximum' employment as the single *goal* of national policy. There are in fact three broad *objectives or criteria* of action set forth . . . Our profession has further work to do toward conceptual clarification." The ideal of "full employment" is one thing on which there has been international agreement (see the United Nations report, *National and International Measures for Full Employment*, Lake Success, 1949, pp. 5 ff.). But clarification, implementation, and resolution of conflicting objectives remain on the agenda of unfinished business (see Jacob Viner, "Full Employment at Whatever Cost," *Quarterly Journal of Economics*, LXIV [August 1950], 388 ff.).

For recognition of how all the various criteria of monetary policy have overlapped in time and space, see Mints, *op. cit.*, pp. 271–272.

151 The *real* concept of economic growth has *re*entered the arena of *monetary* analysis after a half-century of neglect, bringing with it a renewed promise of clarification and possibility of compounded confusion.

152 William Blacker, *The Evils Inseparable from a Mixed Currency, and the Advantages to Be Secured by Introducing an Inconvertible National Paper Circulation, throughout the British Empire and Its Dependencies, under Proper Regulation*, London, 1839, p. 12.

153 Hawtrey recommended restoration of a modified "gold standard" under which gold would be managed so as to stabilize the value of money in terms of commodities (*Monetary Reconstruction*, London, 1923, pp. 22, 132). "It is natural to ask, in the face of advocacy of this kind," Keynes commented, "why it is necessary to drag in gold at all" (*A Tract on Monetary Reform*, p. 174). What had been attempted in the 'twenties was articulated in the 'thirties: "We now know that the value of gold can be controlled by a suitable regulation of the World's monetary demand for gold. This *alters the whole relation between currency and gold*. Our ultimate purpose is now to *give our currency a fixed value in terms of commodities*" (Roy L. Garis, *Principles of Money, Credit, and Banking*, New York, 1934, p. 281 [italics mine]). "The changed attitudes of the people in much of the civilized world, while emphatically demanding a gold base for their money systems, make necessary a high degree of rational monetary control" (James Harvey Rogers, "Introduction" [to] Puxley, *op. cit.*, p. 3).

154 Steiner and Shapiro, *op. cit.*, p. 45.

155 Davidson, *op. cit.*, p. 22.

156 Bernstein, *op. cit.*, p. 54: "If government or the central bank is prepared to buy or sell gold without restrictions at a fixed price, or at a price varying within narrow limits, the country may be said to be

206

on a gold standard." Such *may* be said, but what *should* be said is that this is a *gold policy*, not a gold standard (see *supra*, pp. 66–67). "Convertibility into gold will not alter the fact that the value of gold itself depends on the policy of the Central Banks" (Keynes, *A Tract on Monetary Reform*, p. 170).

157 Halm, *Monetary Theory*, p. 208 (italics mine): "Our discussion of the different backing systems shows, however, that the gold standard may be interpreted more loosely [than the "orthodox," or "automatic," version], depending on the amount of discretion reserved for the monetary authority. Even the strictest backing requirements leave room for some 'play.' The central bank can try to accumulate 'excess' or 'buffer' reserves. *Such systems may still be gold standard systems as long as the monetary authorities buy and sell gold at a fixed price and in unlimited amounts.*"

158 Even "Mr. Gold Standard," himself, appeared to recognize this: "It is often difficult to fix the exact date at which a country actually gave up the gold standard, because the *date of the* de jure *departure from gold was usually later than that of the* de facto *departure; while the latter,* which is more important, was commonly not a *jump* but a *slide"* (Kemmerer, *Gold and the Gold Standard*, p. 120 [first italics mine]). However, his statement was not as significant as it sounded because his list of departures from gold began with the year 1929, the United States' departure being dated March 1933 (*ibid.*, pp. 120–121). Others, with a more detached view of the gold standard were more consistent in this respect: "A regulated non-metallic standard has slipped in unnoticed. *It exists.* Whilst economists dozed, the academic dream of a hundred years, doffing its cap and gown, clad in paper rags, has crept into the real world by means of the bad fairies—always so much more potent than the good—the wicked Ministers of Finance" (Keynes, *A Tract on Monetary Reform*, p. 173). "The breakdown of the more or less automatic gold standard system is perhaps to be traced not to the formal departures from the standard in 1931 and after but to the practice of disregarding central bank reserve ratios upon which its survival may well have depended" (Whittlesey, *op. cit.*, p. 305). See also: Cassel, *op. cit.*, p. 75; Rogers, *America Weighs Her Gold*, p. 97; "Note of Dissent," *Report of the Gold Delegation of the Financial Committee*, Geneva, 1932, p. 73; Madden and Nadler, *op. cit.*, p. 15; Agger, *op. cit.*, p. 193; Nurkse, *op. cit.*, pp. 105–106; Frank D. Graham, "Commodity-Reserve Currency: A Criticism of the Critique," *Journal of Political Economy*, LI (February 1943), 75; Scammell, *op. cit.*, p. 10; and Chandler, *op. cit.*, 3rd edn., pp. 390–391.

159 *Supra*, n. 61 of this chapter.

160 Although this recognition was delayed by the intensity of the orthodox reaction to Keynes' opposition to restoration of the gold standard in the 'twenties, "managed currency" (a phrase Keynes "is credited with having coined" [Fisher, *Stable Money*, p. 87]) is no longer regarded as a dirty word, but, rather, as a fact. "The monetary system of this country must be a Managed System.—It is not advisable, or indeed practicable, to regard our monetary system as an automatic system, grinding out the right result by the operation of natural forces aided

by a few maxims of general application and some well-worn rules of thumb" (*Report of the Committee on Finance & Industry* [Macmillan Report], London, 1931, p. 118). See also: Royal Institute of International Affairs, *op. cit.,* pp. 209–210, 213; Dowrie, *Money and Banking,* pp. 111, 492, 494; Hawtrey, *The Gold Standard in Theory and Practice,* p. 242; Beyen, *op. cit.,* p. 12; Woodworth, *op. cit.,* p. 21; Chandler, *op. cit.,* 2nd edn., pp. 107, 717–718; Day, *op. cit.,* p. 496; Halm, *Economics of Money and Banking,* 2nd edn., p. 60.

161 "Gold was believed to be an automatic standard and therefore free from interference by politicians" (Lionel D. Edie, *Dollars,* New Haven, 1934, p. 25).

162 Samuelson, *op. cit.,* p. 164: "Such an automatic mechanism is often contrasted with a so-called 'discretionary' system. Now over the years I have struggled with this distinction and for the life of me I am unable to isolate any real logical difference, either at the philosophical or pragmatic level. It is not simply that such a mechanism is set up by discretion, is abandoned by discretion, and is interfered with by discretion—although this consideration is itself enough to destroy the notion of a genuine difference of kind. But even my efforts to establish a logically rigorous difference of degree has not met with success." However surprising it may seem in retrospect, the point had already been conceded by the two most dedicated defenders of the pure, unrestricted gold-coin standard, Edwin Walter Kemmerer and Walter E. Spahr. Kemmerer said, "In modern times even gold standard currencies are nearly all more or less managed through central bank operations such as changing discount rates, 'open market operations' and the manipulation of exchange funds" (*Money,* p. 101, n. 1). Later he elaborated: "A popular idea, but a fallacious one, is that metallic-money standards, like the gold standard, are entirely automatic in their operation, and that paper-money standards are entirely managed and not automatic at all. *All monetary standards in modern times are more or less managed. It is not a question of the presence or absence of monetary management, but rather of the extent and character of that management*" (*Gold and the Gold Standard,* p. 213 [italics mine]). Spahr, too, conceded that the monetary system must be managed, even under a gold standard. He attributed the past troubles of the gold standard to neither inherent defects nor management, per se, but to "improper management" (Walter E. Spahr *et al., Economic Principles and Problems,* 2nd edn., I, New York, 1934, 409). "In the past," he added "too much stress has been laid upon the 'automatic' features or operations of the gold standard. In the future, more stress doubtless will be placed upon the *desirability of better control of it*" (*loc. cit.*). See also the reference to Spahr, *supra,* n. 74 of this chapter. Further documentation, though amply available, would be anticlimactic.

163 Modern recognition that all monetary systems are managed has inspired attempts to restate the basic issue: "The real question is not, therefore, whether the government shall have great powers over the monetary system—it has them whether it wants them or not. The real question is whether it will recognize its inevitable possession of many powers, and *whether it will use them wisely and in a coordinated way*

208

to achieve socially desirable objectives" (Chandler, *op. cit.,* 2nd edn., p. 718 [[italics mine]). Curtis and Townshend had earlier expressed the issue in terms of whether or not money is managed with the "conscious *consideration of the best interests of the community"* (*op. cit.,* pp. 8–9 [italics mine]). Even back in the 'twenties, Edie had said, "The question is not whether the money standard can or should be managed, but *how bankers and governments can make certain that the policies of management are wise and sound"* (*Money, Bank Credit, and Prices,* p. 63 [italics mine]). A criterion of monetary management is necessary in order to resolve all such statements of the issue. Some recognition of this appears to be implicit in the literature, e.g., "The real difference between the two outstanding monetary conceptions of the present time is whether or not monetary policy can and should be consciously and predominantly directed toward the stabilization of a price level, and if so, whether or not there is in a monetary organization which is so oriented any necessity—or indeed room—for a metallic standard of value" (Pasvolsky, *op. cit.,* p. 30). "The question, therefore, is not, 'Shall we have a managed currency?' The question is: 'To what end shall it be managed?' In whose interest shall it be managed? *According to what rules* or principles or philosophy and by what methods shall it be managed?" (Lombard, *op. cit.,* p. 157 [italics mine]).

164 Whittlesey, *op. cit.,* p. 563 (italics mine): "Certain unresolved questions relating to the general approach to monetary policy recur again and again. There is the question, for example, of 'rules vs. authorities in monetary policy'. . . . The issue is the historic one of government by laws or government by men. The *answer turns partly on the possibility of finding a sufficiently clear and lasting 'rule' of monetary conduct, partly on the ability of central bankers to adapt themselves wisely to changing economic conditions."*

165 Per Jacobsson's description of the evolving "monetary standard" amounts to an argument that we are working toward a workable set of monetary rules (by which he means policies) without any criterion of workability (*op. cit.,* pp. 8 ff.). See also Smith, *op. cit.,* p. 200. It is, of course, to be expected that the monetary managers, themselves, would favor their own freedom of action and oppose the imposition of criteria by which their work could be judged. The Federal Reserve Board, for example, rejected all criteria of monetary policy even when the United States was supposed to be on a gold standard (*Annual Report, 1923,* pp. 31–39). Their position, however, is justified as long as their powers are not commensurate with their responsibilities.

166 Smith, *op. cit.,* p. 201: "Quite apart from the more technical problems involved in discretionary management of the monetary system, there are the problems of sufficient knowledge and wisdom to carry out these policies effectively, of bringing to the leadership of the central bank and treasury men with the requisite knowledge and wisdom, and of leaving them sufficiently free from political pressures and routine administrative duties. There is the further problem of gaining public acceptance for decisions made by a group of administrators

which must often run counter to the immediate interests of important economic groups."

167 This concept and the terminology associated with it helps to clarify the issues and resolve the apparent differences between Mints and Robertson (D. H. Robertson, "Stable Money," *Utility and All That,* London, 1952, pp. 201–202, 204–205).

168 New York, 1940, pp. 185–199 (italics mine). In the first and second editions of his later text, the section heading was changed from "Criteria" to "Guides to Monetary Policy" (*The Economics of Money and Banking,* New York, 1948, p. 710; *ibid.,* 2nd edn., p. 718), but at least one of the "guides" is still called a "criterion" (*ibid.,* p. 720). The chapter was dropped from the last edition, and the material was more or less integrated into chapters on "Monetary Standards" and the history of "Monetary Policies" (*ibid.,* 3rd edn., pp. 363 *et passim*).

169 Chandler, *Introduction to Monetary Theory,* p. 185 (italics mine). His list of the "guides" that "have been proposed" (*ibid.,* pp. 185–199) corresponds closely to those suggested above (cf. *supra,* p. 81). However, it should be noticed that Chandler's terminology fits the name of the chapter ("Objectives . . .") better than it does the section heading ("Criteria . . ."). For example, "stabilization of the price level" connotes a realizable "objective," whereas the cognate "criterion" of monetary policy would be a "stable price level."

170 *The Wage-Price Issue,* Princeton, 1960, pp. 9, 10 (italics mine).

171 *Op. cit.,* p. 364 (italics mine). See also *ibid.,* p. 546. Shaw's similar views were similarly expressed: "Gold movements and the Reserve banks' reserve ratios, as well as commodity prices, were rejected as primary *guides to policy.* The *criterion of policy* was declared to be the maintenance of 'sound credit conditions,' although it was not clear whether this would mean adherence to the banking principle of varying the money supply with cyclical change in national income or to the competing principle of offsetting cyclical forces" (*op. cit.,* p. 430 [italics mine]).

172 Stokes and Arlt, *op. cit.,* p. 111 (italics mine).

173 *Op. cit.,* 2nd edn., p. 735.

174 Fisher, *Stable Money,* p. 22 (italics mine). Fisher documents the statement by quotations from Ricardo's *Proposals for an Economical and Secure Currency,* pp. 7 and 22 (see *The Works and Correspondence of David Ricardo,* IV, 54–55, 64). For further evidence of the universal relevance of the concept of a monetary standard under discussion, see [John Stuart Mill], "The Currency Question," *Westminster Review,* XLI (June 1844), 581.

175 *Dollars,* p. 280 (italics mine). Even before the debacle of 1931, James had said, "Before the war the gold reserve was considered of fundamental importance as a *guide* to central banking policy, and now that it has proved to be inadequate to meet the situation, central banks throughout the world are forced to seek new *guides* that will prove more satisfactory" (*op. cit.,* p. 334 [italics mine]). See also Robertson, *Money,* p. 151; and Kjellstrom, *op. cit.,* p. 41.

176 *Op. cit.,* p. 426 (italics mine).

177 *The Economics of Money and Banking,* 3rd edn., p. 367 (italics mine).
178 "The Problem of Economic Instability," *American Economic Review,* XL (September 1950), 532 (italics mine).
179 *Supra,* pp. 49, 54.
180 Fisher, *Stable Money,* pp. 2–3 *et passim.*
181 *A Tract on Monetary Reform,* p. 187.
182 *Ibid.,* p. 186.
183 *Ibid.,* pp. 186–187 (italics mine). Similar conceptualization was implied in his later work (*A Treatise on Money,* I, 16).
184 *A Tract on Monetary Reform,* pp. 187–188.
185 *Ibid.,* p. 188 (italics mine). This seems to imply that the criterion of monetary policy is irrelevant to the nonmonetary policies that might be required to deal with the trade cycle.
186 *Loc. cit.* Later Keynes applied the term "Consumption Standard" to such use of a consumer price index (*A Treatise on Money,* I, 57). "Consumer goods standard" would have been a more felicitous expression (see *ibid.,* pp. 57–63).
187 *Gold Standard or Goods Standard,* Adelaide, Australia, 1934, p. 6 (italics mine). See also: Edwin Cannan, *Modern Currency and the Regulation of Its Value,* London, 1931, pp. 34–35; Lombard, *op. cit.,* pp. 24–27, 32, 143–144; Morgan-Webb, *op. cit.,* pp. 6, 158, 165, 173–174.
188 *Op. cit.,* p. 4. "Even in the decade 1920–30, when the United States was *otherwise on a full gold standard,* the price index was apparently a factor of at least some importance, at times, in the current determination of credit policy by the Federal Reserve System" (*loc. cit.* [italics mine]).
189 Arthur F. Burns, *Prosperity without Inflation,* New York, 1957, p. 72.
190 Woodworth, *op. cit.,* p. 61.
191 *Loc. cit.* (italics mine). Later he added that "price stability . . . should be one of the guiding factors, but by no means the only *criterion, of monetary policy*" (*ibid.,* p. 64 [italics mine]).
192 *Economics of Money and Banking,* 1st edn., p. 246 (italics mine).
193 *Ibid.,* p. 55 (italics mine). Notice that these two sentences explicitly equate "criterion of monetary management" with monetary "standard." See also J. E. Meade, *The Control of Inflation,* Cambridge, 1958, pp. 46–47.
194 Nurkse, *op. cit.,* p. 106 (italics mine): "And price stability itself has come to be widely regarded as an inadequate *criterion of policy.*" This statement is documented by reference to the *Federal Reserve Bulletin,* September 1937, p. 828. See also *ibid.,* p. 827. For reservations concerning the national income variant of the goods standard, see Pritchard, *op. cit.,* pp. 740–741.
195 Halm, *Economics of Money and Banking,* 1st edn., p. 246 (italics mine): "We cannot rely exclusively on price stability as the *criterion of monetary policy.*" Shaw's " 'demand standard' of monetary control" is simply an output variant of the goods standard. He proposes the long-run level of output as the referent for monetary policy (Edward S. Shaw, "Money Supply and Stable Economic Growth," *United States Monetary Policy,* ed. Neil H. Jacoby, pp. 60–61, 64, 68).

211

196 *Money, Income, and Monetary Policy,* p. 450. It might be argued that interest rates continued to be *a* criterion of monetary policy until the accord in 1951.

197 *Op. cit.,* p. 64 (italics mine). The monetary-policy criterion of a stable "Labour Power of Money" had been called by Keynes an "Earnings Standard" (*A Treatise on Money,* I, 63).

198 Such a standard does not appear to be feasible in modern society, but it should be recalled that classicists regarded the gold standard as merely the closest practicable approximation to the labor standard (*supra,* pp. 53–54).

199 Coulborn, *op. cit.,* p. 169 (italics mine). To this recommendation, however, he appended a warning: "Yet we must remember, too, that it is not just 'employment' pure and simple that we seek; we want employment at a reasonable standard of life; to take an extreme example, we could easily employ everyone [in England] by stopping imports of food, but whether they could scratch from the soil enough to keep themselves alive is doubtful" (*loc. cit.*).

200 *Economics of Money and Banking,* 1st edn., p. 247 (italics mine). Meanwhile, a section of Thomas' chapter on *"Standards* of Credit and Monetary Policy" was entitled "Full Employment as a *Criterion* for Monetary and Credit Policy" (*op. cit.,* 2nd edn., p. 754 [italics mine]).

201 *Op. cit.,* p. 494. These criteria "as to when to do what" (*loc. cit.*) in the field of money are based on the premise that "the primary business of monetary policy—or more broadly, of monetary-fiscal policy—is economic stabilization" (*ibid.,* p. 411). Structural unemployment and growth are interpreted as real economic problems to be attacked primarily by nonmonetary policies. See also *ibid.,* pp. 414–415.

202 *Supra,* pp. 86–87. The Macmillan Report explained the "automaticity" claimed for the traditional gold standard in the following manner: "The sense in which the gold standard can be said to be automatic is thus very limited; it is automatic only as an *indicator* of the need for action and of the end to be achieved" (*op. cit.,* p. 21 [italics mine]).

203 *Supra,* p. 87.

204 *Supra,* pp. 91–92.

205 The distinction between the criteria, a fine one in the beginning, ultimately became a pronounced enough disparity to constitute the *de facto* departure from the gold standard that ultimately made preservation of the *de jure* gold standard impossible (see *supra,* pp. 92–93). The vicious circle of self destruction operating at that time is implicit in an observation of Halm's: "The experiences of the Federal Reserve make it obvious that gold is worse than useless in guiding a country's monetary policy once the equilibrating gold flow has ceased to operate" (*Economics of Money and Banking,* 1st edn., p. 244). See also *supra,* n. 143 of this chapter.

206 *Stable Money,* p. 1 (italics mine). See also Angas, *op. cit.,* p. 190.

207 *Monetary Theory,* p. 208 (italics mine). See also Nurkse, *op. cit.,* pp. 105–106. Cf. Lindholm, Balles, and Hunter, *op. cit.,* p. 51 (italics mine): "The decision of a central bank to change the interest rate was dictated entirely by the gold-reserve position of the nation [prior to

1914]. The effect of this relatively simple *guide* to a relatively simple action was to keep domestic prices in line [with foreign prices] . . . The gold standard operated largely on the basis that the nation's monetary reserves would be completely utilized and that, gold being established as the monetary reserve, the inflow and outflow of gold would set the quantity of money." Whittlesey also distinguished the traditional concept of the gold standard with later practice in a manner implying that, in any case, the monetary standard was, regardless of its label, the guide followed by the monetary authorities: "According to the traditional theory of the gold standard, the primary function of central bank reserves is to serve as an automatic regulator of the money supply. . . . A tendency of gold to move in one direction or another was looked upon as constituting the best possible *guide to the policies that should be followed by the central bank"* (*op. cit.,* p. 304 [italics mine]). Under the heading, "Gold Movements as *Guides* to Policy," Stokes and Arlt explained that according to the traditional gold standard the level of gold reserves constituted the criterion of monetary policy (*op. cit.,* p. 500 [italics mine]).

208 *Supra,* nn. 181–185 of this chapter.

209 *American and Monetary and Banking Policies,* p. 252 (italics mine).

210 Ervin P. Hexner, "The New Gold Standard," *Weltwirtschaftliches Archiv,* LXXXV (1960), 7–8, 28–30.

211 See Per Jacobsson's address at the annual meetings of the International Monetary Fund and International Bank for Reconstruction and Development, September 18, 1961, *International Financial News Survey,* XIII (September 29, 1961), 301; and Ervin P. Hexner, "Das Problem der Internationalen Liquidität und die Inanspruchnahme der Finanziellen Mittel des Internationalen Währungsfonds durch die Vereinigten Staaten," *Weltwirtschaftliches Archiv,* LXXXVII (1961), 219.

212 Halm, *Economics of Money and Banking,* 1st edn., p. 248 (italics mine): "We must mention one other important *criterion of monetary policy:* the country's balance of payment."

213 Miroslav A. Kriz, *Gold in World Monetary Affairs Today,* Essays in International Finance No. 34, Princeton, 1959, p. 27.

214 Jacques Rueff, "Gold Exchange Standard a Danger to the West," *Times* (London), June 27, 1961, p. 16; *ibid.,* June 28, 1961, p. 16; *ibid.,* June 29, 1961, p. 17. Cf. *supra,* nn. 124 and 125, and see *supra,* n. 145 of this chapter. Recognition of the difficulties, if not the dangers, of such double reporting of reserves is not new (see League of Nations, *Second Interim Report of the Gold Delegation to the Financial Committee,* pp. 13–14, 19; and Mlynarski, *op. cit.,* pp. 19–20).

215 Kriz, *Gold in World Monetary Affairs Today,* p. 27 (italics mine). The speciousness of the alleged analogy to the former guidance of monetary management by gold reserves is demonstrated by the very author who makes the claim: "Conversely a money supply related to *international reserves* has proved flexible enough *to enable the authorities to retain full control over domestic currency"* (*loc. cit.* [italics mine]). In other words, economists now admit that they have been wrong and ignorant laymen have been right, all along: We *can* have our cake and eat it, too! How this differs from the former orthodox

view of external stability, and the means for its maintenance is indicated by the following statement of Edie's: "Nevertheless, if this step is taken [external convertibility], let us be careful to avoid the past mistake of setting up the external stability of a national currency as the end all and be all of its monetary policy. Students of the subject are familiar with the Bank of England's extreme philosophy to the effect that the supreme test of discount rate policy or of open market policy is the effect on the foreign exchange rate and upon the movement of gold. . . . This philosophy has meant in practice a tendency to make a fetish of the exchange rate as something to be defended at all costs, even at the cost of a deflationary collapse of the domestic economy" (*Dollars*, pp. 79–80).

CHAPTER VII

1 T. W. Hutchison, *A Review of Economic Doctrines 1870–1929*, Oxford, 1953, p. 28 (italics mine).

2 *Supra*, pp. 55–56. See also Hutchison, *op. cit.*, p. 40.

3 "Monetary economics has been dormant for two decades. Other aspects of economic analysis have left it far behind. It is so becalmed in an intellectual doldrum that no gentle breeze of inquiry can stir it" (Edward S. Shaw, "Money Supply and Stable Economic Growth," *United States Monetary Policy*, ed. Neil H. Jacoby, New York, 1958, p. 71).

4 " 'Nothing,' says Montesquieu, 'ought to be exempt from variation as that which is the common measure of all things. *Trade* is in itself uncertain; and it is a great evil to add a new uncertainty to it' " (quoted by Robert William Dickinson, *Vexata Quaestio; Being Two Addresses on the Depreciation of the Currency*, London, 1843, p. 13 [italics mine]).

5 John Maynard Keynes' comment on the monetary orthodoxy of the 'twenties—which preceded the financial debacle of the 'thirties—has lost none of its validity: "All those—and in the financial world they are many—who have reasons for wishing to appear 'correct,' are compelled to talk foolishly" (*A Tract on Monetary Reform*, London, 1923, p. 145).

6 Edward S. Shaw, *Money, Income, and Monetary Policy*, Chicago, 1950, p. 17: "Some national monetary systems have no standard; or, in the jargon of the literature, they are on an 'inconvertible paper standard.' " This fact has been implied by others (Eugene E. Agger, *Money and Banking Today*, New York, 1941, pp. 49, 65–66; Lester V. Chandler, *The Economics of Money and Banking*, 2nd edn., New York, 1953, p. 106). Use of the term "inconvertible currency" instead of "inconvertible paper standard" may imply recognition that the so-called paper standard

is a misnomer (International Monetary Fund, *International Reserves and Liquidity,* Washington, 1958, p. 5).

7 "Now it does not change facts to call them by different names and yet terms influence ideas" (Howard S. Ellis, "Some Fundamentals in the Theory of Velocity," *Readings in Monetary Theory,* ed. Friedrich A. Lutz and Lloyd W. Mints, New York, 1951, p. 124). "Words are subject to an evolution which marks the course of ideas, just as—going one step further back—ideas follow the material progress of man" (Alexander Del Mar, *The Science of Money* [2nd edn., London, 1896], p. 8).

8 In their revision of Horace White's *Money and Banking* (6th edn., Boston, 1935, p. 105 [second italics mine]), Charles S. Tippets and Lewis A. Froman noted Irving Fisher's claim that his compensated dollar "puts the 'standard' in the gold standard. Kemmerer maintains that a nation cannot be on gold unless it has a *fixed* price for gold and describes the Fisher plan as a commodity-price-index standard. *Which of these two authorities is correct is largely a matter of how the gold standard is to be defined.*" The issue was left unresolved.

9 "Balance-of-payments equilibrium" is used here in the Nurksian sense (Ragnar Nurkse, *Conditions of International Monetary Equilibrium,* Essays in International Finance, No. 4, Princeton, 1945, p. 7). However, other interpretations of equilibrium may be used as the policy referent. Good or bad, whatever is actually used as the criterion of monetary policy is the monetary standard—as long as it is so used.

10 To the possible objection that stabilization of the price level, per-capita income, or employment are alternative monetary species of the general economic objective of cyclical stabilization, rather than alternative standards, I answer that such terminology is acceptable and in no way inconsistent with mine. A brief explanation will, it is hoped, make this clear. Since none of these specific objectives are attainable in a free society, they are too general to be much help in day-to-day policy decisions. Policy makers need a criterion of the chosen form of stabilization in order to keep their course pointed toward the target even though a "bull's eye" cannot be expected. The criteria corresponding to the above-mentioned monetary objectives would be, respectively, "a stable" (instead of "stabilization of") price level, per-capita money income, or employment level relative to the labor force. To be useful referents for policy decisions, they would have to be defined as variations confined within specified limits. Increasingly aggressive monetary action could be called for as deviation from the norm passed additional benchmarks. It must also be remembered that in order to achieve our economic objectives, monetary policies must be supplemented by appropriate non-monetary economic policies.

11 The question lately raised about the compatibility of this dualism (Chandler, *op. cit.,* pp. 719–720) would have been disposed of long ago.

12 "It was patent that existing gold reserves would be insufficient if any substantial part of these liabilities had to be liquidated in gold. The gold exchange standard, therefore, was held to be particularly advantageous in reducing the demand for gold and in providing an 'economy' in its use" (Raymond P. Kent, *Money and Banking,* 3rd edn., New

York, 1956, p. 42). "The shortage of gold that the gold exchange standard was designed to meet was frequently discussed at the time" (A. C. L. Day, *Outline of Monetary Economics,* Oxford, 1957, p. 495).

13 Even the United States Treasury Department, in distinguishing the "present monetary system of the United States" from the "gold standard system in operation prior to April 1933," says only that "the present system *is sometimes described as* a 'gold bullion standard' or a 'modified gold standard' system" (*Facts about Money* [mimeographed release of the Treasury Department], December 1960, p. 16 [italics mine]).

14 The fixed price of gold is no longer regarded as the means of determining the quantity or value of money (Charles R. Whittlesey, *Principles and Practices of Money and Banking,* 2nd edn., New York, 1954, pp. 545–546).

15 For a good, brief discussion of this dilemma, see J. Herbert Furth, "The Dilemma of U. S. Monetary Policy," *Pennsylvania Business Survey,* May 1962, pp. 4–6.

16 Howard S. Ellis, "The Rediscovery of Money," *Money Trade and Economic Growth,* [Essays] in Honor of John Henry Williams, New York, 1951, p. 265.

17 *Economics of Money and Banking,* Homewood, Ill., 1956, pp. 127–128 (italics mine).

18 Ellis, "The Rediscovery of Money," *op. cit.,* p. 265; J. Whitney Hanks and Roland Stucki, *Money, Banking, and National Income,* New York, 1956, p. 498; Chandler, *op. cit.,* 3rd edn., p. 438.

19 Chandler, *op. cit.,* 3rd edn., p. 437 [italics mine].

20 Day, *op. cit.,* p. 537.

21 Shaw, *Money, Income, and Monetary Policy,* p. 629.

22 Albert Gailord Hart, *Money, Debt, and Economic Activity,* 2nd edn., New York, 1953, p. 494.

23 Neil H. Jacoby, "Contemporary Monetary Issues," *United States Monetary Policy,* p. 7: "Would the United States get a better monetary regulation under a specific statutory rule than under the discretionary exercise of broad powers by the Federal Reserve authorities? Is public uncertainty about monetary policy helpful or hurtful to the process of economic growth and stability? Has our experience with discretionary monetary management since 1914 provided a fair test of present arrangements?" Some expressly prefer the widest possible latitude for the discretion of central-bank officials within the general objective of undefined "stability" (see E. A. Goldenweiser's statement in opposition to Jacob Viner's position, United States Congress, Joint Committee on the Economic Report, Subcommittee on General Credit Control and Debt Management, *Monetary Policy and Management of the Public Debt,* Senate Document No. 163, 82nd Congress, 2nd Session [popularly known as the Patman Report in honor of the subcommittee chairman, Representative Wright Patman of Texas], p. 41).

24 Hans Glückstadt, *Theory of the Credit Standard,* London, 1932, pp. 44–45: "*The world's amount of money, the value of money and the level of calculation are, therefore, determined by the credit capacity of the world, and for so long as no factor for regulating this credit capacity is available we are operating a standardless monetary system. A problem*

216

encompassing the whole world is thus placed before us, not by economists but by hard facts and necessity, a problem upon the correct solving of which the welfare of the world depends." See also Jacob Viner's statement, *Monetary Policy and Management of the Public Debt,* Senate Document No. 163, 82nd Congress, 2nd Session, pp. 40–41. Actually, Goldenweiser's answer to Viner (*supra,* n. 23 of this chapter) was substantially irrelevant. They both agreed on the general economic objective of stability. Viner was pleading for price-level stability as a criterion of stability. A "stable price level" is, in fact, a general enough policy guide to require all the discretion that can be expected from public officials.

25 It has been said that "the criteria of a good monetary standard" are "found in our final economic objectives" (George Walter Woodworth, *The Monetary and Banking System,* New York, 1950, p. 47).

26 "Full employment" and "price-level stability"—often referred to as objectives—are viewed as facets of the stability objective (American Economic Association Committee on Public Issues, "The Problem of Economic Instability," *American Economic Review,* XL (September 1950), 505–506). Depending on how "full employment" is defined, it may be implicit in the other objectives, as well, with the exception of the conservation of natural resources. For other reasons why "full employment" is not listed as a separate objective, see *supra,* Chapter VI, nn. 199, 201; n. 10 of this chapter; and *infra,* n. 43. Although my list of objectives is more detailed than that of either the American Economic Association Committee on Public Issues (*op. cit.,* pp. 505–507) or Kenneth Boulding, I have added only "conservation of natural resources" to the "major objectives of economic policy" (Kenneth E. Boulding, *Principles of Economic Policy,* Englewood Cliffs, 1958, p. 19).

27 American Economic Association Committee on Public Issues, *op. cit.,* pp. 506–507. See also *infra,* n. 29.

28 Shaw, *Money, Income, and Monetary Policy,* pp. 395, 398, 424; Hart, *op. cit.,* p. 411. "Monetary policy operates within cycles and not primarily from a longer term viewpoint" (United States Congress, Joint Economic Committee, *Employment and Unemployment,* 87th Congress, 2nd Session, Washington, 1962, p. 13).

29 Shaw, *Money, Income, and Monetary Policy,* pp. 422–423; Boulding, *op. cit.,* pp. 221–223. This proposition is broad enough to include the cyclically passive monetary policy advocated by Milton Friedman on the assumption that, in the present state of our knowledge and institutions, positive counter-cyclical monetary policies are more apt to be destabilizing than stabilizing (*A Program for Monetary Stability,* New York, 1960, p. 23). Some of the incompatibility that observers have found in our objectives is accounted for by a failure to realize the limitations (1) of economic policies in reaching noneconomic social goals (e.g., peace), and (2) of monetary policies in attaining nonmonetary economic goals. Thus, economic objectives are not distinguished from more general social aims, and monetary objectives are not differentiated from more general economic ends. This confusion is implied by the following statement:

217

The broad objective of monetary policy is the same as that of economic policy in general. In substance, it is the attainment of the highest material well-being of society (as measured, say, by the average standard of living) that is compatible with such political and social goals as national security, freedom of the individual, and equality of opportunity for all. *Attainment of these recognized goals is not the sole responsibility of monetary policy* (Whittlesey, *op. cit.,* p. 418).

Indeed it is not the *sole* responsibility of monetary policy! Nor is it the *primary* responsibility. Monetary policy has little responsibility for the attainment of such "political and social goals." Although realization of broad social aims may be obstructed by bad monetary policies, sociopolitical fulfillment cannot be accomplished by even the best *monetary* policies. Later Whittlesey virtually conceded this, but only after he had, perhaps unintentionally, implied much more (*loc. cit.*). Attempts to reach nonmonetary objectives by monetary means are destined for frustration, and such results as are produced may be so perverse as to create or exaggerate the appearance of conflict among the objectives sought. The apparent inconsistency (Woodworth, *op. cit.,* p. 564) might be substantially reduced and the problem of weighting objectives (*loc. cit.*) simplified if the hierarchy of goals were more generally and consistently recognized. "The problem of harmonizing the standard with the objectives" (*loc. cit.*) might then be less troublesome. Some of the argument about competing objectives reduces to different preferences concerning criteria of monetary policy which are based on different interpretations of economic "stability" (see, for example, Henry C. Wallich's summary of the controversy in "Postwar United States Monetary Policy Appraised," *United States Monetary Policy,* pp. 98–102). Shaw's "Money Supply and Stable Economic Growth," *op. cit.,* pp. 66–71, is also relevant.

30 Instead of blaming President Roosevelt's inconsistency, Sir Charles Morgan-Webb attributed the failure of the London Economic Conference in 1933 to incomprehension of the two different meanings of stabilization prevailing at the conference: (1) stable exchange rates (external stability of the value of money, the continental view) and (2) stable price level (internal stability of the value of money, the United States view). (See *The Rise and Fall of the Gold Standard,* New York, 1934, pp. 130–131.) On the other hand, T. E. Gregory expressed the conflicting versions in terms of internal stability only: "It is no longer the *stabilization of prices,* but increased *stability in general* which now attracts economists as constituting the true aim of monetary policy" (*The Gold Standard and Its Future,* 3rd edn., London, 1934, p. 163 [italics mine]).

31 This was accomplished under the nineteenth-century gold standard by having the value of the monetary unit fixed in terms of a common commodity (gold) by more than one country. "The gold standard can best be regarded as a device for maintaining the stability of the exchange rates" (Geoffrey Crowther, *An Outline of Money,* 2nd edn., London, 1948, p. 277). See also J. W. Beyen, *Money in a Maelstrom,* New York, 1949, pp. 25, 27.

32 In either case if the external change is structural rather than cyclical

218

or temporary, there will be a domestic reallocation of resources. The ease of this adjustment will vary directly with the mobility of resources, which is primarily nonmonetary and, therefore, not peculiarly affected by internal or external monetary policies. Advocates of internal, in contrast to external, stabilization maintain that in their program this microeconomic adjustment (to a relative change in the prices of imports and exportables) is uncomplicated by the macroeconomic adjustment (to changes in the quantities of imports and exports and in the volume of income and employment) imposed on the domestic economy by fixed exchange rates. Partisans of external stabilization attach less significance to the macro aspects of the adjustment.

33 The desire is not new; witness the following statement of great depression vintage: "The United States should strive to attain a *monetary standard which accomplishes both internal and external stability.* This means a rejection both of the old point of view of the Bank of England which emphasized stability of foreign exchanges to the neglect of price level considerations, and of the view of the extremist commodity dollar and managed currency schools which emphasizes stability of the internal price level to the neglect of stability in the foreign exchanges. *The objective of the future should be stability in* both fields . . ." (Lionel D. Edie, *Dollars,* New Haven, 1934, p. 279 [italics mine]). At the same time, this desire is not old enough to merit the veneration it has received. The traditional gold standard's prevention of "errant monetary authorities and commercial bankers from indulging in the grossest excesses of inflation and deflation" (Chandler, *op. cit.,* 2nd edn., p. 719) should by no means be confused with a program for stabilizing the domestic price level.

34 Proposals have ranged from various types of "managed gold standards," which obscured rather than resolved the issue by resort to the ambiguity, "stable price system" (Roy L. Garis, *Principles of Money, Credit, and Banking,* New York, 1934, p. 307), to Robert Triffin's plan for converting the International Monetary Fund into an international central bank, and the counterproposals thereto.

35 L. L. B. Angas, *The Problems of the Foreign Exchanges,* New York, 1935, pp. iii, 11–12:

> Money cannot be "sound" (i.e., stable) both externally and internally —Stable money and stable exchanges are mutually incompatible—A choice must be made of the lesser evil.
>
> . . . .
>
> Instability of exchanges is the *price* of monetary stability; instability of money is the *price* of stabilized exchanges.
>
> Alternatively, government interference with foreign trade and international finance is the *price* of trying to secure *sound* money, in both senses.

See also *ibid.,* pp. 9, 13, 67–69.

36 R. G. Hawtrey, *The Gold Standard in Theory and Practice,* 5th edn., London, 1947, p. 238.

37 Richard W. Lindholm, John J. Balles, and John M. Hunter, *Principles of Money and Banking,* New York, 1954, pp. 63–64.

38 *Ad hoc* enlargement of the International Monetary Fund and other

schemes for modifying its *mechanism* without including provisions for assuring appropriate domestic policies fall into this category.

39 Royal Institute of International Affairs, *The Future of Monetary Policy*, London, 1935, pp. 148–149; Day, *op. cit.*, pp. 492–494; W. M. Scammell, *International Monetary Policy*, London, 1957, p. 5, 310–315. Actually, capital flows were at least as important a part of the nineteenth-century equilibrating mechanism as internal resource reallocation (*ibid.*, pp. 5, 311–313).

40 John Maynard Keynes, *A Treatise on Money*, II, New York, 1930, 336: "Owing to her immensely large holdings of gold, the United States is able to obtain, to a great extent, the combined advantages of a local and of an international standard . . ." However, this relative immunity from foreign influence despite stable exchange rates appears to be coming to an end (see the statement of Walter W. Heller, *International Payments Imbalances and Need for Strengthening International Financial Arrangements*, Hearings before the Subcommittee on International Exchange and Payments of the Joint Economic Committee, United States Congress, June 19, 1961, Washington, 1961, pp. 45–46).

41 Such is the rationale of the recent enlargement of the International Monetary Fund and the proposals for giving it the power to create international reserves.

42 Frank D. Graham, *Fundamentals of International Monetary Policy*, Essays in International Finance, No. 2, Princeton, 1943, pp. 11, 14.

43 Interpretation of the United States Employment Act of 1946 as enunciating the objectives of *monetary* policy represents a confusion of monetary and general economic objectives (Per Jacobsson, *Towards a Modern Monetary Standard*, The Stamp Memorial Lecture, London, 1959, p. 11). The degree of resource utilization cyclically and secularly maintained in a free and open society is determined by the degree to which the general economic objectives listed above are achieved. Including "maximization of consumer satisfaction" among the objectives of *monetary* policy represents a similar confusion (Hanks and Stucki, *op. cit.*, pp. 467–474).

44 "The distinction between [general] economic and monetary policy is not always clearly made . . . Monetary policy is but a division, though a major one, of the broader field of economic policy" (Hanks and Stucki, *op. cit.*, p. 466).

45 See *supra*, Chapter VI, n. 48.

46 Hanks and Stucki, *op. cit.*, p. 480; Leland J. Pritchard, *Money and Banking*, Boston, 1958, pp. 489–490; Lawrence Smith, *Money, Credit, & Public Policy*, Boston, 1959, pp. 562–565.

47 Few have improved on Ricardo's statement of the case for independence of the central bank (*The Works and Correspondence of David Ricardo*, ed. Piero Sraffa with the collaboration of M. H. Dobb, Cambridge, 1951–1955, IV, 282–285). This kind of independence did not exist then; nor does it now. Ricardo's premises were long-run. In a short-run cyclical frame of reference, coordination appears to supercede independence (D. H. Robertson, *Money*, 2nd edn., New York, 1929, p. 193; Lloyd W. Mints, *A History of Banking Theory in Great Britain and the United States*, Chicago, 1945, pp. 280–281). The Radcliffe Report under-

scored the issue without resolving it (*Economist,* August 22, 1959, pp. 508–509).

48 Failure to resolve this issue to date has resulted from its traditionally wrong formulation as a question of independence versus coordination on policy *decisions* rather than on the *criteria for* policy decisions (see, for example, Mints, *op. cit.,* p. 272).

49 Evidence that the public acts on principles it does not completely understand is furnished by the calendar, the clock, and the sanitation standard observed in modern communities (Norman Lombard, *Monetary Statesmanship,* New York, 1934, p. 5).

50 Lester V. Chandler, *An Introduction to Monetary Theory,* New York, 1940, p. 185; United States Congress, Joint Economic Committee, *Employment and Unemployment,* pp. 13–14.

51 The bimetallist heterodoxy was overwhelmed (see [S. Dana Horton], *The Parity of Moneys,* London, 1888, pp. 26–27), and the conventional denial of any causative significance in money has been traditionally documented by lifting out of context John Stuart Mill's observation that "there cannot, in short, be intrinsically a more insignificant thing, in the economy of society, than money" (*Principles of Political Economy,* ed. Sir W. J. Ashley, London, 1936 [reprint of 1909 edn.], p. 488).

52 Keynes himself was not as guilty of this paradoxical lopsidedness as his followers (see *supra,* Chapter VI, nn. 184, 185).

53 Ironically, appreciation of this fact (League of Nations, *Report of the Gold Delegation of the Financial Committee,* Geneva, 1932, pp. 56–57; "Objectives of Monetary Policy," *Federal Reserve Bulletin,* XXIII [September 1937], 828) declined as its truth was reinforced by the decreasing mobility of resources and increasing structural rigidity resulting from the quest for security by businessmen, farmers, and workers (see Jacobsson, *op. cit.,* p. 9, for some relevant observations).

54 Will E. Mason, "The New Inflation and the Middle-Class Crisis," *Problems of United States Economic Development,* II, New York, 1958, 156–157; Charles L. Schultze, *Recent Inflation in the United States,* Study Paper No. 1, Study of Employment, Growth, and Price Levels, Joint Economic Committee, Congress of the United States, 86th Congress 1st Session, Washington, 1959, pp. 8–10.

55 Ludwig von Mises has furnished one of the few explicit descriptions of the institutional requirements of "the gold standard" in modern society (*The Theory of Money and Credit,* 2nd edn., trans. H. E. Batson, New Haven, 1953, pp. 219, 438, 448, 450–451). The virtual impossibility of their accomplishment today needs no elaboration.

56 Realistically, the choice today appears to be limited to standards implying either a secularly stable (see Wallich, *op. cit.,* p. 102) or rising price level (see the various and sundry pronouncements of the Cambridge [Mass.] school).

57 Mason, *op. cit.,* pp. 153–156; Schultze, *op. cit.,* p. 10.

58 See *supra,* Chapter VI, n. 201.

59 A fortuitous, coincidental reshuffling of reserves such as to obviate this necessity cannot be realistically expected.

60 Appreciation of these facts antedated the Triffin Proposal (see Royal

221

Institute of International Affairs, *op. cit.,* pp. 18–19, 122–123).

61 This seems possible among nations on roughly the same level of economic development. More general application is less clear. The possibilities for maintaining viable relations between variously developed countries and for extending the area of feasibility for the balance-of-payments standard needs study. In any event, the present failure to rationalize the financial requirements of developed and underdeveloped nations has been described as "monstrous and unnecessary" (A. C. L. Day, "The World's Payments System," *International Payments Imbalances and Need for Strengthening International Financial Arrangements,* Hearings . . . Joint Economic Committee, 1961, p. 326).

62 "The basic rules of the game today are very like those of the old gold standard . . ." (*ibid.,* p. 325). It ought to be pointed out that the "basic rules of the game" are even more completely ignored today than they were before the last collapse of the so-called gold standard. Preservation of the rules and neglect of their internal application will ultimately prove the inadequacy of international reserves in the future as in the past. "Just as in the late twenties, there was repeated discussion of the gold shortage, so in recent years, there has been steadily increasing discussion of the shortage of international liquidity . . ." (*loc. cit.*). "A country which finds itself in external economic difficulties with a balance-of-payments deficit *is normally expected to deal with its troubles by internal action taken to reduce domestic spending and incomes*" (*loc. cit.* [italics mine]). But the fact is that this is *not* normally done. This sort of self-discipline is only rarely manifested. Preservation of fixed exchange rates in the face of these circumstances means growing imbalances. Is it any wonder that "the total amount of internationally acceptable currency in the world is less than the total amount which all countries, taken together, would like to hold" (*ibid.,* p. 326)? It is unrealistic to expect a nation today to accept mass unemployment as the only corrective for fundamental disequilibrium (*loc. cit.*). "Yet it is this policy which is demanded, particularly from the key currencies, in the new gold standard system" (*loc. cit.*). Day concludes that "the full gold standard rules are nonsense today" (*loc. cit.*). Their nonsensicality is underscored by the fact that they are generally ignored.

63 *International Payments Imbalances and Need for Strengthening International Financial Arrangements,* Hearings . . . Joint Economic Committee, 1961, p. 175–176.

64 *Ibid.,* p. 176.

65 Royal Institute of International Affairs, *op. cit.,* p. 213 (italics mine): "Theoretically, the possibilities of combining internal and external stability through management [of the monetary system] are much greater than is often supposed, but practical difficulties remain. It would be important to introduce an element of elasticity into any international system, in order to enable it to withstand the strain. *The possibility of working any international system will depend on how far it can provide for particular countries economic security against the impact of change.*" The added italics epitomize the erroneous doctrine that undermined the old gold standard and has continued to thwart efforts to re-

222

establish a viable international monetary system. Securing the various nations against the impact of change makes an international monetary system based on fixed exchange rates unworkable. Such a system will function only if the constituent countries have the will and the means to expedite rather than obstruct the adaptation of their internal economies to the changes imposed upon them from abroad.

INDEX
(Subject)

Abstract money (*see* Money, Types of).

Abstract standards (*see* Monetary standards, species of).

Accord of 1951, 109, 195 (n. 46).

Adjustment to external change, 119, 219 (n. 32). *See also* Stabilization.

American Economic Association, Committee on Public Issues, 95.

Antibullionism: Agreement with bullionist concept of a monetary standard, 24. Denial external drain required monetary restriction, 85–87. Disagreement with bullionist species of monetary standard, 24, 48, 85–86. Fallacy of (*see* Fallacy of equivocation). Ultimate triumph over bullionism, 54, 170–171 (n. 60).

Antibullionists, 24–25, 48, 171 (n. 60).

Austrian school, 62, 175–176 (n. 46). *See also* Value theory, Austrian.

Balance of payments, 204 (n. 143), 213 (n. 212). Deficit in, 222 (n. 62). Equilibrium of, 74, 215 (n. 9).

Balance-of-payments standard, 82, 99, 116–118, 213 (n. 212), 222 (n. 61). *See also* Monetary standard, generic concepts of, Workable concept.

Balance of trade, 89.

Bank Act of 1844 (U.K.), 85, 88, 199–200 (n. 76), 200 (n. 81).

Bank credit, 87–88, 191 (n. 17), 193 (n. 32).

Bank deposits, 12, 43, 57, 89, 126 (n. 48), 193 (n. 32). Classical view of, 44, 159 (n. 10). And the money supply, 80, 85, 95, 103, 108, 190 (n. 12), 191 (n. 17). *See also* Bank Act of 1844 (U.K.); Money, Types of; Parity, Internal.

Bank of England, 85, 88, 91, 158 (n. 8), 197 (n. 62), 202 (n. 129), 219 (n. 33). Discretionary reserve ratio of, 88. External nineteenth-century orientation of, 214 (n. 215). As nineteenth-century world central bank, 89–91. *See also* Sterling (exchange) standard.

Commercial loan theory of banking, 78, 191 (n. 16). *See also* "Real bills" doctrine.

Commission on Money and Credit, 121 (n. 4).

Committee on Coinage, Weights, and Measures, U.S. Congress, 137 (n. 76), 138 (n. 83), 142 (n. 113).

Committee on Finance and Industry (*see* Macmillan Report).

Commodity money, 15, 35, 43, 81, 105, 157 (n. 224), 171 (n. 60), 200 (n. 80), 202 (n. 116).

Commodity standards, 18, 68, 131 (n. 23), 145 (n. 136), 149 (n. 170), 171 (n. 60), 184 (n. 33), 194 (n. 45). *See also* Goods standard; Monetary standards, species of.

Commodity theory of money, 37, 76, 79, 103, 190 (n. 15), 191 (n. 15). *See also* Monetary theory, Classical; Monetary theory, Neoclassical.

Commodity-reserve standard, 18, 29, 31, 81, 106, 115–116.

Compensated dollar plan, 36, 73, 133 (n. 34), 136 (n. 69), 149 (n. 170), 171 (n. 60), 215 (n. 8). Confused with tabular standard, 149 (n. 167). As implementation, not abrogation, of gold standard, 133 (n. 34), 149 (n. 173).

Conferences: International Monetary (Paris, 1878), 143 (n. 116). International Economic (Genoa, 1922), 188 (n. 83), 192 (n. 20), 205 (n. 147). World Economic (London, 1933), 69, 218 (n. 30). Bretton Woods (1944), 121 (n. 4).

Convertibility, 44, 86–87, 90, 123 n. 28), 191 (n. 17). Classical rationale of, 101. Modern restriction to external application, 36–37, 72–73, 187–188 (n. 78), 205 (n. 143). *See also* Gold reserves, Reversal of roles.

Convertible paper, 43, 102, 184 (n. 37). *See also* Credit money; Money, Types of; Paper money.

Credit conditions, sound, 92, 94, 210 (n. 171).

Credit money, 12, 15, 43–44, 85, 103, 130 (n. 15), 190 (n. 12), 191 (n. 17). Classical concept of, as *replacement* for standard money, 60, 158–159 (n. 8), 177 (n. 60). Modern insignificance of distinction from standard money, 35, 37–38, 102–103. Neoclassical concept of, as *supplement* to standard money, 36, 50, 78–79, 102–103, 154 (n. 204). And obsolescence of "money-material requirements," 8, 126–127 (n. 48). Types of, 190 (n. 14), 199 (n. 74). *See also* Monetary management, Required under traditional gold standard by credit-media augmentation of money supply; Parity, Internal; Standard money, Value of, result not cause of value of credit money; Standard of value, Destruction of concept.

Cunliffe Committee, 203 (n. 134).

Currency, 43, 78, 80, 95, 148 (n. 156), 151 (n. 181), 158 (n. 7), 186 (n. 54), 199 (n. 74), 202 (n. 124), 206 (n. 153). *See also* Convertibility; Monetary terminology, traditional.

Currency controversy, 1, 25, 204 (n. 143).

Currency principle, 98, 141 (n. 108).

Currency school, 25, 89, 91.

Currency system, mixed, 25, 72, 85.

Debt management policy, 195 (n. 48). Fiscal-economy orientation of U.S. Treasury, 108. A species of monetary policy, 113, 195 (n. 48).

Depreciation of money, 48, 151 (n. 182), 169 (n. 55). *See also* Money, Value of.

227

Depression, 15, 79, 107.
Devaluation, 36, 154 (n. 206).
Direct controls vs. open-ended international reserves or flexible exchange rates, 117. *See also* Stability; Stabilization.
Discount rate, 89, 191 (n. 16), 214 (n. 215). *See also* Gold standard, Management of; Monetary management; Monetary policy; Sterling (exchange) standard.
Dollar problem, 112.

Economic theory, traditional limitation of term, 62.
Employment, 97, 104, 212 (n. 199), 217 (n. 26). *See also* Full employment; Monetary standards, species of, Modern, employment standard; Stabilization, Internal.
Employment Act of 1946, 109, 206 (n. 150).
Equilibrium (*see* Balance of payments, Equilibrium of).
Exchange rates: Fixed (stable), 82, 98, 111, 117, 192 (n. 20), 204–205 (n. 143), 218 (n. 31), 219 (nn. 32, 33), 220 (n. 40), 222 (n. 62), 223 (n. 65). Flexible, 107, 110–111, 117, 214 (n. 215). Pegged but adjustable, 118. *See also* Gold reserves, Reversal of roles; Gold standard; Stabilization.

Fallacy of equivocation, 24, 50, 169 (n. 56).
Federal Reserve Act, 201 (n. 102).
Federal Reserve Bank of New York, 188 (n. 85).
Federal Reserve bank reserves (*see* Reserves, Central bank).
Federal Reserve Board, 88, 128 (n. 56), 169 (n. 56), 170 (n. 57), 191 (n. 16), 201 (n. 103), 204 (n. 139), 205 (n. 146), 211 (n. 194), 221 (n. 53). Guided vs. discretionary exercise of broad powers, 209 (n. 165), 216 (n.

23). Justification for rejection of specific guides, 108. *See also* Monetary authorities.
Federal Reserve Policies: Nebulous relation to gold reserves, 91–92, 108, 127–128 (n. 53), 128 (n. 56), 204 (n. 139). Variety of guides to, 91–92, 108. *See also* Monetary authorities, Coordination vs. independence of central bank and treasury; Monetary policies; Fiscal policy.
Federal Reserve System, 91–92, 153 (n. 195), 211 (n. 188).
Fineness of standard metal, 14–15.
Fiscal policy: A species of monetary policy, 108, 113, 195 (n. 48). Independence of vs. coordination with monetary policies, 95, 108–109. *See also* Monetary authorities, Coordination vs. independence of central bank and treasury.
Flight from the currency, 86.
Foreign exchange (*see* Exchange rates; Reserves, International).
Full employment, 83, 206 (n. 150), 217 (n. 26), 217–218 (n. 29). *See also* Employment.

Gold: External drain of, 87, 108, 205 (n. 143): bullion and currency controversies concerning monetary policies appropriate to, 87; modern policy dilemma of, 108. Internal drain of, 87. Now instrument of, rather than guide to, policy, 183 (n. 27), 185 (n. 53), 212 (n. 205). Value of, more result than cause of value of money, 37, 71, 155–156 (nn. 216, 217), 198 (n. 72).
Gold bullion, 78, 133 (n. 35), 156 (n. 216).
Gold bullion standard, 5, 91, 94, 186 (n. 59), 216 (n. 13). International, 125 (n. 41), 203 (nn. 131, 135). Purpose of, 79, 90, 192 (n. 19). Restricted (limited or modi-

fied), 18, 32, 37, 90, 125 (n. 41), 133 (n. 35).

money supply, 88–89, 91, 108, 204 (n. 139), 205 (n. 147), 210 (n. 171), 216 (n. 14). Distinguished from price-level stabilization, 219 (n. 33). Elimination of distinction from paper standard, 70, 73, 105. Equilibration under, 89, 128 (n. 56). Excesses of claims for and against, 69. Fixed exchange rates of, 218 (n. 31). As a genus, 71, 186 (n. 59), 187 (n. 62). As identification of money with gold, 77, 131 (n. 21), 144 (n. 133), 183 (n. 26), 196 (n. 57). Incompatible with modern objectives, 8, 185 (n. 46), 222 (n. 62). Institutional requirements of, 221 (n. 55). International, 203 (n. 135). Limited (modified, restricted), 20, 91, 187 (n. 73): difficulty of distinguishing between modification and abandonment, 69, 71–73; stabilization of money in terms of something other than gold, 206 (n. 153). Managed, 73, 80, 198 (n. 68), 204 (n. 140), 219 (n. 34): broad latitude for discretion, 89, 104; distinction between managements of old and new gold standards, 199 (n. 74); indistinguishable from paper standard, 73, 105; not actually a gold standard, 32, 82, 186 (n. 54), 194 (n. 43); system managed, not the standard, 66, 78, 198 (nn. 71, 72), 208 (n. 162), 187 (n. 75), 199 (n. 74). Management of, 25, 87, 182 (n. 17), 187 (n. 68), 199 (n. 75), 204 (n. 139), 208 (n. 162). Meaning according to workable concept of a monetary standard, 106. Necessary conditions for, 92, 122 (n. 16), 123 (n. 28), 135 (n. 50), 183 (n. 26), 196 (n. 57). Neoclassical defense of: paradox in, 155 (n. 215); paradoxical acceptance of antibullionism and affirmation of commodity theory, 54, 92, 170 (n. 60), 191 (n. 15); as a rea-

sonably stable standard of value, 54, 76–77, 143–144 (n. 129) (*see also* Antibullionism, Ultimate triumph of). Provisional, 125 (n. 41). Redefinition as a substitute for restoration, 69–70. Regulated, 8, 22, 73, 117–118, 128 (n. 57), 150 (n. 174), 170 (n. 58), 188 (n. 83), 206 (n. 153). As a species, 71, 186 (n. 59). Standard of value vs. standard of weight, 149 (n. 173). Sufficient conditions for, 69, 92. Traditional, 72, 83, 85, 99, 125 (n. 41), 149 (n. 173), 185 (n. 52), 187 (n. 65), 193 (n. 32), 199 (n. 74), 213 (n. 207), 218 (n. 31), 219 (n. 33): absence of gold reserves against deposits, 193 (n. 32); form vs. substance, 185 (n. 52); function of gold reserves, 200 (n. 80); managerial discretion in, 87; recognized as managed, 84–85, 105, 197 (n. 61), 198 (n. 72), 199 (n. 74). *See also* Gold (exchange) standard; Monetary management; Monetary standard, generic concepts of, Classical; Monometallism; Sterling (exchange) standard.

Gold Standard Act of 1900 (U.S.), 26, 137 (n. 76).

Gold Standard Defense Association, 142 (n. 110).

Gold-coin standard, 78, 85, 98, 123 (n. 16), 186 (n. 59), 187 (n. 65), 208 (n. 162). *See also* Gold standard, Traditional.

Gold-standard system, 66, 69, 98, 198 (n. 68), 207 (n. 157). Replacement for the classical gold standard (of value), 91, 216 (n. 13). *See also* Gold (exchange) standard, new; Gold standard, limited, managed, regulated; Monetary standard, generic concepts of, Modern.

Government, 77, 84, 101, 200 (n. 80), 206 (n. 156), 209 (n. 164).

Greenback, 1, 25.

Growth, economic, 79, 92, 95. And employment, 79. Obstruction by uncertainty relative to monetary policy, 119. Revival of interest in, 206 (n. 151). And stability, 212 (n. 201), 216 (n. 23).

Historical school, 62.
Hoards, 87. *See also* Plate, as a store of value.

Inconvertibility, 136 (n. 57). New interpretation of, 72–73, 188 (n. 78). Viewed by classicists as temporary condition affecting circulation but not standard, 43–44, 48, 192 (n. 25).
Inconvertible (paper) standard (*see* Paper standard).
Inflation, 96.
Interest rate, 89, 92, 196 (n. 58).
International Monetary Fund, 99, 108, 181 (n. 10), 203 (n. 129), 205 (n. 143), 215 (n. 6), 219 (n. 38). Proposed modifications of, 111–112, 219 (n. 34). Rationale of enlargement of, 113, 220 (n. 41). Reason for necessary modification of, 117.
International Monetary Fund Agreement, 11, 99, 107. Balance-of-payments standard implied in, 106. Gold policy, not gold standard, implied in, 108, 118.

Jevonsonian paradox, resolution of: His terminology as consistent with classicism, 28, 30, 151 (n. 183). Jevons not an "Austrian," 59, 61–62, 175–176 (n. 46), 179 (nn. 66, 70). Jevons' value theory a refinement, not a refutation, of classical theory, 59–60, 176 (n. 47), 177 (n. 58), 178 (n. 62), 178–179 (n. 65), 179 (nn. 66, 68), 179–180 (n. 70). Monetary classicism, evidence of his consistency, not inconsistency, 59–

61, 103, 175 (n. 44), 177 (n. 60). Reasons for misconstruction of Jevons as "Austrian," 60–61, 104, 176 (nn. 47, 50), 177 (n. 57), 178 (n. 64), 179 (n. 68), 180 (n. 70).
Joint Economic Committee, U.S. Congress, 125 (n. 41), 216 (n. 23), 217 (n. 28), 220 (n. 40), 221 (n. 50), 222 (n. 61).

Labor theory of value, 45, 47, 53–54, 60, 161 (n. 25), 172 (n. 1), 176 (n. 47).
Legal tender, 184 (n. 37).
Lender of last resort, 86, 90.
Liquidity, international: Gold as a source of and problem in, 185–186 (n. 53). Proposals for expansion of, 119, 205 (n. 143). Shortage of, 222 (n. 62). *See also* Gold reserves; Reserves, International.
Liquidity preference, 87.

Macmillan Report, 208 (n. 160), 212 (n. 202).
"Managed currency," 2, 68, 84, 198 (n. 72), 209 (n. 163), 219 (n. 33). A policy, not a standard, 95–96. Transition of, from a dirty word to a respectable misnomer, 72–73, 197 (n. 65), 198 (n. 68), 207 (n. 160), 208 (n. 162). *See also* Gold standard, Managed; Monetary management.
Measure of value, 28, 30, 48, 53, 58, 62, 65, 135 (n. 50), 137 (n. 83), 142 (nn. 111, 114), 151 (n. 183), 154 (n. 206), 156 (n. 216), 159 (n. 11), 163 (n. 35), 164 (n. 38), 168 (n. 52). Denial of application to money, 47, 164 (n. 37), 166 (n. 44), 167 (n. 45). As link between classical value and monetary theories, 47, 53–55, 157–158 (n. 4), 162 (n. 28), 164 (n. 37). *See also* Standard of value, Distinction from "unit of account" and "measure of value."

231

Medium of exchange, international, 118.

Metallism, 76. *See also* Bimetallism; Gold standard; Monometallism.

Monetary authorities, 77. Absence of a common guide, 114. Coordination vs. independence of central bank and treasury, 108, 113, 197 (n. 62), 200 (n. 80), 220 (n. 47), 221 (n. 48).

Monetary economics, dormancy of, 214 (n. 3).

Monetary management, 91, 95, 199 (n. 74), 213 (n. 215). Conflicting purposes of, 85. Criteria of, 209 (n. 163), 211 (n. 193). Denial this distinguishes paper from gold standard, 198–199 (n. 72). Inescapability of, 84, 89–90, 93, 208 (n. 162), 208–209 (n. 163). Nineteenth- and twentieth-century monetary systems differ in objectives, not existence, of management, 205 (n. 145). Permitted under traditional gold standard by variable central-bank reserve ratios, 88. Present chaos of decision-making in, 109. Recurrent issues of, under nineteenth-century gold standard, 87. Required under traditional gold standard by credit-media augmentation of money supply, 85, 87–90, 199 (n. 74), 200 (n. 80). Tools of, 88. *See also* Credit money, Neoclassical concept of, as *supplement* to standard money; Parity, Internal, causal sequence reversed by triumph of neoclassical quantity theory over commodity theory; Standard money, Value of, result not cause of value of credit money; Standard of value, Destruction of concept.

Monetary management, discretionary, 73, 216 (n. 23). Difficulties of, 93, 101. Implicit absence of a monetary standard, 194 (n. 40). Latitude increased by excess reserves, 205 (n. 143).

Monetary objectives (*see* Objectives, Monetary).

Monetary policies, 7–8, 67, 72, 84, 89, 92, 109, 116, 128 (n. 59), 194 (n. 40), 198 (n. 71), 205 (n. 143), 214 (n. 215), 215 (n. 10). Must be supplemented by nonmonetary policies, 113–114, 211 (n. 185), 218 (n. 29), 218–219 (n. 32), 221 (n. 53). Need for distinction from nonmonetary policies, 113. Relationship to monetary objectives and standard, 82–83.

Monetary policy, 6, 81, 83, 91, 93, 96, 106, 110, 124 (nn. 30, 33), 124–125 (n. 35), 127–128 (nn. 52–54), 129 (n. 61), 188 (n. 1), 195 (nn. 52, 53), 196 (nn. 57, 58), 200 (n. 80), 209 (nn. 163, 164), 212 (n. 205), 216 (n. 23), 217 (n. 29). Absence of ascertainable criteria of, 183 (n. 27). Complicating factor in issues of, 10. Concept of, 82. Dilemmas of, 11–12, 118. Discretionary, 101. Independence of vs. coordination with fiscal policy, 95 (*see also* Monetary authorities). Internal, 204–205 (n. 143). Necessity for criteria of, 120. Obsolescence of limiting term's coverage to central-bank policy, 113, 195 (n. 48). Possible criteria of, 95, 97–99, 105, 107, 113, 195 (n. 53), 209 (n. 165), 210 (nn. 169, 171), 211 (nn. 185, 195), 213 (n. 212), 218 (n. 29). Primary purpose of, 212 (n. 201). Short-run orientation of, 217 (n. 28).

Monetary requirements, modern subordination of, 193 (n. 34).

Monetary standard: Ambiguity of species, 4–5, 7, 68, 125 (n. 40). Confusion of: with monetary objectives, 6, 84, 105, 124 (n. 35), 188–189 (n. 1); with monetary objectives and policies, 6–7, 9, 12, 84–85, 124 (n. 33), 196 (n. 58); with monetary policies, 6, 67, 71–

72, 76, 84, 104, 123 (n. 28), 124 (nn. 30, 32, 33), 127 (n. 52), 194 (n. 40), 196 (n. 57), 209 (n. 165); with monetary system, 64–67, 104, 126 (n. 47), 182 (n. 19), 216 (n. 13). Inattention to generic concept of, 3, 5–10, 65, 105, 122 (nn. 9, 15), 128 (n. 59), 128–129 (n. 61), 194 (n. 45). Issue of, 27, 95, 118–120, 209 (nn. 163, 165). "Management" of, 66. National vs. international types of, 81–82, 106, 115–117. Necessity for, 10, 105, 209–210 (n. 166). Obsolescence of received concepts of, 10, 101–106. Prerequisites for selection of, 109–115. Present U.S.: actual absence of, 109, 118; possibility for adoption of, 109; variety of names for, 73, 125 (n. 41). Question of desirability of, 109. Reduction to absurdity, 103, 136 (n. 60). Relevance to policies and objectives, 7, 10, 82–84, 129 (n. 61).

Monetary standard, generic concepts of, 3–4, 10, 13, 30, 64, 66–69, 77, 79–80, 102, 104, 121 (n. 4), 133 (n. 34), 182 (n. 19), 194 (n. 45). Classical concept, 12, 21, 23–26, 42–44, 48–50, 78–79, 102, 144 (n. 133), 159 (n. 11), 194 (n. 41): limitations of, 12, 29–33, 39; a matter of substance, 23, 102; *reductio ad absurdum* of (in modern setting), 33, 39–40, 103 (*see also* Gold standard, Classical rationale of, inverted by neoclassicists). Modern concept, 68, 75–81, 105, 193 (n. 40): inconsistencies with both classical and modern doctrine, 78–81; not classificatory basis actually used, 80. Postclassical concept, 34–36, 103: an attempt to accommodate idea of standard to economic changes, 11–12; no escape from absurdity, 38; not classificatory basis actually used, 38–39; rationalization of "paper standard," 157 (n. 224) (*see also* Paper

standard). Preclassical concept, 14–17, 22, 102–104, 130 (nn. 11, 17): deficiency of, 14–18; empty legalism or confusion of standard with policy, 11; a matter of convenience, 102; not classificatory basis actually used, 20; revival of, 11, 15, 20, 27, 39–40, 104; separated mechanism of monetary system from substance of monetary theory, 16. Workable concept, 81–82, 105–107: cure for conceptual anarchy in monetary matters, 84; implicit use of, 92–100, 105; permits recognition of absence of a standard, 81; resolves independence-vs.-coordination-of-central-bank-and-treasury issue, 113; resolves "rules-vs.-authorities" issue, 93, 113; resolves terminological issues, thus clarifying substantive issues, 106.

Monetary standards, paradoxical terms for: Compensated standard, 18, 31, 149–150 (n. 173) (*see also* Compensated dollar plan). Discretionary standard, 20. Flexible standard, 133 (n. 32), 136 (n. 69). Gold insolvency standard, 5. Inconvertible managed gold standard, 5, 73. Inconvertible paper money gold standard, 5, 73. Irredeemable paper money standard based on gold, 5. Limping standard, 17, 80, 132 (n. 28). Managed inconvertible gold bullion standard, 5, 68. Managed inconvertible gold standard, 73. Managed irredeemable paper standard based on silver, 5. Manipulated gold-loan standard, 5, 90. Non-fixed inconvertible paper standard, 5, 125 (n. 41). Provisional gold standard, 5, 125 (n. 41).

Monetary standards, species of: Anticlassical (abstract ["ideal"]), 24, 29, 33, 48, 145 (n. 136), 146 (n. 141), 166 (n. 44), 171 (n. 60). Classical (concrete): labor

233

standard, 18, 20, 81, 107, 115; metallic, 43 (*see also* Bullion standard; Gold bullion standard; Gold coin standard; Gold standard; Monometallism; Silver standard). Modern (abstract): commodity-price-index standard, 215 (n. 8); consumption standard, 211 (n. 186); credit standard, 18; currency exchange standard, 18; demand standard, 211 (n. 195); deposit standard, 105; earnings standard, 212 (n. 197) (*see also* labor standard); employment standard, 81, 97, 107, 115–116; gold parity standard, 18; gold reserve standard, 18, 20, 125 (n. 41); gold settlement standard, 18; goods standard, 81, 95–97, 107, 115–116, 133 (n. 34), 196 (n. 53), 211 (nn. 194, 195) (*see also* demand standard); index-number standard, 18, 29; interest-rate standard, 18, 97, 195 (n. 46); market-basket standard, 97; multiple standard, 5, 18, 29–31, 80, 131 (n. 23), 138 (n. 87), 150 (n. 173); parallel standard, 18; price index standard, 18, 20, 96; stable-price-level standard, 18, 20, 96–97 (*see also* Balance-of-payments standard; Gold bullion standard, Restricted; Gold [exchange] standard, new; Gold standard, Regulated; Inconvertible standard; Monetary standards, paradoxical terms for; Sterling [exchange] standard). Postclassical (confusion of abstract and concrete): fiat standard, 183–184 (n. 32) (*see also* Bimetallism; Gold bullion standard, Restricted; Gold exchange standard; Gold standard, Limited; Gold standard, Managed; Paper standard). Workable: presently feasible standards, assuming primacy of external stability, 115–116; presently feasible standards, assuming primacy of internal stability, 116–

118; reinterpretation of conventional terms for standards, 106–107.

Monetary system, 34, 70–71, 81, 216 (n. 24). Confusion with monetary standard (*see* Monetary standard, Confusion of). Distinguished from monetary theory, 16. And general vs. monetary objectives, 114, 218 (n. 29). Management of, 85–86, 91, 197 (n. 61), 198 (n. 68), 199 (n. 74), 208 (n. 163), 222 (n. 65). Relics of gold standard in, 193 (n. 40). Requirements for, 126 (n. 47).

Monetary terminology, traditional: Classical differentiation of "money," "currency," and "circulation," 158 (n. 7). In general, 39–44. Obsolescence of, 10, 39–46, 49–52, 63, 102–104. Persistence of, 10, 40, 42, 51, 56–58, 63–64, 104–105. Resulting confusion of substantive and terminological issues, 9–10, 30, 44, 64, 67, 74, 83–84, 104–106, 125 (n. 41), 126 (n. 44). *See also* Monetary standard, Confusion of; Money; Standard of value.

Monetary theory, 12, 16, 22, 52, 55–59, 103. Classical: alleged discrepancy with value theory, unfounded, 52, 56–58; application of classical value theory to money, 52, 55–57, 60; explanation of supply of and demand for money, 55–57, 78–79, 174 (n. 21); unrecognized need for revision of, 10, 63, 103 (*see also* Classical school, Not guilty of doctrinal dichotomy; Money, Concepts of, classical). General: immunity to developments in value theory, 10; inconsistency with value theory, 52, 59; lag of, 62, 180 (n. 72). Neoclassical: application of term "neoclassical" to monetary theory, 174 (n. 23); dichotomization of economic theory, 10–12, 57, 62; divesting quantity theory of its classical

234

short-run application, 56–58; elimination of classical distinction between long- and short-run doctrines, 56–58; methodological confusion of "short run" and "long run," 56–58, 174 (n. 28); removal of quantity theory from its classical value-theory context, 55–58, 63, 78–79; reversal of causal sequence between value of gold and value of currency, 36, 71, 155–156 (nn. 216, 217) (*see also* Commodity theory of money; Monetary theory, Classical, alleged discrepancy with value theory; Parity, Internal).

Monetary unit, 16, 18–19, 22, 24, 47–49, 54, 65, 67, 95, 97, 105, 134 (n. 43), 137 (n. 79), 155–156 (n. 216), 164 (n. 37), 168 (n. 48), 170 (n. 57), 171 (n. 60), 187 (n. 62), 196 (n. 57).

Money, 5, 10, 12, 14, 24, 28, 46–50, 62, 70, 75–76, 84, 98, 103, 109, 114, 125 (n. 40), 126 (nn. 42, 47), 131 (n. 17), 133 (n. 35), 135 (nn. 49, 50), 136 (nn. 56, 59, 60), 137 (n. 76), 150–151 (n. 181), 151 (n. 189), 152 (n. 190), 159 (n. 15), 160 (n. 17), 164 (n. 37), 165 (nn. 38, 39), 166 (n. 44), 167 (n. 45), 169 (n. 56), 170 (n. 57), 171 (n. 61), 174 (n. 21), 177 (n. 60), 194 (n. 45), 196 (n. 57), 201 (n. 102), 219 (n. 35), 221 (n. 51). Assumed commodity origin of: influence on contemporary thought, 40, 157 (nn. 225, 228); present irrelevance to abstract moneys ignored, 40, 171 (n. 60). Concepts of: classical, 42–43, 55, 60, 157 (n. 4), 158 (nn. 6, 7), 159 (n. 11); modern, 80, 134 (n. 43); neoclassical, 44, 57–58, 80; unorthodox, 134 (n. 43). Material of, 8, 126–127 (n. 48), 127 (n. 49). Quantity of (*see* Money supply). Substitutes for, 36, 43–44, 158 (n. 6). Types of: abstract, 40, 43, 81, 105, 135 (n.

51), 160 (n. 19); fiat, 145 (n. 136), 157 (n. 224); full bodied, 19, 44, 140 (n. 100); inconvertible, 19, 184 (n. 37), 214 (n. 6); metallic (coin), 20, 92; modern insignificance of distinction between standard and nonstandard, 35–38; nonstandard, 20, 35–38, 78, 104, 123 (n. 28); representative, 190 (n. 14). Value of: cause, not result, of value of gold, 36, 71, 155–156 (nn. 216, 217); in gold, 48, 77, 104, 111, 169 (n. 55), 183 (n. 26), 216 (n. 14); in goods, 15, 22, 35, 48, 58, 78, 142 (n. 111), 151 (n. 182), 154 (n. 206), 156 (n. 216), 171 (n. 60), 192 (n. 25); in moneys, 15, 21, 81, 102, 111. *See also* Commodity money; Credit money; Paper money; Paper standard money; Parity, Internal; Standard money; Token money.

Money supply, 37, 85, 90, 102, 105, 124 (n. 33), 174 (n. 21), 193–194 (n. 40), 210 (n. 171), 213 (nn. 207, 215). Absence of a regulating principle for, 81, 108. Need for criteria for management of, 94.

Monometallism, 25, 29, 78, 124 (n. 33), 127 (n. 52), 138 (n. 90), 151 (n. 186), 167 (n. 45), 190 (n. 15), 191 (n. 15). *See also* Bimetallic controversy; Gold standard.

National Bureau of Standards, 45.
National Industrial Conference Board, 144 (n. 133), 169 (n. 56), 203 (n. 131).
Neoclassical school, 51–52, 174 (n. 23).
Neomercantilism: Need for distinguishing between monetary and nonmonetary problems and remedies, 113–115, 218 (n. 29). Paradoxes in conversion of old heterodoxy into new orthodoxy, 114, 185 (n. 46).
Note issue, 44, 78, 87, 135 (n. 50).

Objectives: All-embracing socio-political: compatibility and priority of, 217–218 (n. 29); limitations of economic means to, 217–218 (n. 29). General economic: compatibility and priority of, 110, 117, 218 (n. 29); democratic version of, 110; limitations of monetary means to, 110–114, 215 (n. 10), 217–218 (n. 29). Monetary: concept of, 82, 109–111; confused with more general goals, 217–218 (n. 29), 220 (n. 43); confused with policies, 7–8, 83; confused with policy guides (standards), 7–8, 82–83, 195 (n. 52), 205 (n. 145); limitations of nonmonetary means to, 113, 217–218 (n. 29); relationship to monetary policies and standard, 82–83; relationship to more general objectives, 110–111 (*see also* Monetary standard, Confusion of, with monetary objectives).

Overtrading, 87.

Paper money: Classical interpretation of, 42, 158 (n. 6). Most token form of tangible money, 19. *See also* Money, Types of; Paper standard money.

Paper standard, 4–5, 14, 20, 29, 35, 38, 40, 66, 70, 72–73, 78, 80, 94, 120, 125 (n. 41), 131 (n. 17), 136 (n. 56), 189 (n. 8), 208 (n. 162). The concept: limbo nature of, 105; negative nature of, 19, 28, 39, 44, 68–69, 127 (n. 52), 135 (nn. 49, 50, 51), 136 (n. 55), 184 (n. 33); prevalence of, 160 (nn. 20, 21); significance of, 48, 106, 135 (n. 49), 145 (n. 136), 159 (n. 11), 214 (n. 6). The term: contradictory nature of, 28, 43, 68, 104–105; rationalization of, 157 (n. 224), 159 (n. 15); reduction of, to absurdity, 19; unclassical nature of, 48, 159 (n. 11).

Paper standard money, 18, 72.

Parity, 2, 16, 103, 160 (n. 19), 186 (n. 53), 196 (n. 57). External, 14. Internal: causal sequence reversed by triumph of neoclassical quantity theory over commodity theory, 35–36, 44, 102–104, 156 (n. 216), 190 (n. 15); classical concept of, 35–37; conventional rationale of, 35; irony of, 37–38; modern irrelevance of, 37, 153 (n. 195), 155 (n. 214). *See also* Credit money, Neoclassical concept of as *supplement* to standard money; Monetary management, Required under traditional gold standard by credit-media augmentation of money supply; Monetary theory, Neoclassical reversal of causal sequence between value of gold and value of currency; Standard money, Value of, result not cause of value of credit money; Standard of value, Destruction of concept.

Plate, as a store of value, 174 (n. 21).

President's Council of Economic Advisors, 114.

Price index, 95–96, 150 (n. 173). *See also* Monetary standards, species of, Modern (abstract).

Price-level stability, 49, 83, 92, 95–98, 210 (n. 169), 215 (n. 10), 217 (nn. 24, 26). Ambivalent usage of term, 196 (n. 58). Assumed by classicists to be unattainable, 32. Inadvisability of exclusive attention to, 195 (n. 53), 211 (nn. 194, 195). *See also* Price-level stabilization; Stability, Internal.

Price-level stabilization, 6, 18, 32, 195–196 (n. 53), 209 (n. 163), 215 (n. 10), 219 (n. 33). Ambivalent usage of term, 83, 210 (n. 169). As an objective, 29. *See also* Price-level stability; Stabilization, Internal.

Public policy, democratic division of labor in, 113–115.

Pseudoclassical school, 52.

236

Psychological school (*see* Austrian school).

Quantity of money, 77–79, 96, 101, 104, 190–191 (n. 15), 192 (n. 26), 199 (n. 74), 200 (n. 80), 216 (n. 14). *See also* Money supply.
Quantity theory, 52, 55–57, 78, 191 (n. 15). *See also* Monetary theory, Classical; Monetary theory, Neoclassical.

Radcliffe Report, 220 (n. 47).
"Real bills" doctrine, 79, 89–90, 191 (n. 17), 193 (n. 32). *See also* "Banking principle" of note issue; Commercial loan theory of banking.
"Received doctrine," meaning of, 161 (n. 23).
Reductio ad absurdum, 33, 38, 103.
Report of the Monetary Commission of the Indianapolis Convention, 142 (n. 110), 147 (n. 145), 150 (n. 178), 156 (n. 223), 159 (n. 14), 163 (n. 34), 197 (n. 66).
Reserve ratio, 88, 95, 204 (n. 143), 207 (n. 158), 210 (n. 171).
Reserves: Bank, 57, 86–88, 157 (n. 225). Central bank, 87–89, 201 (n. 102), 205 (n. 143), 213 (n. 207). International, 111, 116–118, 192 (n. 20), 205 (n. 143), 220 (n. 41), 222 (n. 62). Silver, 80. *See also* Convertibility; Gold reserves.
Royal Commission on Relative Values of Precious Metals (U.K.), 140 (n. 107), 143 (n. 114), 153 (n. 201), 163 (n. 37), 165 (n. 39).
Royal Institute of International Affairs, 181 (n. 8), 182 (n. 18), 199 (nn. 74, 75), 202 (n. 128), 208 (n. 160), 220 (n. 39), 222 (nn. 60, 65).
"Rules-versus-authorities" issue, 84, 87, 92–94, 113, 208 (n. 162), 209 (n. 164). *See also* Monetary

standard, generic concepts of, Workable concept, resolves "rules-vs.-authorities" issue.

Silver, 54–55, 60, 98, 127 (n. 48), 130 (nn. 10, 17), 137 (n. 83), 142 (nn. 110, 114), 155 (n. 215), 191 (n. 15).
Silver standard, 43, 81, 106, 151–152 (n. 189), 196 (n. 57).
Specie payments, resumption of, 2, 25, 54.
Specie régime, 66. *See also* Gold standard.
Stability: External stability: criteria of, 98, 115–117; of the economy, 111; monetary standards appropriate to, 115–116; of money, 111–112; new view of, 213–214 (n. 215). External vs. internal stability: conflict of objectives, 112, 116–120, 205 (n. 148), 213–214 (n. 215), 218 (nn. 29, 30), 219 (nn. 33, 35), 220 (n. 40), 222 (n. 62); nineteenth-century idea of relative attainability, 98; twentieth-century desire for both, 111–112, 222–223 (n. 65); ultimate compatibility vs. simultaneous attainability of, 112, 118. Internal stability: criteria of, 97–98, 115–117, 215 (n. 10), 217 (n. 24); of the economy, 86, 91–92, 97, 110–111, 218 (n. 29); incompatibility with fixed exchange rates and limited international reserves, 117; monetary standards appropriate to, 115–117; of money, 98, 110, 219 (n. 33). *See also* Price-level stability; Stabilization.
Stabilization: External stabilization: meaning of, 111; necessitates internal flexibility, 111, 120–121; premises of, 111, 219 (n. 32). External vs. internal stabilization: conflict of objectives, 111–113, 205 (n. 148), 218 (n. 30); relative priority and relation to monetary standard, 120. Internal

237

stabilization: meaning of, 110; necessitates external flexibility, 111, 120; premises of, 111–112, 219 (n. 32). *See also* Price-level stabilization; Stability.

Stabilization of money: In terms of one commodity *and* many, 54, 107. In terms of one commodity *or* many, 49, 95–97, 111, 196 (n. 53). In terms of other moneys (*see* Stability, External). *See also* Price-level stabilization; Stability; Stabilization.

Standard bullion (metal), 14–15, 36, 80, 129 (n. 4), 155 (n. 216), 160 (n. 18), 199 (n. 74).

Standard coin, 15, 135 (n. 54), 177 (n. 60).

Standard of deferred payments, 30, 58, 132 (n. 26), 137 (n. 72), 146 (n. 144), 166 (n. 40).

Standard of the coinage, 129 (n. 4), 130 (n. 10), 190 (n. 15).

Standard measure of value (*see* Standard of value).

Standard money, 16–18, 20, 22–23, 27, 33, 38, 44, 66–67, 78, 85, 92, 102–103, 130 (nn. 11, 15), 130–131 (n. 17), 133 (nn. 35, 37), 135 (n. 54), 136 (n. 55), 137 (n. 76), 138 (n. 83), 151 (n. 186), 152 (n. 191), 154 (n. 204), 157 (n. 224), 160 (nn. 18, 19), 189 (n. 8), 190 (n. 15). Change from standard for relative valuation of goods to standard for valuation of money in terms of goods, 154 (n. 206). Change of, without changing standard of value for goods, 36. Concepts of: classical, 42, 158 (n. 5); neoclassical, 130 (n. 8); preclassical, 129 (n. 5). Difficulties in identification of, 133 (n. 36). Modern irrelevance of, 19, 35, 103–105, 131 (n. 23), 134 (n. 43), 136 (nn. 57, 59). Not necessarily identical with standard of value, 34, 36. Value of, result not cause of value of credit money, 36–37, 155 (n. 215). *See also* Credit

money, Neoclassical concept of, as *supplement* to standard money; Monetary management, Required under traditional gold standard by credit-media augmentation of money supply; Parity, Internal, causal sequence reversed by triumph of neoclassical quantity theory over commodity theory; Standard of value, Destruction of concept.

Standard of value, 18, 22–23, 25, 28, 31, 36, 38, 42, 45–46, 48, 51, 54, 63, 65–67, 78, 103–104, 132 (n. 26), 136 (n. 72), 137 (nn. 76, 79), 141 (n. 108), 143 (n. 114), 144 (n. 129), 144–145 (n. 133), 145 (nn. 136, 139), 146 (n. 144), 147 (n. 147), 148 (n. 156), 150–151 (n. 181), 151 (n. 183), 152 (n. 191), 156 (nn. 216, 217), 158 (n. 8), 163 (n. 35), 164 (n. 38), 166 (n. 40), 168 (n. 48), 169 (n. 56), 172 (n. 62), 175 (nn. 38, 44), 194 (n. 41). Anti-classical-neoclassical confusion of, with unit of account, 24, 33, 38–39, 47, 49, 145–146 (n. 141), 156 (n. 216), 169 (n. 56). Concepts of: classical, 12, 21, 23–24, 29–30, 43, 48, 63, 102, 142 (n. 110), 162 (n. 28), 168 (n. 53), 175 (n. 38); modern, 15, 21–22, 130 (n. 15), 137 (n. 76), 152 (n. 190); neoclassical, 49–50, 58, 170 (n. 57); preclassical-anti-classical, 24–25. Denial of abstract concept of, 24–25, 48, 140 (n. 103). Destruction of concept, 45–48, 50, 57–58, 103, 163–164 (n. 37), 166 (n. 44), 168 (n. 48), 173 (n. 2). Distinction from "unit of account" and "measure of value," 24–25, 28, 30, 45–49, 59, 61–63, 167 (n. 45), 168 (n. 52). Invalidity of yardstick analogy, 46, 164–165 (n. 38), 165–166 (n. 39), 167 (n. 45). Necessity for intrinsic value of, 25, 33, 38–39, 156 (n. 223), 171 (nn. 60, 61). Neoclassical anomaly of variable value of, 20, 50, 59, 142 (n. 111), 152 (n. 195), 165 (nn. 38, 39), 169–170 (n. 57), 171 (n. 62), 186 (n. 54). Postclassical distinction from standard money, 22–23, 138 (n. 83), 154 (n. 206). Species of: commodity other than gold, 26, 28–30, 33–34, 50, 59, 61, 69, 138 (n. 89), 209 (n. 163); Gold, 25–27, 35–36, 48, 91, 137 (n. 73), 141 (nn. 108, 109), 149 (n. 173), 155 (n. 214), 175 (n. 43), 186 (n. 54); money, 15, 50, 137 (n. 79), 150–151 (n. 181), 156 (nn. 216, 217), 157 (n. 4), 165 (n. 38); paper, 28, 39. Survival of term, 58. Terminological issue of, 162 (n. 28), 163 (n. 37). *See also* Credit money, Neoclassical concept of, as *supplement* to standard money; Gold standard; Measure of value; Monetary management, Required under traditional gold standard by credit-media augmentation of money supply; Monetary standard, generic concepts of, Classical concept; Paper standard; Parity, Internal.

Sterilization, 110.

Sterling (exchange) standard, 90–91, 202–203 (n. 129), 203 (nn. 131, 135). *See also* Gold standard, Traditional.

Symmetallism, 29, 81, 106, 137 (n. 83), 148 (n. 150).

Tabular standard, 17, 80, 131 (n. 23), 132 (n. 24), 149 (nn. 167, 170), 193 (n. 37). Of deferred payments, 132 (n. 26), 148 (n. 156), 150 (n. 173), 175 (n. 43). Genesis of, 131 (n. 24). Of value, 30–31, 148 (n. 156), 148–149 (n. 158).

Token money, 19, 102, 127 (n. 49), 135 (nn. 54, 55).

Treasury policies (*see* Monetary authorities; Monetary policies; Monetary policy).

Triffin proposal, 222 (n. 60).

Unemployment, 212 (n. 201), 215 (n. 10). *See also* Employment; Full employment.

Unilateral payments, 87.

Unit of account, 28, 47–49, 123 (n. 28), 145–146 (n. 141), 169 (n. 56), 171 (n. 60). International, 118. Money as, 46, 167 (n. 45). *See also* Standard of value, Distinction from "unit of account" and "measure of value."

Unit of value, 21, 142 (n. 111), 152 (n. 190). *See also* Unit of account.

U.N. report on full employment measures, 206 (n. 150).

U.S. Constitution, 21.

U.S. Treasury Department Reports, 132 (n. 27), 141 (n. 109), 182 (n. 18), 188 (n. 85), 216 (n. 13).

Utility, Marginal, 16, 45, 52, 58, 61–63, 161 (n. 24), 162 (n. 28), 163 (n. 37), 176–177 (n. 52), 179 (n. 70).

Utility theory of value (*see* Value theory, Austrian).

Value: Common denominator of, 46–48, 167 (nn. 44, 45) (*see also* Standard of value, Distinction from "unit of account" and "measure of value"). Denial of absolute, 164 (n. 37). Exchange, 4, 49, 161 (nn. 26, 27), 162 (n. 28), 163 (n. 37), 167 (n. 45). Intrinsic, 46, 50, 161 (n. 25), 164 (n. 37), 171 (n. 61), 172 (n. 1), 172–173 (n. 2), 194 (n. 45): denial of, 12, 58, 62–63, 161 (n. 26), 164 (n. 37), 172 (n. 63); implied by classical value theory, 45–46, 51, 161 (n. 25), 162 (n. 28); persistence of notion, 58, 63, 161 (n. 24), 172 (n. 63) (*see also* Labor theory of value). Objective vs. subjective, 57–58, 161 (nn. 24, 26), 164 (n. 37). Use, 45, 161 (n. 24).

Value theory, 10, 12, 55, 59, 61, 180 (n. 72). Austrian, 52, 57–59, 62,

175–176 (n. 46), 179 (n. 70). Classical, 52–54, 60, 81, 104, 173 (n. 8), 176–177 (n. 52), 177 (nn. 55, 58), 179 (n. 66), 179–180 (n. 70). False appearance of irrelevance to monetary theory, 103. Modern, 45, 63, 81, 103. Schools of, 172 (n. 1), 175–176 (n. 46). *See also* Austrian school; Classical school; Labor theory of value; Monetary theory, Classical, unrecognized need for revision of; Monetary theory, Classical, alleged discrepancy with value theory; Neoclassical school; Pseudoclassical school.

War of standards, 1–3, 121 (n. 3), 167 (n. 45).

INDEX
(Author)

241

242

money, 153 (n. 200). Monetary policy: gold and, 95, 154 (n. 202), 193 (n. 36), 205 (nn. 139, 142, 143), 205 (n. 143); independence vs. coordination of central bank and treasury, 216 (nn. 18, 19); monetary management, 136 (n. 62), 182 (n. 17), 188 (n. 79), 192 (n. 21), 202 (n. 120), 208 (n. 160), 209 (n. 163), 221 (n. 50); substitution of "policies" for "standards," 128 (n. 59), 182–183 (n. 22), 196 (n. 58). Species of monetary standards: differences within as well as among categories, 183 (n. 30); gold, 70, 182 (n. 16), 185 (nn. 51, 52), 186 (n. 58), 187 (n. 62), 199 (n. 72), 200 (n. 80), 207 (n. 158), 215 (n. 11), 219 (n. 33); gold bullion, 192 (n. 19), 202 (nn. 119, 121); gold exchange, 192 (n. 20); inconvertible (paper), 135 (n. 51), 183 (n. 31), 184 (nn. 35, 41), 214 (n. 6); procedure for identification of, 123 (n. 17); sterling, 90. Standard of value, 154 (n. 201), 166 (n. 39), 168 (n. 48). Terminology, 41–42, 195 (n. 47).

Cline, Denzel Cecil, 136 (n. 62), 182 (n. 22), 186 (n. 58), 200 (n. 80).

Conant, Charles A., 65, 123 (n. 27), 131 (n. 23), 132 (n. 28), 136 (n. 57), 143 (n. 128), 145 (n. 136), 149 (n. 159), 155 (n. 210), 161 (n. 26), 165 (n. 39), 172 (nn. 62, 63), 183 (n. 29), 185 (n. 45).

Condliffe, J. B., 198 (n. 71).

Copleston, Edward, 139 (n. 97).

Coulborn, W. A. L., 3, 125 (nn. 35, 41), 128 (n. 55), 132 (n. 29), 134 (n. 40), 136 (n. 61), 185 (n. 52), 188 (n. 84), 201 (n. 109), 203 (n. 134), 212 (n. 199).

Cross, Ira B., 137 (n. 77), 184 (n. 37).

Crowther, Geoffrey, 122 (n. 14), 134 (n. 39), 153 (nn. 197, 200), 154

(n. 208), 156 (n. 216), 185 (n. 52), 186 (n. 54), 190 (n. 12), 192 (n. 29), 204 (n. 142), 218 (n. 31).

Cummings, John, 174 (n. 15), 193 (n. 32).

Currie, Lauchlin, 187 (nn. 67, 68, 72, 73), 189 (n. 12), 192 (n. 29), 205 (n. 143).

Curtis, Myra, 205 (n. 148), 209 (n. 163).

Darwin, George H., 178 (n. 64).

Davidson, David, 203 (nn. 134, 135), 206 (n. 155).

Day, A. C. L., 128 (nn. 58, 60), 181 (nn. 10, 12, 15), 182 (nn. 18, 19), 201 (nn. 105, 106), 203 (nn. 131, 136), 208 (n. 160), 216 (n. 20), 220 (n. 39), 222 (nn. 61, 62).

Del Mar, Alexander, 153 (n. 201), 159 (n. 10), 162 (n. 27), 165 (n. 39), 172 (n. 63), 215 (n. 7).

Dick, Ernst, 134 (nn. 44, 46).

Dickinson, Robert William, 214 (n. 4).

Disraeli, Benjamin, 140 (n. 107).

Donaldson, John, 3, 96, 122 (n. 9), 153 (n. 195), 154 (n. 202), 182 (n. 18), 185 (n. 53), 205 (n. 148).

Dowrie, George William, 98, 128 (n. 57), 133 (n. 37), 136 (n. 63), 137 (n. 77), 147 (n. 147), 150 (n. 173), 152 (n. 191), 153 (n. 196), 154 (n. 208), 156 (nn. 216, 218, 219), 166 (n. 39), 172 (n. 62), 193 (n. 35), 199 (n. 74), 200 (n. 78), 204 (nn. 138, 143), 208 (n. 160).

Dunbar, Charles F., 193 (n. 32).

Durbin, E. F. M., 195 (n. 49).

Eckard, E. W., 177 (n. 56), 179 (nn. 68, 70).

Edgeworth, F. Y., 148 (n. 150).

Edie, Lionel D., 94, 143 (n. 128), 170 (n. 58), 181 (n. 16), 182 (n. 21), 185 (n. 52), 202 (nn.

244

as system, 181 (n. 10), 186 (n. 53), 198 (n. 68), 207 (n. 157), 207–208 (n. 160); workable, 96–97, 211 (n. 195), 212 (n. 205), 213 (n. 212). Incongruity of managing gold standard independently of gold supply, 193–194 (n. 40). Limping standard, 193 (n. 38). Monetary standard and value of money, 189 (nn. 7, 8). Policy guides: identification with goals, 96–97, 124 (n. 35), 125 (nn. 36, 38), 195 (n. 51), 196–197 (n. 58); lack of, 108–109; suggestions for, 98. Terminological issues, 133 (nn. 35, 37), 134 (n. 41). Variation of goods value of gold standard of value, 154 (n. 202), 199 (n. 74).

Hamilton, Alexander, 21, 147 (n. 148).

Hanks, J. Whitney, 65, 123 (n. 21), 136 (n. 59), 166 (n. 39), 169 (n. 56), 182 (n. 19), 183 (n. 22), 184 (n. 33, 34), 186 (n. 59), 187 (n. 76), 195 (n. 52), 216 (n. 18), 220 (nn. 43–46).

Hansen, Alvin H., 190 (n. 14).

Hardy, Charles O., 202 (n. 117).

Harris, Joseph, 129 (n. 5), 130 (n. 10), 151 (n. 187), 153 (n. 197), 158 (n. 4), 164 (n. 38), 192 (n. 30).

Harrod, Roy, 205 (n. 143).

Hart, Albert Gailord, 97, 116, 124 (n. 33), 125 (n. 39), 196 (n. 53), 216 (n. 22), 217 (n. 28).

Hawtrey, R. G.: Art of central banking, 86, 200 (n. 83). Gold standard: as limitation on money supply, 190 (n. 12); monetary management under, 199 (n. 73), 200 (n. 80), 202 (n. 114), 208 (n. 160); as a moral principle, 184 (n. 45); recommended modification of, 206 (n. 153), 219 (n. 36); variability of gold reserves, 201 (nn. 94–98). Monetary standard, 157 (n. 223), 181 (nn. 10, 11, 15). Standard money, 153 (nn. 197, 200), 154 (n. 202).

Standard of value, 140 (n. 103), 152 (n. 191).

Hayek, F. A. von, 72, 128 (n. 54), 154 (n. 204), 187 (n. 75), 200 (n. 78), 201 (n. 91).

Helfferich, Karl, 65, 130 (n. 12), 135 (nn. 50, 54), 161 (nn. 24, 26), 163 (n. 37), 165 (n. 39), 167 (nn. 44, 45), 181 (nn. 6, 7), 197 (n. 61).

Heller, Walter W., 197 (n. 64), 220 (n. 40).

Helm, Elijah, 155 (n. 215), 191 (n. 15).

Hepburn, A. Barton, 143 (n. 128).

Herries, Edward, 200 (n. 81).

Hexner, Ervin P., 121 (n. 4), 137 (n. 77), 185 (n. 49), 213 (nn. 210, 211).

Higgs, Henry, 180 (n. 72).

Hobson, J. A., 134 (n. 46).

Holdsworth, John Thom, 122 (n. 14), 123 (n. 18), 125 (n. 41), 149 (nn. 158, 170), 150 (n. 175), 152 (n. 191), 153 (n. 200), 154 (n. 208), 156 (n. 218), 157 (n. 226), 160 (n. 20), 168 (n. 47), 187 (nn. 64, 68), 188 (n. 88), 194 (n. 45), 199 (n. 72).

Horner, Francis, 197 (n. 62).

Horton, S. Dana, 13, 14, 26, 129 (n. 3), 150 (n. 181), 163 (n. 37), 221 (n. 51).

Howard, Earl Dean, 133 (n. 37), 143 (n. 128), 150 (n. 178), 166 (n. 39).

Huizinga, J. H., 144 (n. 133).

Hunter, John M. (see John J. Balles).

Huskisson, William, 168 (n. 52).

Hutchison, T. W., 214 (nn. 1, 2).

Jack, D. T., 133 (n. 37), 143 (n. 128), 169 (n. 56).

Jackson, George N., 165 (n. 38), 166 (n. 44).

Jacobsson, Per, 126 (n. 43), 197 (n. 58), 198 (n. 68), 209 (n. 165), 213 (n. 211), 220 (n. 43), 221 (n. 53).

Jacoby, Neil H., 61 (n. 129), 214 (n. 3), 216 (n. 23).

James, F. Cyril, 122 (n. 14), 128 (n. 57), 144 (n. 133), 146 (n. 141), 153 (nn. 200, 201), 154 (n. 202), 155 (n. 214), 156 (n. 216), 169 (n. 56), 182 (n. 18), 198 (n. 68), 210 (n. 175).

Jerome, Edward, 186 (nn. 54, 58), 201 (n. 95), 202 (n. 127).

Jevons, H. Stanley, 177 (nn. 56, 57).

Jevons, H. Winefred, 177 (n. 56).

Jevons, W. Stanley: Bank of England as world central bank, 202 (n. 127). On importance of classification, 126 (nn. 42, 44). Marginal utility, 58. Monetary standard as standard of value, 26, 142–143 (n. 114). Money: declining importance of requirements for money material, 126–127 (n. 48); functions of, 28, 30, 46–47, 58–59, 103, 145 (nn. 139, 140), 146 (n. 144), 151 (n. 183), 166 (n. 40); significance of, 193 (nn. 30, 31); standard vs. token, 19. Monometallist, 26, 146 (n. 143), 147 (n. 147). Paradox of his monetary classicism, 58. Resolution of Jevonsonian paradox: his value theory not anticlassical, 59–62, 103–104, 175–180 (nn. 37–41, 46–72), 192 (n. 26). Standard and policy, 124 (n. 32). Standard of value: distinction from standard money, 154 (n. 207); as monetary standard, 26, 142–143 (n. 114) (*see also* Jevons, W. S., Money, functions of). Tabular standard, 30, 132 (n. 24), 148–149 (n. 158). Value, 161 (nn. 26, 27), 175 (n. 36).

Johnson, Harry G., 125 (n. 41).

Johnson, Joseph French, 124 (n. 33), 133 (n. 37), 143 (n. 128), 150 (n. 178), 157 (n. 224), 166 (n. 39), 190 (n. 12).

Jome, Hiram L., 130 (nn. 7, 14), 154 (n. 201), 166 (n. 39), 169 (n. 56), 182 (n. 16), 185 (n. 47), 186 (n. 55), 198 (n. 68), 204 (n. 141).

Joplin, Thomas, 139 (n. 96), 140 (n. 100).

Jordan, William Leighton, 129 (n. 4), 137 (n. 83), 138 (n. 86), 140 (n. 107), 142 (n. 111), 143 (n. 124), 147 (nn. 146–149), 153 (nn. 196, 197).

Judson, Lewis W., 162 (nn. 29, 30, 32, 33).

Kelly, Patrick, 130 (n. 6), 162 (n. 31).

Kemmerer, Edwin Walter: Credit money as supplement to, instead of substitute for, standard money, 159 (n. 13). *De facto* vs. *de jure* departure from gold standard, 207 (n. 158). Distention of quantity theory to long run, 174 (n. 31). Implicit artificiality of internal parity dogma, 155 (nn. 210, 215). Monetary standard: implied conception of, as combination of standard money and standard of value, 152 (n. 191); implied conception of, as system, 181 (nn. 11–13); implied standard-money concept of, 131 (n. 23); implied standard-of-value concept of, 138 (n. 84), 148 (n. 153), 156 (n. 218); neglect of genus, 122 (nn. 14, 15); rationalization of term "paper (fiduciary) standard" by terminological distinction between "standard" and "primary" money, 157 (n. 224); species of, 123 (n. 27), 186 (n. 59), 188 (n. 81), 202 (n. 122), 215 (n. 8). Standard of value: use of false analogy of physical measurements, 166 (n. 39); variability of, 152 (n. 195), 154 (n. 201). Tabular standard distinguished from monetary standard, 132 (n. 26). Vacillation between automaticity and management of gold standard, 188 (n. 81), 198

246

Lawrence, Joseph Stagg, 132 (n. 24), 137 (n. 81), 143 (n. 128), 197 (n. 60).
Layton, Walter T., 143 (n. 128).
Leacock, Stephen, 7.
Leffler, Ray V., 4, 126 (n. 46), 130 (n. 15), 133 (n. 34), 136 (n. 69), 154 (nn. 206–208), 156 (n. 216), 160 (n. 19), 168 (n. 48).
Lehfeldt, R. A., 73, 135 (n. 49), 150 (n. 174), 152 (n. 189), 153 (n. 201), 166 (n. 39), 187 (n. 69), 191 (n. 17).
Leith-Ross, Sir Frederick, 205 (n. 143).
Lindholm, Richard W. (see John J. Balles).
Linton, Edward D., 140 (n. 100).
Liverpool, Lord, 158 (n. 5).
Lohman, Philipp H. (see Delmas R. Cawthorne).
Lombard, Norman, 124 (n. 35), 192 (n. 20), 196 (n. 58), 197 (n. 66), 202 (n. 127), 209 (n. 163), 211 (n. 187), 221 (n. 49).
Lowe, Joseph, 131 (n. 24).
Luthringer, George Francis (see Denzel Cecil Cline).
Lutz, Friedrich A., 203 (n. 129), 204 (n. 140).

MacDonnell, Sir John, 127 (n. 48).
Maclaren, James, 141 (n. 108).
MacLeod, Henry Dunning, 122 (n. 5), 163 (n. 37), 165 (n. 39), 172 (n. 63).
Madden, John T., 130 (n. 14), 184 (n. 43), 201 (n. 93), 202 (n. 122), 204 (n. 142).
Magee, James Dysart, 138 (n. 84), 161 (n. 24), 166 (n. 39).
Marshall, Alfred, 27, 29, 61, 132 (n. 31), 137 (n. 83), 147 (n. 147), 148 (nn. 150, 151), 149 (nn. 163, 164), 153 (n. 201), 157 (n. 226), 178 (n. 65), 179 (nn. 66–68).
Marx, Karl, 52.
Mason, Will E., 139 (n. 92), 145 (n. 135), 157 (n. 3), 159 (nn. 8,

9), 169 (n. 54), 186 (n. 54), 201 (nn. 87–89), 221 (nn. 54, 57).
Meade, J. E., 211 (n. 193).
Melville, L. G., 96.
Menger, Karl, 163 (n. 37), 176 (n. 46).
Mikesell, Raymond, 189 (n. 2).
Mill, James, 24, 140 (n. 103), 163 (n. 36), 173 (n. 8).
Mill, John Stuart: Bank deposits regarded as commercial credit, not as part of currency, 159 (n. 10). Concept of monetary standard: as criterion of monetary policy, 210 (n. 174); as standard of value, 141 (n. 108). Gold standard: advocacy of, 26; interpretation of, 141 (n. 108), 162 (n. 28), 173 (n. 14). On importance of classification, 126 (n. 42). Member of banking school, 87, 98, 201 (n. 89). Monetary theory: elasticity of money supply explained by alternative uses of precious metals as money or plate, 174 (n. 21); position of money supply function explained by cost of producing or obtaining precious metals, 174 (nn. 22, 29); quantity theory, an application of market supply-demand analysis to money, 174 (n. 20); value of money explained in same manner as value of any other commodity, 174 (n. 19). Money: claimed insignificance of, related to quantity in analytical long run, 193 (nn. 30, 31), 221 (n. 51); convertible credit money a substitute for, not supplement to, standard money, 158 (n. 6); inconvertibility viewed as affecting circulation, not standard, 159 (nn. 8, 9); interpretation of, 158 (nn. 6–8). Not the last of the classicists, 175–176 (nn. 46, 47). Overtrading and commercial crises, 200 (n. 86). Standard of value: classical realization standard for relative valuation of goods did not imply stable value of

249

Poor, Henry V., 121 (n. 1), 174 (n. 34).
Prather, Charles L., 123 (nn. 19, 20), 125 (n. 41), 126 (nn. 46, 47), 132 (n. 27), 144 (n. 133), 146 (n. 141), 151 (n. 183), 156 (n. 216), 159 (n. 12), 168 (n. 47), 170 (n. 57), 183 (n. 26), 184 (n. 37), 186 (n. 58).
Preston, Robert E., 130 (n. 11).
Pritchard, Leland J., 122 (nn. 4, 16), 125 (n. 40), 150 (n. 175), 152 (n. 192), 156 (nn. 219–222), 157 (n. 229), 159 (n. 12), 170 (n. 57), 183 (n. 25), 187 (nn. 65, 66, 71), 188 (n. 88), 189 (n. 10), 194 (n. 45), 195 (n. 48), 211 (n. 194), 220 (n. 46).
Probyn, Lesley, 138 (n. 86), 190 (n. 15).
Puxley, H. L., 167 (n. 46), 168 (n. 47), 185 (n. 52), 199 (n. 74), 205 (n. 148).

Raithby, John, 140 (n. 100).
Reed, Harold L., 121 (n. 4).
Ricardo, David: Bullion standard proposal, 79, 94, 139 (n. 96). Case for independence of central bank, 220 (n. 47). Concept of monetary standard: as criterion of monetary policy, 210 (n. 174); as standard of value, 23–25, 139 (nn. 93, 96), 192 (n. 23). Distinguished from Jevons in form, not substance, 178 (n. 65). Exchange value, 165 (n. 39). Gold standard: gold reserves viewed as guide to central bank policy, 200 (n. 80); rationale of, 173 (n. 14); remained the standard during inconvertibility, 48–49, 158–159 (nn. 8, 9, 11), 169 (n. 55), 192 (n. 25). Harmony of monetary and value theory, 173 (nn. 5, 7), 176 (n. 52), 192 (nn. 24, 26). Money: claimed irrelevance of its quantity, related to analytical long run, 193 (n. 30); convertible credit money a substitute for, not

supplement to, standard money, 158 (n. 6); inconvertibility as a principle instead of expedient, viewed as paper currency without a standard, 159 (n. 11); inconvertibility viewed as affecting circulation, not standard, 48–49, 158–159 (nn. 8, 9, 11). Policy implications of external drain, 87. Standard of value: denial of anti-bullionist abstract notion of, 24–25, 48; distinction from exchange value, 162 (n. 28); distinction from unit of account, 168 (n. 52); interpretation of, 162 (n. 28).
Ridgeway, William, 130 (n. 9).
Rist, Charles, 145 (n. 133), 153 (n. 197), 154 (n. 201), 191 (n. 17).
Robertson, Sir Dennis H., 20, 67, 77, 125 (n. 41), 132 (n. 28), 136 (nn. 70, 71), 153 (n. 197), 156 (n. 216), 185 (n. 45), 205 (n. 147), 210 (nn. 167, 175), 220 (n. 47).
Robey, Ralph, 140 (n. 107), 143 (n. 114), 153 (n. 201), 163 (n. 37), 165 (n. 39).
Rogers, James E. Thorold, 153 (n. 200).
Rogers, James Harvey, 204 (n. 139), 206 (n. 153), 207 (n. 158).
Rogers, Raymond, 131 (n. 19), 154 (n. 208).
Roll, Erich, 176 (nn. 46, 48), 178 (n. 63).
Rooke, John, 132 (n. 31).
Roosevelt, President Franklin D., 218 (n. 30).
Rostow, W. W., 154 (n. 208), 155 (n. 214), 166 (n. 39).
Rueff, Jacques, 213 (n. 214).
Rufener, Louis A., 123 (n. 26), 126 (n. 47), 188 (nn. 90, 93).

Sadeque, Abdus, 132 (n. 28), 144 (n. 133).
Salomons, Sir David, 141 (n. 108), 142 (n. 114), 191 (n. 15), 201 (n. 95).

Samuelson, Paul, 197 (n. 64), 208 (n. 162).

Scammell, W. M., 202 (n. 127), 220 (n. 39).

Schultze, Charles L., 221 (nn. 54, 57).

Schumpeter, Joseph, 173 (n. 3), 176 (n. 46), 178 (n. 63), 180 (n. 72).

Scitovsky, Tibor, 119, 125 (n. 41).

Scott, William A., 126 (n. 47), 135 (nn. 54, 55), 146 (n. 142), 153 (n. 200), 154 (n. 202), 157 (n. 225), 184 (n. 38).

Scrope, G. Poulett, 131 (n. 24), 141 (n. 108), 148 (n. 158), 151 (n. 183), 165 (n. 38).

Seaver, Charles H., 196 (n. 57).

Seligman, Edwin R. A., 161 (n. 24), 179 (n. 68).

Senior, N. W., 176 (n. 52).

Shapiro, Eli, 206 (n. 154).

Shaw, Edward S.: Bank of England as world central bank before 1914, 203 (n. 129). Chaos of decision-making in monetary management, 216 (n. 21). Concept of monetary standard: conflict of, with notion of limited gold standard, 193 (n. 40); interpretation of, as a policy, 194 (n. 40); interpretation of, as principle limiting money supply, 76–77, 121 (n. 4), 124 (n. 33); interpretation of, as standard of value, 194 (n. 41); virtual disappearance of term and concept, 128 (n. 58), 128–129 (n. 61). Dormancy of monetary economics, 214 (n. 3). Federal Reserve policy: association with "real bills" doctrine, 191 (n. 16), 193 (n. 32); interest rate on government securities as criterion of, 97, 195 (n. 46), 205–206 (n. 149); neglect of reserve ratio as guide to, 193 (n. 32); "sound credit conditions" as guide to, 210 (n. 171). Gold standard: confusion with gold policy, 186 (n. 54); *de facto* abandonment of, 73; modern tendency to call any mone-

tary use of gold a gold standard, 185 (n. 52). Relative attainability of goals by monetary means, 217 (nn. 28, 29). Species of monetary standards: credit standard, 134 (n. 47); currency exchange standard, 134 (n. 42); demand standard, 211 (n. 195); gold settlement standard, 134 (n. 38); modern American limping standard, 132 (n. 28); paper standard as absence of a standard, 214 (n. 6); sterling exchange standard, 203 (n. 131).

Sherbrooke, Lord, 147 (n. 147).

Sherwood, Sidney, 6, 124 (n. 30), 135 (n. 54).

Shibley, George H., 142 (n. 111), 146 (n. 144), 147 (nn. 147, 148), 174 (nn. 16, 17).

Sidgwick, Henry, 126 (n. 44), 159 (n. 10).

Simons, Henry C., 197 (n. 59).

Smith, Adam, 101, 139 (n. 91), 151 (n. 183), 158 (n. 6), 164 (n. 38), 173 (nn. 10, 12–14).

Smith, J. Allen, 132 (n. 31), 134 (n. 45), 148 (nn. 152, 155), 149 (n. 165), 150 (n. 176), 175 (n. 41).

Smith, Lawrence, 16, 122 (n. 16), 123 (nn. 22, 23), 125 (n. 41), 133 (n. 34), 136 (nn. 58, 60, 68), 137 (nn. 78, 80), 154 (n. 201), 181 (n. 12), 182 (n. 18), 184 (n. 35), 186 (n. 56), 188 (nn. 91, 92, 95), 193 (n. 34), 195 (n. 48), 196 (n. 57), 209 (nn. 165, 166), 220 (n. 46).

Smith, Thomas, 139 (n. 99), 140 (n. 100).

Smith, W. Henry, 147 (n. 149).

Soddy, Frederick, 183 (n. 27).

Southard, Frank A., Jr., 181 (n. 15), 198 (n. 71), 201 (n. 106).

Spahr, Walter E., 125 (n. 41), 156 (n. 218), 172 (n. 63), 187 (n. 64), 188 (n. 86), 189 (n. 10), 199 (n. 74), 208 (n. 162).

Spann, Othmar, 176 (n. 46).

Sprague, Oliver M. W., 181 (n. 15).

Sproul, Allan, 203 (n. 131).

Stafsing, O. I., 128 (n. 57).
Steiner, William Howard, 4, 126 (n. 46), 129 (n. 4), 130 (n. 14), 132 (n. 26), 168 (n. 48), 169 (n. 56), 182 (nn. 19, 22), 183 (n. 24), 200 (n. 79), 206 (n. 154).
Steuart, Sir James, 25, 164 (n. 38), 171 (n. 60).
Stigler, George J., 176 (n. 47).
Stokes, Milton L. (see Carl T. Arlt).
Strover, Carl, 137 (n. 77), 197 (n. 65).
Stucki, Roland (see J. Whitney Hanks).
Swart, Philip F., Jr., 181 (n. 15), 198 (n. 71), 201 (n. 106).

Tatham, W. P., 141 (n. 109), 159 (n. 10).
Taussig, F. W., 174 (nn. 15, 31), 181 (n. 11).
Taylor, F. M., 16, 121 (n. 4), 137 (n. 77), 138 (n. 87), 145 (n. 141), 146 (n. 142), 149 (n. 158), 156 (n. 223), 157 (n. 224), 191 (n. 15).
Taylor, John, 161 (n. 25), 162 (n. 31).
Taylor, Overton H., 173 (n. 3).
Teller, James H., 141 (n. 109), 142 (n. 111), 161 (n. 26), 165 (nn. 38, 39), 167 (n. 45), 191 (n. 15).
Temple, Sir Richard C., 151 (n. 181).
Thomas, Rollin G., 94, 123 (n. 17), 125 (n. 35), 131 (n. 17), 136 (n. 59), 137 (n. 79), 170 (n. 57), 181 (n. 12), 182 (n. 18), 192 (n. 20), 196 (n. 58), 212 (n. 200).
Thornton, Henry, 137 (n. 73), 197 (n. 62), 200 (nn. 81, 84), 201 (nn. 88, 95).
Todd, John A., 186 (n. 58), 202 (nn. 117, 126).
Tooke, Thomas, 87.
Torrens, Robert, 140 (n. 103), 165 (n. 39).
Tourgée, Albion W., 127 (n. 52), 153 (n. 201), 161 (n. 26), 167 (n. 45).

Towne, Edward Cornelius, 143 (n. 128), 147 (n. 145), 184 (nn. 44, 45).
Townshend, Hugh (see Myra Curtis).
Triffin, Robert, 205 (n. 143), 219 (n. 34), 221 (n. 60).
Turgot, Anne Robert Jacques, 127 (n. 48), 162 (n. 34).

Veeder, Nicholas, 147 (n. 150).
Villard, Henry H., 173 (n. 3).
Viner, Jacob, 139 (n. 92), 206 (n. 150), 216 (n. 23), 217 (n. 24).

Walker, Francis A., 28, 30, 46–47, 56, 142 (n. 111), 145 (n. 140), 146 (n. 144), 148 (n. 150), 149 (n. 161), 166 (nn. 40–43), 167 (nn. 44, 45), 168 (n. 51), 175 (n. 40).
Wallich, Henry C., 195 (n. 51), 218 (n. 29), 221 (n. 56).
Walras, Auguste, 176 (n. 46).
Walras, Leon, 176 (n. 46).
Ward, William, 202 (n. 114).
Warren, George F., 37, 155 (n. 209).
Webster, Daniel, 141 (n. 109).
Westerfield, Ray B., 122 (n. 16), 123 (n. 27), 126 (n. 47), 130 (n. 14), 131 (n. 23), 132 (n. 29), 134 (n. 40), 154 (nn. 201, 202), 167 (n. 46), 181 (n. 12), 182 (n. 17), 198 (n. 67), 201 (n. 99), 204 (nn. 141, 142).
White, Horace, 122 (n. 14), 126 (n. 46), 130 (n. 8), 132 (n. 27), 136 (nn. 55, 62), 137 (n. 74), 142 (n. 110), 147 (n. 145), 148 (n. 156), 168 (n. 47), 181 (n. 16), 184 (n. 38), 192 (n. 19), 215 (n. 8).
Whittlesey, Charles R.: Concept of monetary standard: explicit concept as standard money, 131 (n. 17); implicit concept as criterion of monetary policy, 213 (n. 207). Gold standard: called a "system,"

252

A NOTE ON THE TYPE USED IN THIS BOOK

The text of this book was set on the Linotype in a face called
TIMES ROMAN, designed by STANLEY MORISON for *The Times*
(London), and first introduced by that newspaper in the middle nineteen thirties.

The book was composed, printed, and bound
by Kingsport Press, Inc., Kingsport, Tennessee.
Typography and binding design by
MAXINE SCHEIN